Praise for

'... a well-written compelling tale'
Judges' report, Davitt Awards

'The story she tells ... is a useful challenge to any
tendency to simple moral indignation'
Sydney Morning Herald

'This is a fascinating book, a terrific read, and an
excellent reminder of who tells the stories, and whose
stories are forgotten'
South Coast Register

'... what's ... interesting is Caroline Overington's
even-handed appraisal of Collins's alleged crime(s)
that led her to become the last woman hanged in
New South Wales in 1889'
Launceston Sunday Examiner

Caroline Overington is a writer and journalist. She is the author of nine books and has twice won Australia's most prestigious award for journalism, the Walkley Award. She lives in Sydney, Australia, and Santa Monica, USA.

For more about the author, visit
carolineoverington.com

LAST
WOMAN
HANGED

The terrible, true story
of Louisa Collins

CAROLINE OVERINGTON

HarperCollins*Publishers*

HarperCollins*Publishers*
First published in Australia in 2014
This edition published in 2016
by HarperCollinsPublishers Australia Pty Limited
ABN 36 009 913 517
harpercollins.com.au

HarperCollins*Publishers*
Level 13, 201 Elizabeth Street, Sydney NSW 2000, Australia
Unit D1, 63 Apollo Drive, Rosedale, Auckland 0632, New Zealand
A 53, Sector 57, Noida, UP, India
1 London Bridge Street, London SE1 9GF, United Kingdom
2 Bloor Street East, 20th floor, Toronto, Ontario M4W 1A8, Canada
195 Broadway, New York NY 10022, USA

National Library of Australia Cataloguing-in-Publication data:

Overington, Caroline.
    Last woman hanged / Caroline Overington.
    978 1 4607 5093 3 (pbk.)
    978 1 4607 0362 5 (ebook)
    Notes: Includes bibliographical references.
    Collins, Louisa, 1848–1889.
    Women murderers — New South Wales.
    True crime stories.
364.15230944

Cover design: Design by Committee
Cover image: Darlinghurst Gaol and Court House, Sydney, 1870 by Charles
Pickering/ State Library of NSW (SPF/253, a089253)
Spine image: Photograph of Louisa Collins from State Records NSW (NRS 2138,
Darlinghurst Gaol photographic Description Book, [3/6050 p.84], Reel 5103)
Typeset in Adobe Caslon Pro by Kirby Jones
The papers used by HarperCollins in the manufacture of this book are a natural,
recyclable product made from wood grown in sustainable plantation forests.
The fibre source and manufacturing processes meet recognised international
environmental standards, and carry certification.
Printed and bound in Australia by Griffin Press

*This book is dedicated to the memory of those
women who fought so hard to save Louisa,
and for so many of the rights
that women enjoy today.*

Contents

Introduction

On 8 January 1889, Louisa Collins, a 41-year-old mother of ten children, became the first woman hanged at the Darlinghurst Gaol and the last woman hanged in New South Wales.[1]

Dark-eyed, dark-haired, plump-of-figure, beautiful — all these words had been used to describe Louisa. Also: *drunk*. Louisa liked to drink brandy and she liked to drink beer and when she got drunk she liked to dance by the light of the lamp, even as her many children crawled on the dirty floor around her feet.[2]

Louisa had twice been married, and — unlucky for some — she had twice been widowed. Over six tense months in 1888, the centenary year in New South Wales, she was tried not once, but four times for the murder of one or the other of her husbands.

Some of the strongest evidence against Louisa came from her only daughter, tiny fair-haired May, who was just ten years old when first asked by a judge of the Supreme Court to take the stand with a Bible in her hand and testify against her mother.[3]

The execution of Louisa Collins was ghastly, not only because executions generally are, or because Louisa was a woman, but because the hangman in New South Wales at that time, the gruesome Nosey Bob, was inept. He misjudged the length of the drop, and nearly tore Louisa's head off. So terrible was the scene — Louisa was left to dangle for twenty minutes, with blood dripping from a gaping wound in her throat — that no woman would ever again be hanged in New South Wales.

The first question this book seeks to answer is perhaps the most obvious one: did she do it? Was Louisa guilty? This requires a rigorous examination of the original evidence, including trial notes and forensic reports, most of which are stored at State Records New South Wales.

The aim throughout has been to ensure that everything recorded here — as opposed to anything that might have been said about Louisa at the time — is true: therefore, if a character says or does something on these pages, it is because they were recorded as saying or doing so, at the time of Louisa's trials.

That said, all evidence must be read in its historical context: Louisa Collins died at a time when women were in no sense equal under the law, except when it came to the gallows. Women could not vote. They could not sit in parliament. There were no female judges — and no female jurors either.

The space available for women to have their say — to express an opinion about capital punishment, for example — was limited. The space available to them to exercise real power, in a legal and political sense, was non-existent. Also important is the fact that Louisa was a poor woman, in debt even to the undertaker. The Crown, by contrast, was equipped with the best of the colony's barristers, for all four trials.

A story like this one, where both the stakes and the body count are high, inevitably features heroes and villains. To some extent, it will be for the reader to decide the category into which Louisa should fall. What is certain is that two of the colony's most powerful men — the premier, Sir Henry Parkes, and His Excellency, the governor, Lord Carrington — ultimately declined to intervene on Louisa's behalf. In their absence, it fell to the little people — many of them women — to find the moral courage to try to save her life. Their argument was both passionate and compelling, and may today seem obvious: that a legal system comprised only of men — male judges, all-male jury, male prosecutor, governor and premier — could not with any integrity hang a woman.

The tenacity of these women would not, in the end, save Louisa Collins, but it would ultimately carry women from their homes in the new colony of New South Wales all the way to Parliament House. Little more than a decade after Louisa was hanged, Australian women would become some of the first in the world to get the vote. They would take seats in state parliaments, and in Canberra. They would become doctors, lawyers, judges, premiers — even the prime minister.

Besides being the true story of one woman's life, this book should be read as a letter of profound thanks to that generation of Australian suffragettes who fought so hard for so many of the rights that women enjoy today. Their first steps into the political arena may have been tentative, but a wave rose in their wake and it would prove unstoppable. The delight and surprise in researching their lives was in discovering that some of their descendants — as well as some of Louisa's — still walk among us. Surely their spirit does, too.

Caroline Overington
Sydney, 2014

CHAPTER 1

The Early Years

According to various sources, Louisa Collins was just thirty-two years old when she was hanged at the Darlinghurst Gaol in 1889 — or else she was thirty-nine or perhaps forty. Not even prison officials could seem to make up their minds.[1]

In fact, if the official records are correct, Louisa must have been forty-one years old when she died. Her baptism certificate makes plain that she was born Louisa Hall on 11 August 1847 at Belltrees, near Scone, and no amount of lying about her age, which Louisa had a habit of doing, could make a difference to that date.[2]

Typically enough for the time, Louisa's father, Henry Hall, was a convict. The particulars document attached to his file describes him as having a scar over his eye and a pock-marked, ruddy complexion. He was also short — and a thief.[3] Louisa's mother, Catherine King (sometimes recorded as Catherine Ring), was a free settler who arrived in Australia on the *Fairlie*. Upon Henry securing his ticket of leave — and permission to marry[4] — the couple went to live and labour at Belltrees.

Belltrees. It even sounds beautiful — and it is. A pastoral station situated on the Hunter River, Belltrees has for more than seven generations been managed, and then owned, by one of Australia's most successful families, the Whites.[5] The centrepiece of the property today is a magnificent homestead of fifty-two rooms wrapped in a iron verandah, all of it cast at Morpeth. Stallions are kept there; the great-great-grandsons of the original Whites today tend cattle, and play polo. When Louisa was born, Belltrees was very different: it comprised only the original homestead, which still stands, a trading store and a few small cottages scattered across the fertile plains.

Given its distance from Sydney — more than 250 kilometres — the shepherds and labourers who lived on the station had to be entirely self-sufficient. They grew their own vegetables (turnips, onions, carrots) and killed their own meat. One of the closest main towns, Scone, had one church, a courthouse constructed of hand-made bricks, and a population of just sixty-three.[6]

Louisa was perhaps the second of at least seven children born to Catherine and Henry Hall[7] and, from her birth on Belltrees through puberty, she learned all a girl of her station needed to know. Perhaps surprisingly, that included how to read, write, and do basic arithmetic, but she was also taught to dust shelves, knead bread and peel potatoes.

When Louisa reached what was known as a 'suitable age' — about fourteen — she took the position for which she had been trained: she became a domestic.

Louisa's first employer was a solicitor in Merriwa, a town slightly more developed than Scone. By the 1860s, when Louisa went to live there, Merriwa had three inns, five stores, two blacksmiths, several tailors and shoemakers — and a dour butcher, whose name was Charles Andrews.

Charles and Louisa. As matches go, theirs was an odd one. According to one report, in Sydney's *Evening News*, Louisa was, in her early girlhood, 'the pet of the village' and by age sixteen she had 'developed all the qualities of a country coquette', able with her 'winning ways' to attract many 'youthful sweethearts'.[8]

She was, in other words, a pretty little flirt.

Poor Charles was, in contrast, a tragic figure. Born on or about 25 August 1833, he had sailed to Australia with his parents at the age of fifteen.[9] His first job, fresh off the *Canton*,[10] was as a carter (literally, carting goods around manure-strewn streets of Sydney with a hand-drawn wagon and, later, carting skins for the wealthy wool merchant, Mr Simeon Lord[11]). By almost every account but the formal one, Charles soon married[12] and had a child, but his first wife died and the boy was taken from his care. Then, just a few years before he married Louisa, Charles suffered another tragedy: his father, Richard Andrews, at first tried to drown himself in four feet of water at the bottom of a 12-foot well; and, when that failed, cut his own throat in a fit of madness,[13] and died in Sydney Hospital.[14]

How did two such different people — grieving Charles the slaughterman, and the pretty town pet — get together? Apparently it was Louisa's mother who made the match, telling neighbours that she believed Charles would be an excellent alliance for her daughter.[15] On paper, that probably made sense: Charles was hard-working, sober and honest. Like so many others in the town of Merriwa, he was also passionately in love with Louisa.

Did Louisa love him back? From this distance, it's hard to tell, but it doesn't seem so. In years to come, Louisa would complain to neighbours that Charles had always been boring. She liked to dance and he didn't. She liked to drink and he would scold her for getting drunk. And yet, when Charles offered his dark-haired, dark-eyed sweetheart the security of marriage, Louisa accepted (or, more likely, her mother made sure that she accepted).

The couple were married, by Church of England rites, on 28 August 1865 at the local Church of the Holy Trinity.[16] Charles was thirty-two, widowed, and already a father, albeit to a child he never saw. Louisa, who gave her occupation as domestic servant, had turned eighteen just seventeen days earlier.

The couple stayed in Merriwa for some years. Charles continued to work as a butcher, while Louisa began having children. By the 1870s, they had moved to Muswellbrook, where the bushranger Captain Thunderbolt was known to roam.

Were they happier in Muswellbrook than in Merriwa? Once again, it's hard to say. Charles had work (in 1876, eleven years after the marriage, the *Maitland Mercury* reported that he had been granted a licence to slaughter in his own yard[17]) but money was short, the family was often in debt[18] and there is some evidence that Louisa began to drink quite heavily and they began to squabble.[19] The question is whether Louisa came at any point to loathe Charles enough to slowly poison him to death — and it's a critical question, not only for the purposes of this book, but because if such an allegation could ever be proved, she would very likely hang.

Capital punishment had, regardless of gender, been the standard response to the crime of murder since the arrival of the First Fleet. The preferred method was hanging, which was for years done before crowds of enthusiastic onlookers, and often with startling ineptitude. Take, for an example, the first public hanging in the colony of South Australia.[20] Given it was the first, mistakes were bound to happen — but still. The year was 1838, and the condemned man's name was Michael Magee.[21] He was twenty-four years old and had been brought to the court in clanking irons, accused of firing a shot at the local sheriff, Mr Samuel Smart. The shot missed, leaving nothing but a gunpowder graze on Mr Smart's cheek — but the judge decided that Magee should hang.

Three immediate problems arose.

First, Magee was a Roman Catholic and would therefore need to see a priest before he died, but there seems to have been no Catholic priest in the colony of South Australia in 1838. The judiciary pondered this problem for a day or so before deciding that a local tradesman — fellmonger or blacksmith, the record does not say — would have to do (Magee reportedly agreed to this arrangement, not, one supposes, that he had much choice).

The second problem was more serious: besides having no Catholic priest, the colony had no executioner.

Again, the judiciary pondered. The sheriff's name was mentioned, but given he had also been the intended victim of Magee's poorly timed shot, this was considered 'unseemly' and so the job was put to tender.

Who, now, would take five pounds to execute Michael Magee?

Nobody came forward.

Who now will take *ten* pounds to execute this man?

Still no takers.

By the day of the hanging — it was a Wednesday — all of Adelaide was agog with curiosity. Would the execution go ahead and, if so, who would be the hangman? Everyone wanted to know and so, in the hours immediately after sunrise, at least 1000 people — women and children included — rose from their beds and began to make their way across fields to the hanging place to see what might happen.

Officials had decided that Magee should hang from a tree on the banks of the Torrens River. The tree was chosen both because it had a thick, horizontal bough over which the noose could be thrown, and because it was the only such tree on government land.

Perhaps because of the pretty location, many people had decided to bring picnics, and before long the riverbank was filled with spectators. Then, shortly after nine a.m., the mood turned serious: through the trees, people could see a procession leaving the distant gaol. (It wasn't really a gaol; it was more a timber shed. A proper gaol wouldn't be built for a year, and it would be run for decades by a man so fat that when he died his corpse would have to be carried out through a window.)

The procession comprised mounted police and a cart led by two horses, one in front of the other. Upon the cart sat a timber coffin — and upon the coffin sat Magee. If that were not bad enough, also sitting on the coffin was the hangman.

Who was he? Well, it was hard to be sure. To keep his identity a secret, the hangman had stuffed his clothes with padding, so he looked like he had a huge hump, and he covered his face with a horrible hand-made mask painted white around the eyes. The closer the hangman got to the crowds on the riverbank, the more enormous and repulsive he seemed. Women gasped and children screamed, the 'thrill of horror creeping through their veins'.

In an effort to keep people from crowding too close to the hanging tree, the judiciary had set up a temporary enclosure, like a sheep pen, around its base. They had also saddled an extra horse so the hangman could make a quick getaway after the job was done.

With Magee's cart now parked inside the pen, the execution was, as they say, good to go. The noose was placed over Magee's head and a cap was drawn over his face. Prayers were concluded. A motion was made that all was ready and then, after 'a whip or two of the leading horse', the cart upon which Magee still sat was drawn away. Many in the crowd shut their eyes, as well they might, because 'here commenced one of the most frightful and appalling sights that ever perhaps will be again witnessed in the colony'. Either the horse was moving too slowly or else the hangman had bungled the noose, but instead of having his neck instantly broken, Magee started to slide gently off the coffin until he was hanging by his throat in the air, screaming, 'Oh God! Oh Christ! Save me!'

Now it was time for men to gasp. The hangman —
still in his mask and lumpy costume — got on the saddled
horse and bolted.

'Fetch him back!' the crowd cried, so mounted police
took off at full speed. Magee, meanwhile, was uttering
the same piercing cries: 'Lord save me! Christ have mercy
upon me!' Nobody knew what to do. Some cried, 'Cut him
down!' Others urged the marines to shoot Magee dead
with their muskets to at least put an end to his misery, and
all the while, Magee's hands were up the rope as he madly
tried to save himself, while his body twisted 'like a joint of
meat before the fire'.

Finally, the hangman was brought back. Inspiration
had struck and, with a 'fiendish leap', he threw himself
upon Magee's body and proceeded to hang himself from
the condemned man's legs, pulling him toward the ground
until Magee could no longer cling to the rope and began to
suffocate. By some counts, it took thirteen long minutes for
Magee to die this way. Many in the crowd were horrified.
Others waited for the body to be cut down and then carried
on with their picnic.[22]

CHAPTER 2

A Dour and Boring Man: Louisa's first husband

It is often said that history is written by winners but, at least until recently, it was written by men. In Australia in the nineteenth century, newspapers were edited and the stories were penned by men, and since only men could vote, and only men could take seats in parliament, it was mostly men they wrote about. Women were engaged in the life of the colony — they owned businesses and employed staff and did extraordinary work for charitable causes — but their lives were also very often dominated by pregnancy and childbirth, over and over again.

Louisa Hall — by now Louisa Andrews — did not escape that fate. According to records held by the New South Wales Registry of Births, Deaths and Marriages, she gave birth to her first child, a boy called Herbert, in 1867.[1] A second child — a boy, Ernest — was born after 1868 and died before 1872.[2] A third son, Reuben, arrived in 1871. He was followed by Arthur in 1873; then by Frederick in 1875; and by Louisa's only daughter, May, in 1877.[3]

By 1878, Charles had hit on hard times and the family was forced to move to Sydney so he could find work. Their first stop was a place called 'Berry's paddock', near today's suburb of Waterloo (Berry was Mr John Sugden Berry, who owned a bone dust, or fertiliser, factory[4]). By the 1880s, the family had moved again, this time to Botany, and it was here that Louisa had another three children: Edwin, who was born in 1880; David, who was born and died in 1881; and baby Charles, who arrived in 1883.[5]

The family's move to Botany made sense. While the suburb was foul-smelling and swampy, there was work there, mainly in factories associated with the wool industry.

A former convict, Simeon Lord, had been the first to see Botany's potential as an industrial site. Upon winning his freedom, he had taken commercial leases over huge tracts of land, and then proceeded to dam the streams, build sheds, and take in wool for washing, drying and packing. It wasn't long before Simeon was one of the richest men in the colony. Others followed his lead, among them Geddes and Sons, a firm that built its wool sheds on a ten-acre site that would today be bounded by Botany Road to the west, Randwick Racecourse to the east, and Surry Hills to the north.

At the peak of its operations in the late 1880s, Geddes employed more than 100 men, whose job it was to load large skips with soapy water and use their hands to create a continuous, vigorous movement to rid the wool of dirt, grease and ticks. Once clean, the wet wool had to be carried out in baskets and spread across the drying grounds, where it would be hand-turned before being packed, weighed and bundled off to England.

Charles had experience working for Simeon Lord, and upon moving to Botany he was sure he would be able to find work at Geddes, and find work he did. Indeed, the record suggests that Charles Andrews would become one of Geddes' most reliable employees. His boss, Mr Alexander Geddes, would tell the judge at one of Louisa's trials that Charles had worked for him for more than six years, and that he had found him to be a sober, honest, good-hearted man 'who earned for himself the respect and esteem of all who knew him'.[6]

The same could not be said for Louisa, mainly because Louisa liked to drink. To be fair, so did many people, and in fact Botany was home to one of New South Wales's grandest drinking establishments, the Sir Joseph Banks Hotel and Pleasure Gardens. This was not your average pub. It had a 1000-seat dining room, an archery range and a running track (besides foot races, the hotel sponsored speed tree-climbing events, with local Aborigines pitted against new settlers). There was also a private zoo with Australia's only elephant, a Bengal tiger, and a Himalayan bear.[7]

As the wife of a poor wool-washer, Louisa did not socialise at the Sir Joseph Banks. She obtained her liquor from the much more modest, timber-posted Amos Pier Hotel just three doors from her house.

The address at which Louisa, Charles and their children lived was No. 1 Pople's Terrace. The house was one of a row of small, weatherboard cottages built on land so swampy it was known as Frog's Hollow. The front door was accessible only via a rickety bridge over a swamp, while the back door was separated from the fetid bay only by a 'split-rail fence, and a few feet of scrub'.[8] In total, the house had four rooms, and Louisa had eight mouths to feed — nine if you count her own. Living conditions were deplorable: there was no real system for the disposal of sewerage, and drinking water came from a shared pump behind the row of cottages.

Charles did his best to try to improve his family's situation, at first by taking whatever hours were on offer at Geddes, and later by taking in boarders. By late 1886, there were at least six adults living at No. 1 Pople's Terrace, as well as the couple's children — a chaotic situation that Louisa seems to have greeted with what might be termed lusty approval.[9]

'Her relations with the boarders were soon the scandal of Frog's Hollow,' declared the *Evening News*, in a lengthy article published after her death, before adding: 'In fact, the boarders whom the Andrews family had living with them were all at various times favoured by the attentions of their landlady.'[10]

One boarder in particular had caught Louisa's eye: Michael Peter Collins, son of Ballarat farmer James Collins, and his wife, Margaret (née Lennie).[11] Michael was somewhere between twenty-five and twenty-seven years old when he arrived in Botany. The one photograph of him that survives shows him to be a strong, muscular man, with centre-parted hair and a neat moustache.

Louisa was at least a decade older. Still, it seems that the couple fell in love, or at least into bed.

Like Charles, Michael had travelled to Botany in

search of work, and he'd found it at Geddes, where he was responsible for carting sheep skins from the slaughterhouses on Glebe Island to the sheds at Botany. Like scouring, carting was dirty work and it wasn't unknown for carters to gather of an evening at the Amos Pier to drink until they vomited.

By some accounts, this was how Louisa met Michael Collins: the two of them got drunk together at her local pub, after which she invited Michael to become a boarder.

According to neighbours, it was obvious to everyone — except perhaps poor Charles — that they had become lovers. 'They would go down to the bay and canoodle in the bushes,' cried the *Evening News*. They conspired to meet at the tram stop, and got caught 'KISSING IN THE CARS [capitals in original]'.[12]

Given the flagrant nature of the affair, it was surely only a matter of time before the gossip reached Charles, who confronted his wife. Louisa denied wrongdoing, but Charles nonetheless instructed Michael — and all the other boarders — to immediately leave the house. A sheepish Michael complied, finding lodgings at another boarding house down the road but then, on 16 December 1886 — an important day in the context of the trial ahead — Charles returned home unexpectedly to find Michael sitting in his front room. Outraged, he took the law into his own hands and kicked Michael into the street.

One of Louisa's sons, Arthur, who was then about fourteen, was alarmed and asked his father what he was doing, but Charles refused to shame his wife, saying: 'Oh, I don't want to tell you what for.'[13]

Now it was Louisa's turn to be furious. She ran to the police station at Botany to complain that her husband had been 'fighting and rowing with the boarders' and threatening to throw her into the street as well.[14] Such a development would have been calamitous: Louisa had no income and there were at least five children still at home (Louisa's eldest, Herbert, by then twenty years old, had gone north to Adamstown, near Newcastle, to look for work, while her second eldest, Reuben, who was around sixteen, was also often away, either working or looking for work).

The policeman on duty that evening was Constable George Jeffes. He went to No. 1 Pople's Terrace, perhaps expecting to find a fist fight underway, but all was quiet. One of Louisa's neighbours, James Law, confirmed that Charles had earlier been in a jealous rage, but Michael Collins had scarpered and, when approached at his new lodgings, insisted on taking the matter no further.[15]

Louisa had been warned, and yet she could not help herself. According to the *Evening News*, whose reporting relied on the accounts of scandalised neighbours, she continued to see Michael, and in fact began 'carrying on her shameless doings with even greater energy'.[16] Louisa's children — already somewhat neglected — grew lean and dirty, and her husband, Charles, had the sympathy of everyone in the street.

What happened next is, of course, what matters most: just six weeks after Charles threw Michael out of the house, Charles became sick. The sickness came on suddenly. On Friday, 26 January 1887 — now called Australia Day, it was then called Anniversary Day — Charles called on a friend, a Mr Bullock, to say he was going to kill a pig on Saturday. Would Mr Bullock like a piece for Sunday dinner? Mr Bullock happily accepted — who doesn't like a piece of pork? — but Saturday came and went, and so too did Sunday, and the pork was not forthcoming. By Monday, everyone knew the reason: Charles was gravely ill.[17]

Louisa sent for the doctor. The one who came, Dr Thomas Morgan Martin, was relatively young at thirty-three years of age, and new to the colony, having arrived from Ireland only a year earlier. His practice was in College Street in Sydney, which was about fifty minutes from Botany by horse-drawn tram.

Dr Martin visited Charles at Pople's Terrace at eight p.m. on the day after Anniversary Day.[18] Charles complained of severe pain in the stomach, constant vomiting and diarrhoea. Dr Martin prescribed a mixture of powders, and Louisa sent one of her children to the chemist to get the prescription filled, but although Charles took the medicine, he remained on his sickbed.

As was customary, friends came to visit, among them Charles Sayers, who was the local grocer, and Constable Jeffes.[19] Louisa was present throughout, tending to her husband with what seemed to some to be indifference, and to others a quiet tenderness. One thing that stuck in the minds of many of the neighbours was the fact that Louisa seemed quite certain that her husband was going to die. In fact, on 29 January — just two days after Charles fell sick — Louisa went running around the neighbourhood, trying to find adult men to witness her husband's will (the signature of a woman, in 1887, wouldn't have held water).[20]

One of the doors upon which she knocked was answered by Mrs Margaret Collis. 'She asked if Mr Collis or any of the other men were at home,' Mrs Collis would later tell the court. 'I said, no, but my brothers will be home at dinnertime.'

'That won't do,' Louisa cried. 'I've been to Sydney and got the Will drawn up and I want a witness to see him [Charles] sign his name.'

Mrs Collis was alarmed, saying: 'He's not that bad, is he?'

'Yes!' Louisa cried. 'He will never get out of bed again! And it will save me trouble to get the Will signed before he dies.'[21]

Louisa returned to Charles's bedside, but the unsigned will seemed to plague her. Later the same night, she sent one of the children down the road to try to get another neighbour, Mr William Farrer, to come. He was not there, but when he returned home, his wife passed on the message: 'They say that Andrews is dying!' Mr Farrer could hardly believe it: the Charles he knew was a hale and hearty man. He went directly to Louisa's house, where he found Charles in agony. The room was crowded: Louisa and four of her children were there, as was another of Charles's friends, Mr John Stephens.

Charles struggled into a sitting position. Louisa explained that she had been into town, where a clerk had prepared a will. Charles wanted to read it out loud, and have it witnessed. The reading didn't take long: there was some furniture valued at twenty-five pounds, and a small sum of money (eleven pounds, ten shillings) in a savings account at the Bank of New South Wales, plus a life insurance policy with the Mutual Life Association of New South Wales, worth an impressive 200 pounds, boosting the total value of Charles's estate, minus debts, to 214 pounds and ten shillings, an amount equivalent to $20,000 today.[22]

Charles read the will and, in a shaky hand, he signed it. Mr Farrer took the document from him, and added his signature. Mr Stephens did the same. Charles fell back against the bed.

In the hours that followed, and into the next day, many friends came to call, among them Mr Henry Kneller, who had known Charles almost six years. Dazed Charles was lying on a stretcher in the front room. Seeing his friend in the doorway, he called out: 'George Osborn! How are you?' Louisa tried gently to correct him, saying: 'It's Mr Kneller.'[23]

'Mr Kneller,' murmured Charles. 'How are your wife and children?' The words barely came out, and Charles had soon fallen back against his pillow. Mr Kneller stayed for several hours, watching as Charles moaned in pain and gasped for breath.

'I remained until about one p.m. [and] before I left, he gave two or three great gasps,' Mr Kneller said. 'I told [Louisa] I thought he was dying. She then began to cry a little.'[24]

Mr Kneller was not wrong: Charles had fallen ill on 27 January and by 2 February this sad, solid man was indeed dead.

Louisa immediately sent May next door to fetch Mrs Mary Law. Their houses were just steps apart, and Mrs

Law would later recall that Charles had been dead no more than a minute or two by the time she arrived. She also remembered thinking, 'But he wasn't ill more than a week!' and being startled when she turned to offer words of comfort to Louisa, only to see her preparing to go out.

'But where are you going?' Mrs Law said.

'By the next tram to Sydney,' Louisa replied, as if that were the most normal thing in the world to do after one's husband of twenty-seven years has died.

'But why?' Mrs Law said.

'Because I must see the insurance people,' Louisa said, 'and I must let the man at the savings bank know.'[25]

Mrs Law watched, astonished, as Louisa hurried from the house to catch the four p.m. tram into the city.

Quite by chance, on Louisa's way into town she encountered her son Reuben, returning from a week-long search for work. Reuben knew that his father had been sick — he'd wished him well just a week earlier — and so asked his mother: 'How is Father?' and was startled when Louisa coolly said: 'He's dead.'[26]

Reuben rushed to the house. Could it really be true? It was: Charles was lying dead on a stretcher, with only Mrs Law there to care for the weeping children.

'I didn't know that he would die,' Reuben would later tell the police. 'Before this my father had never been ill ... he was a strong, healthy man.'[27]

Having announced her husband's death to the bank and the insurance company, Louisa began making her way home again. En route, she called on a friend, Mrs Ellen Price, to ask if she would accompany her back to Pople's Terrace to prepare Charles's body for burial. (The task of laying out the dead — washing the body, and dressing the corpse — was often the business of women in the nineteenth century, and it was a necessary one, because it would often take extended family some days to travel to pay their respects.)

Like Mrs Law, Mrs Price was startled to hear that Charles had died. She had known that he was ill but not that the sickness was so serious. She immediately agreed to assist Louisa, gathering up her hat and her purse to ride the eight p.m. tram back to Pople's Terrace. Louisa was so composed that Mrs Price began to wonder if she'd perhaps heard wrongly. Perhaps Charles wasn't dead after all? Working up some courage, she ventured a question: 'How is he?' she asked gently.

Louisa turned in surprise. 'I told you,' she said. 'He's dead.'

Six-and-a-half hours after Charles Andrews breathed his last, Louisa and Mrs Price returned to Pople's Terrace. Charles's body was still lying on the stretcher, stiff and cold. Mrs Price was dismayed. Rigor mortis had set in, and she would have to cut Charles's shirt to get it off.

'It's a pity you did not call me earlier,' Mrs Price said.

'I had business in town,' Louisa replied.[28]

Mrs Price set to work, cutting Charles free of his clothes, sponging his body with soapy rags and dressing him for his coffin. According to the *Evening News*, 'during all these mournful proceedings the widow — Louisa — looked on with supreme composure … the body might have rather been a wax figure than the corpse of the man she had called husband for over twenty years'.[29]

By contrast, Reuben was distraught. 'We should send for Herby,' he said, meaning his eldest brother, Herbert, who would, in normal circumstances, now be expected to take up the role as head of the Andrews household, but Louisa, who had begun drinking, wanted nothing to do with that idea, saying: 'I will be in no hurry to let him know.'[30]

This was somewhat odd: by rights, or at least by tradition, Herbert would upon the death of his father automatically inherit all of the estate. In exchange, he would be expected to provide for his mother and her children. Of course, Louisa had already taken care of that: under the will that Charles had signed two days before he died, all of the insurance money would go to her and so, rather than send a message up the Newcastle line to Herbert, who was in Adamstown, working as a butcher, she instead ordered another of her sons, Arthur, out the door to Dr Martin's rooms, to get a death certificate so she could get Charles's body buried.

By Dr Martin's account, he wasn't surprised that Charles had died. He had called on the patient earlier that day, and 'from his condition ... I [did] not expect him to live more than a couple of hours ... [even on the evening before] I thought he would hardly live through the night'.[31] Dr Martin agreed to give the certificate to Arthur but what would he put down as the cause of death?

Not poisoning. He never even considered that, which is actually quite curious. After all, the case had all the signs: Charles had been a healthy man struck down with stomach pains and vomiting, who had died in a matter of days. In addition, poisoning was all over the news at the time, thanks to a product called Rough on Rats.

Rough on Rats wasn't an Australian invention. It had come from the United States. The inventor, Ephraim Stockton Wells — he called himself ES Wells — had been apprenticed, aged twelve, to a chemist, and he later worked as a drug-store clerk, before becoming a union soldier and fighting in the Civil War. Like many soldiers, ES came home alive but broke. According to family legend, he went to bed starving one night and woke to find that his last loaf of bread had been eaten by rats. He swore vengeance, and soon after began the manufacture of his special poison.[32] His new product — made of fine sand, barium oxide, carbon dioxide and arsenic, but mostly arsenic — worked so well that ES's wife jokingly called it 'Rough on Rats'. The name stuck, and the product became a huge success.

Rough on Rats was packaged in a small, round box, usually red in colour, with pictures of dead rats, flat on their backs. As well as being a good chemist, ES was a dab hand at advertising.[33] Rough on Rats was one of the first products to be advertised with a jingle:

> *R-r-rats! Rats! Rats!*
> *Rough on Rats*
> *Hang your dogs and drown your cats*
> *We give a plan for every man*
> *To clear his house with Rough on Rats.*[34]

Some of the earliest ads for Rough on Rats also had lines such as: 'Rough on Rats — a leading cause of cat unemployment!'[35]

Of course, it wasn't long before people figured out that if a little arsenic could topple a rat, a lot might topple a person. In 1882, the *Cortland County Democrat*, a newspaper in Tully, New York, reported the case of a woman found lying on the floor, her face covered with powder that proved to be Rough on Rats. 'She had taken a cup of tea to her room when she retired and after mixing the poison in the tea, drank the mixture and scraped the dregs left in the bottom of the cup with her fingers and ate them,' the newspaper said. 'Her husband is said to be a dissolute, worthless fellow who had abused and ill-treated her times without number.'[36]

Before long, people started to joke about the deadliness of Rough on Rats. A variation of the original advertising jingle went:

> *Willie and three other brats,*
> *Ate up all the Rough-on-Rats*
> *Papa said, when Mama cried,*
> *'Don't worry, dear, they'll die outside.'*[37]

Demand for the product soon spread from the American east coast to all cities with a rat problem, Sydney included. The first advertisements for Rough on Rats in New South Wales newspapers began to appear in 1883–84. They read:

DON'T DIE IN THE HOUSE. — Rough on Rats
clears out rats, mice, beetles, roaches, bed-bugs,
flies, ants, insects, skunks, jack-rabbits, gophers.[38]

By the following year, the wording had changed slightly to better suit conditions in the colony (Sydney didn't really have much of a skunk problem) and there seems little doubt that the product was popular, with advertisements appearing in all the major newspapers.

Unfortunately, just as had happened in the United States, almost as soon as Rough on Rats became available, people as well as rats began consuming it, often in startling circumstances. For example, in November 1886, just two months before the death of Charles Andrews, all the Sydney newspapers carried the story of a merchant named Mr Frederick Berndt, who died after eating Rough on Rats at the posh Grand Hotel on Wynyard Square.

Mr Berndt had been staying at the hotel for about ten months when he sat down at a table in the kitchen to talk to fellow guests. The proprietor of the hotel, Mr Uhde, was also there, handling a plate of sandwiches. He told his guests that he'd spread the bread with Rough on Rats and that he intended to leave it out that night, in the hope of slaying some vermin. He then left the room.

By all accounts, Mr Berndt immediately leapt to his feet, seized one of the sandwiches, made a joke about their landlord never wanting to feed his tenants properly, and chowed on down. 'Why,' he exclaimed, 'it tastes like sand!'

Mr Berndt's friends were alarmed. They were quite sure that Mr Uhde hadn't been joking about poisoning the sandwiches. They — and the panicked Mr Uhde — urged Mr Berndt to take an emetic of salt and water to bring on vomiting but, of course, it was too late: once taken, arsenic is hard to expel and the effect — it essentially rots you from the inside — is near impossible to reverse. Mr Berndt spent the night in a state of agony and near collapse, rallying only long enough to call for his solicitor to make out his will. Shortly before he died, he turned to his brother and said: 'I took that thinking it was …' His last words were never finished.[39]

Mr Berndt's death generated a great deal of negative publicity, not only for the Grand Hotel but for Rough on Rats. One letter writer — they did not always give their names, unfortunately — complained to the *Evening News* that the product was 'simply arsenic, with a slight admixture of charcoal or lamp-black' to give it colour. It was also tasteless, or nearly so, and yet was being sold in three-ounce boxes large enough 'to poison the inhabitants of a good-sized township'.[40]

A plan to bring Rough on Rats under the requirements of the *Poisons Act*, limiting its sale to people known to the pharmacist, was mooted but didn't get far. Just six months later, yet another man was killed by the poison.[41] This second case involved a labourer named Mr William Snelson who, having become 'terribly oppressed by his debts', told his wife that he needed to find a way to make some money, or else he was going to poison himself. His children cried, but their mother calmed them, saying she was quite sure their father wouldn't do such a thing, at which point Mr Snelson went into their kitchen 'and returned to the dining-room with a cup of water, exclaiming: "Won't I?"'[42]

The children rushed out of the room, and soon afterwards they saw their father throw out whatever had been in the cup, which made them think he hadn't taken anything at all. In fact, he'd taken Rough on Rats. The poison burned quickly down his throat and Mr Snelson was soon after seen guzzling water from the pump. After half an hour, he started to vomit and continued to do so until 'he slipped off the bed and rolled under it' at around 4.20 a.m. By morning, he was stiff as a board — with the packet of Rough on Rats still in his trouser pocket.[43]

As with the death of Mr Berndt, it was all over the news. The symptoms in both cases had been similar: a quick death preceded by vomiting and agonising pain. Yet, when Dr Martin went to make out his death certificate for Charles Andrews, he didn't consider poison, and certainly not Rough on Rats. No, in his opinion, the cause of death was something much less exotic: 'acute gastritis'.[44]

CHAPTER 3

Dance All Night: Marriage to Michael Collins

Charles Andrews was buried at Rookwood on 5 February 1887.[1] By tradition, Louisa should have gone to her draper ahead of the ceremony to have dark mourning clothes made, but that was not Louisa's style. On the contrary, her draper, Mr Bullock — the same Mr Bullock who had waited for Charles to bring him a piece of pork — was surprised to see her coming through the door of his little shop requesting not mourning clothes but 'dress material of light colours'.

Astonished, he asked whether she wanted to be fitted for something in black as well.

'Oh no,' Louisa said, 'I can mourn in my heart without carrying my grief in my clothes.'[2]

Louisa seemed to some neighbours to be deliriously happy that Charles was dead. Just two or three days after he was buried, Mrs Price saw Louisa at the tram stop and noted with disapproval that she still 'had no mourning on'.[3] A few days after that, Louisa hosted a party in one of the empty houses at Pople's Terrace — and guess who was with her? The young and handsome Michael Collins. There was food and drink and dancing, with Louisa's children left to run around and help themselves to treats.

'I remember the party,' Louisa's daughter, May, would later tell a judge of the Supreme Court. 'The singing and dancing went on until two or three in the morn.'[4]

One day later, Michael moved back into No. 1 Pople's Terrace. Some neighbours thought it unseemly, particularly because most believed that Michael was not now a boarder, rather that he and Louisa were now 'living as man and wife'. Mrs Law recalled seeing them walking arm-in-arm 'as if already married', prompting her to shake her head and say: 'And the poor man, hardly cold yet.'[5]

Besides inviting her lover to move into her house, it seems that Louisa also used the occasion of her husband's death to go on a bit of a spending spree. On 8 February, just three days after Charles's funeral, she approached Mr William Burnett at the Savings Bank in Sydney, asking to withdraw any money that Charles had deposited there.

'She produced a copy of the certificate of death,' Mr Burnett would later tell the coroner. 'She made a strong appeal to get the money at once as she was greatly in need of it … an exception to the general rules of the bank was made in her case and the money was paid to her at once.'[6]

Louisa used part of the money to clear Michael's debts (he was a hopeless gambler, which would later create problems for them) and she bought him a new watch and chain, and a new suit of clothes. She also purchased new furniture for the house and she began dying her hair.

Then, on 9 April 1887, just three months after Charles's death, Louisa married Michael Collins at St Silas's Church of England near the Waterloo tram terminus. The ceremony was performed by a Reverend H Martin, with a Mrs Caroline Graham and a Mr John Johnstone asked to sign the certificate (both were what was known as 'parsonage witnesses', meaning people who happened to be there as opposed to friends). The bride described herself as a widow (which was true) and as a native of Scone (also true), but she gave her age as twenty-eight, which was patently ridiculous, given her eldest son, Herbert, was by then twenty.

There were some people who wondered what Michael — who put his age down as twenty-six — saw in Louisa. She was plump, which was in those days considered attractive (no longer, alas) plus she liked to drink, dance and sing and to flirt and to giggle, so she was probably fun to be around. Still, the *Evening News* claimed that Michael married her mainly because he was 'attracted by the sum of money derived from [Charles's] life insurance policy'.[7]

There was at least one other reason: although it wasn't reported anywhere, when Louisa walked up the aisle to meet Michael at the altar, she was pregnant.

The couple returned from their wedding to the little house at No. 1 Pople's Terrace but, for reasons that aren't adequately explained in any of the many accounts of Louisa's movements in the months that followed, they didn't stay long, opting to move to a little cottage in Johnson's Lane in Botany instead. Whatever her reasons for moving, Louisa soon began to miss her old neighbourhood. She asked the family that had taken over No. 1 Pople's Terrace to move out but they refused, so she and Michael and the growing family moved into No. 5 instead.

These should have been gay days but they were not. According to the *Evening News*, the couple lived 'in an indolent, unsatisfactory manner, with the wife always drinking and the husband helping to spend what little money there was' (the inheritance seems to have disappeared very quickly).[8] Fights began to break out, especially between Michael, who had for weeks been idle, and Louisa's son Arthur, who expected Michael to try to find a position. Michael's view was that Arthur, who was barely sixteen, could make the money necessary to feed the younger children.

Matters came to a head when Herbert, quite by chance, discovered that his father had died. Sorrow-stricken, he 'at once sought his mother [and upon] reaching the house at Botany he discovered the little children, dirty and uncared for, playing about the untidy house'.[9]

And sitting in the kitchen was Michael Collins. In age, Michael and Herbert weren't quite peers, but almost. Herbert looked at his mother — by now in her forties and pregnant with her tenth child — and demanded to know what her relationship to this man was, but Louisa felt no obligation to explain herself to her son. She answered Herbert in a cool manner: Michael was her husband; she loved him very much. Herbert was shocked. Why hadn't she sent word that his father had died? And what had she done with his father's estate? Louisa shook her head, dismissively. The money was gone.

'The son was thunderstruck,' the *News* said. 'Had his mother given him his share of the money he might have opened a small business in Botany or Waterloo, and helped her to live and keep the children in comparative ease and comfort.'[10] Now what hope was there for any of them with this layabout in the house?

He remonstrated with his mother, who soon became furious. She ordered Herbert out the door. He left without looking back. The next time mother and son saw each other, she would be in prison.

On 28 November 1887, Louisa's first baby with her new husband was born at home in Botany. The birth certificate suggests that she named the child William but changed her mind and called him John. She also fudged some of the dates to make it look like he'd been born nine months after she was married, instead of only seven.

According to the *News*, Louisa failed to display maternal affection for the baby, which seemed to cry a lot. Neighbours who popped in to have a look at him were turned away. Mrs Law, from next door, came for a bit of a peek, but Louisa told her: 'It's only a very little thing.'[11]

Then, one day, when John was about four months old, he started crying in a way that suggested he was neither tired nor hungry but sick. Louisa gave him a teaspoon of castor oil to settle his tummy and he went off to sleep but woke again at around ten p.m., wailing and screaming. Michael got up from bed, lit the lamp and gathered John into his arms, and the baby soon started to laugh and gurgle, apparently delighted by the lamp. Michael carried him to the marital bed, where John took the breast from Louisa and was soon back to sleep. However, at about 11.20 p.m., the baby woke again, 'screaming and suffering great pain'. Nothing Michael could do this time seemed to soothe him and, less than twenty minutes after waking the house, baby John was dead.

Louisa called for a doctor. Once again it was Dr Martin who came. He examined the baby's corpse and concluded that the child had been 'constitutionally delicate'. There was some evidence of teething; John's gums were raw and sore. The only medicine that had been given to him was the castor oil. Dr Martin suspected nothing. He filed a report for the coroner, who concluded:

> About 11.40 p.m., on the 10th April 1888, a
> child named John Collins, aged 4½ months, died
> suddenly at his parents' residence [in] Botany
> Road, Botany ... It appears the deceased suffered
> slightly from a sick stomach for two days previous
> to its death, but the parents did not consider it
> bad enough to call in medical aid. As there are no
> grounds for supposing this child died from any
> but natural causes, an inquest may be dispensed
> with.[12]

For the second time in just fourteen months, Louisa had to call on Mrs Price to wash and dress a corpse in her house. Although she did not then raise the alarm with authorities, Mrs Price would later say she was 'amazed by the child's swollen lips and tongue' and she noted 'the same callousness' that she had seen in Louisa when Charles had died. Still, there was nothing of the magnitude that would 'justify her in speaking to the police' and so she did not. A short time later, the undertaker, John Watters, came with a tiny coffin to take Louisa's tenth child to the Rookwood Cemetery. Despite having cashed her inheritance cheque less than a year earlier, Louisa was by then so broke that she had to bury her baby in grave No. 232 in the paupers' section.

Louisa took the death of yet another of her children in infancy stoically, as all women in all neighbourhoods had to do. By contrast, Michael took the death badly. John had been his first-born and his only son.

'I tried to cheer him all I could,' Louisa would later tell the coroner. 'It was no use. He had a broken-hearted look.'[13]

Some weeks after baby John died, Michael Collins was moved to seek work. We know this because on 23 June 1888, he was carting skins from the slaughter yards at Glebe Island to the sheds owned by Geddes and Sons when he suddenly became ill.[14] He hopped down from the cart and vomited by the roadside. Michael's co-worker, Mr John Walker, at first assumed he must be suffering from the after-effects of drink, but Michael was leaking from the other end as well. He ran into the bushes to pull down his britches. When he came back to the cart, he was clutching his guts and moaning, and seemed to be in agony. Pretty soon afterwards, Michael went home and climbed into his sickbed.

Louisa Collins, as she now was, would later say that she at first assumed that Michael must have been suffering some kind of ailment or contagion and would soon be up and about, but the pain and vomiting would not stop. Still, it was five days before she was able to convince Michael to go with her to see a doctor.

On 28 June 1888, Michael and Louisa left their house at No. 5 Pople's Terrace and headed for the tram stop. On the way they came upon Constable Jeffes, who asked where they were going. Louisa explained that Michael was sick. Constable Jeffes could see that: Michael was near doubled over with the pain. 'What is the matter?' he said, but it was Louisa who answered, saying: 'He has a very bad cold.' It is perhaps worth noting that Constable Jeffes would later say that he was not at all surprised to hear that Michael was on his way to see a doctor because he (Constable Jeffes) had noticed that Michael had been suffering from some kind of sickness, 'like as if he had a sore throat' for 'a few months'.[15]

The couple travelled by tram into Elizabeth Street, where they waited to see a man who would later become an Australian war hero, celebrated for his courage on the beaches of Gallipoli, Dr George Marshall. Michael went into the rooms alone, so Dr Marshall could do some basic tests. He found that Michael's pulse was strong, and he appeared to have no disease of the heart or lungs. There was nothing about Michael's pallor or general appearance to cause alarm. The main thing was he had no appetite, a slight cough, and a terrible pain in his guts. Dr Marshall thought Michael must be suffering 'malaise preceding an attack of fever'[16] and prescribed a few different medicines. They included liquid ammonia syrup and camphor water to make him sweat and help clear his chest and throat of mucus; and some other potions for pain.

Michael thanked the doctor and returned with Louisa to Botany, where he again took to bed. 'I'll be up and about in a day or so,' he told those neighbours who came to check on his progress. In fact, Michael kept getting worse, so much so that Louisa returned to Dr Marshall's offices on 2 July and asked him to accompany her back to Botany to see to her husband again.

'The medicines are not working,' she said. Dr Marshall was surprised. He hadn't been able to diagnosis any particular sickness, but he had still expected Michael to recover quite quickly from whatever ailed him, especially if he'd been taking medicine to rid his body of fever. But no, Louisa said, 'nothing will lie on his stomach. Please, can't you come?'

Dr Marshall hesitated. He had not been paid for Michael's first consultation, and doubted that he'd be paid this time. 'Would it do that I call tomorrow?' he said, but Louisa was adamant.

'No!' she said. 'I fear that he will die in the night.'

The reluctant Dr Marshall accompanied Louisa back to Botany that afternoon, arriving shortly after five p.m. He stayed only a few minutes because he wanted to get the next tram home. Michael was in bed, with a shirt and trousers on, in agonising pain. Dr Marshall examined the sick man's chest with a stethoscope, but his heart seemed strong. He examined his pulse, which was fine, and his tongue, which was clean. In fact, in general condition, Michael seemed much as he'd seemed a few days earlier: he still had a pain in the guts, but by now he also had diarrhoea and was 'passing something like a white of an egg'.[17]

Dr Marshall pondered the matter before asking Michael whether he had eaten any fish or knew of anything likely to disagree with him. Michael said no, so the doctor turned to Louisa and asked the same question: had Michael eaten any tinned fish or was there anything else in his diet that might cause vomiting?

The question seemed to annoy her. 'No!' she said, angrily. 'I know what he has taken and he has not taken fish.'

Dr Marshall looked around the room, scanning for anything that might assist. In the corner, there was a chamber pot. 'Is this you that has vomited this up?' he asked. When Michael said yes, Dr Marshall went to have a closer look. The chamber pot contained three or four ounces of green and smelly vomit and saliva. Dr Marshall poured what he could into a little bottle, and tucked it away for testing.

Turning now to Michael, Dr Marshall said: 'Are you able to pass some urine?' Michael wasn't sure but agreed to try. He got up from the bed and walked unsteadily across the room. There he found the bottle that he had been using to pee. Dr Marshall waited for him to finish, before taking that bottle from him. In the course of scanning the room, he also noticed another bottle — a lemonade bottle — by the bed.

'It is brandy,' Louisa said, 'for the pain.'

Dr Marshall nodded, but still took some of the contents of that bottle for tests, before heading into the kitchen, where he found a third bottle — a medicine bottle — on a shelf. 'Is that the medicine I prescribed?' he said.

'Yes,' Louisa said, 'but why won't the medicines stop the vomiting?'

'They are not directly to stop the vomiting,' Dr Marshall said. They were to ease Michael's pain. Louisa asked whether her husband could have something to stop the vomiting and Dr Marshall agreed to prescribe four more powders[18] to help Michael bring up whatever was ailing him. But in truth, he was perplexed. Michael was apparently in good health — meaning, he was normally a fine figure of a man — yet he hadn't responded to treatment, or even to bed rest. Dr Marshall had considered whether he might be suffering gastro-duodenal catarrh[19] (a disease of the lining membrane of the biliary ducts) but it seemed unlikely in a man so young.

In a search for answers, Dr Marshall later that day called upon a colleague, Dr H Hamilton Marshall, who was also his cousin. The first Dr Marshall subjected the vomit from Michael's chamber pot to some tests — including the Wright's test for arsenic[20] — but nothing of any consequence was found.

Meanwhile Michael's pain intensified, so much so that neighbours from as far away as down the street could hear him moaning and groaning. Many stopped by to see if they could help.

First among the visitors was Constable Jeffes, who would later recall that he had passed Louisa's door at around noon one afternoon and, after calling out 'How is Collins?', Michael himself had summoned him to the bedside.

'How are the pains?' Constable Jeffes said.

Michael said he was in agony, and could not keep anything down.

'You may have caught cold,' Constable Jeffes suggested, 'riding atop the dray, sitting on some wet skins.'

Michael shook his head. No, he said, this was something more serious, and yet he still seemed to think that he would be 'up and about in a day or two'.

When this did not in fact happen, Louisa was again forced to make her way through Sydney's streets in her long skirts to ask Dr Marshall to once more visit the patient.

'She was alarmed about his condition,' Dr Marshall would later tell the coroner, 'but I did not go that day.' Asked why not, Dr Marshall said he still hadn't been paid for the earlier visits. That said, he did go the next day, mainly to prescribe some new potions including bismuth nitric acid (an ancient remedy that is still used as an antidiarrhoeal, in products such as Pink Bismuth); diluted hydrocyanic acid (a highly poisonous substance when undiluted, popular in the nineteenth century as a remedy for both vomiting and spasms); morphine hydrochloride (an opiate used to treat pain) and peppermint water (often used for upset stomachs and diarrhoea).[21]

Unlike the first prescription, which was supposed to make Michael sweat out or cough up his illness, these medicines were meant to be 'sedative and anodyne' — that is, Dr Marshall expected that they would allay irritation, relieve pain and stop the vomiting. He instructed Louisa to fill the prescription as soon as possible, and to direct Michael to gargle the medicine in his throat. Louisa agreed to follow his instructions precisely.

At around four p.m. on 6 July, Dr Marshall returned to Botany to again check on the patient.[22] Upon entering the bedroom, he encountered Louisa 'half-leaning over the bed' as she tried to coax some kind of liquid into Michael's mouth. When Dr Marshall asked her what she was doing, Louisa explained that a neighbour, the grocer Mr Sayers, had told her that Michael was probably suffering from biliousness (an irritable sensation, sometimes caused by a problem with the liver or the gall bladder) and that she should try a vomiting powder, and so she had sent her son Frederick to the chemist with a sixpence.

The chemist, Mr Evan Thomas, was not in the habit of supplying medicines to children, but Frederick handed him a note from his mother, saying: 'Please give bearer a vomiting powder for a man.' Mr Thomas nodded and got to work. Most of his medicines were kept in glass jars behind a raised counter toward the back of his shop, an arrangement designed to deter snatch-and-grabs of dangerous drugs that persists in chemists today. Using special measuring tools, Mr Thomas shook some grains of tartar emetic and fifteen grains of ipecacuanha powder into a piece of chemist's paper and folded it up for Frederick. (Ipecacuanha, which is derived from a plant, induces vomiting. It was a staple of many nineteenth-century homes, where it was used to guard against accidental poisoning, and is still used in some homes today.)

Frederick paid and ran straight home to his mother, who immediately mixed the powder up for Michael.

'I thought it was not likely to be injurious,' Dr Marshall said, and so he did not object as Louisa continued to try to make Michael take it. Finally she succeeded, and a few minutes later, Michael vomited up at least six ounces of green mucus. Dr Marshall opened his leather bag and took another glass bottle — a clean one — and collected what he could. He then turned to the patient: Michael did not look worse than he'd looked a day or so earlier. His pulse was still good. He had a touch of conjunctivitis — an inflammation of the eye — but that had already been coming on during an earlier visit. The patient's main complaint was still the pain in his guts.

Unlike Dr Martin, who had not at any point suspected Charles of being poisoned, Dr Marshall had by this stage begun to wonder whether Michael had taken — or been given — something toxic. The one thing that didn't add up was the fact that he was lingering: as explained earlier, arsenic tends to kill a man quickly, meaning in hours, not days, and certainly not over several weeks. Still, when Michael retched a second time, Dr Marshall collected more of the fresh vomit, not, he would later tell the coroner, 'for the symptoms, but from general suspicions'. He didn't hide from Louisa what he was doing, saying: 'I want this for an arsenic test.'

If Louisa was panicked she did not show it. On the contrary, she went into the kitchen to find a small cup to scoop more vomit out of the chamber. In her absence, Dr Marshall poured all of the vomit into one of his own

bottles and tucked it away. When Louisa returned, he said:
'You should take your husband to the hospital.' (When
the coroner later asked why he'd done that, Dr Marshall
explained that it was partly because it was difficult for him
to travel out to Botany by tram each day, and 'partly I had
asked for my fee and could not get it'.)[23]

As to what Michael made of the suggestion,
Dr Marshall said: 'He made no reply. He was not
communicative. He very seldom was.' That said, he wasn't
surprised that Michael expressed no great desire to go.
'I have met with people prejudiced against going to a
hospital. It is tolerably common,' Dr Marshall said.

Certainly Louisa was dead against it. 'People die in
hospital!' she cried. 'I would rather he died at home if he
is going to die.'

Dr Marshall tut-tutted. 'I didn't think he would die,'
he told the coroner. 'I said he would probably recover if
properly taken care of.'

The following day — Saturday, 7 July — was a chaotic
one, filled with the sound of Louisa wailing as Michael
dipped in and out of consciousness and writhed in pain. A
next-door neighbour, Mrs Ellen Pettit, who had knocked
on the door in the company of her friends Mrs Collis and
a Mrs Saunders, also from the neighbourhood, was so
concerned she ended up staying until well after two o'clock
in the morning.

'When we went there, we met Mrs Collins at the door,
which she kept partially closed,' Mrs Pettit would later say.
'Mrs Collis said: we came to see Mr Collins. [Louisa] took
us into the room and said, do you know who this is, Mick?'

Michael said yes: it's Mrs Pettit and Mrs Collis, 'but I do not know the old lady' (Mrs Saunders). He was, however, in no mood for guests. His throat was burning, and he repeatedly asked Louisa to bring him a drink. The neighbours watched as she came with a cup of cold tea, and then egg and brandy on a spoon, but Michael wanted milk. Louisa asked Mrs Pettit if she would fetch a glass off the mantlepiece, and a very particular glass it was, too: smaller than any other in the house, and probably stolen from the Amos Pier Hotel. Mrs Pettit complied and Louisa took the glass into the kitchen, before coming back with the same glass, now containing what looked like milk. She lifted Michael's head and held the glass to Michael's lips but, after taking just a sip, Michael 'appeared to go off in a fit and remained so for about five minutes. When he came to, he said: "Do you see all the green lights and stars?"'[24]

There were no green lights and stars. Michael Collins was dying.

Louisa called out to her son Arthur to run for Dr Marshall who agreed to go back to Botany that night — but he did not go alone. He arrived instead with a colleague whom Louisa would immediately have recognised: it was Dr Martin, who had tended to Charles when he was sick.

If doctors today comprise a fraternity, then doctors in the nineteenth century were more so. Dr Martin and Dr Marshall not only knew each other, they were friends who compared notes about their patients. So when Dr Marshall mentioned to Dr Martin that he had been treating a man at Pople's Terrace for stomach pains that he couldn't seem to alleviate, Dr Martin was alarmed.

Why, he'd treated a man with similar symptoms at Pople's Terrace not more than a year earlier.

And who was that man?

Charles Andrews.

And did he have a wife?

He did — and her name was Louisa.

It wasn't long before the two doctors figured out that each had treated one of Louisa's husbands. They headed for Botany together, but by the time they arrived, Michael was 'in a very bad state indeed'. Although not yet in a complete stupor — he could answer when asked a question — his eyes had sunk into his head, and Dr Marshall could scarcely find a pulse.

'His skin was cold and clammy,' Dr Marshall said, 'and his face was shrunken. He had hollows in his cheeks, sores on his lips and teeth. He showed great exhaustion. His extremities were cold ... he was [no more than] semi-conscious. He complained of great pain in the stomach, also pain in the left shoulder.'[25]

Dr Marshall knelt by the bed. 'Where did this sickness begin?' he said.

If ever there was an opportunity for Michael to say that he might have been poisoned, it was right then, and you'd think he'd have had his own suspicions: Michael had seen Charles die from a similar illness not much more than a year earlier. Yet he seemed to harbour no doubts about his wife. 'It came on at work,' he replied, his voice weak. 'I cannot think what might have caused it.'

By this stage, Michael had 'not the strength to rise' but Louisa was frantic. She wanted the doctor to see him sitting up, 'as he was all trembles'. She tried to lift Michael in his bed, but Dr Marshall told her to stop. Michael fell back, and from that moment, he wouldn't ever again 'rise and stand on his feet'.

Dr Marshall asked why Louisa had not taken Michael to the hospital.

'If you were sick you would not go to hospital,' she replied, which was probably true. Many people — doctors included — regarded hospitals with suspicion.

'You must give him both brandy and egg,' Dr Marshall said.

'I suppose you think I wouldn't give it him!' Louisa cried.

'Well, you must. He is dying,' Dr Marshall repeated. Placing his hat back on his head, he joined Dr Martin in the other room, before both retreated from the house.

Mrs Pettit watched them go. She was not naïve. She had watched them taking bottles from the kitchen shelves to sniff the contents and now she could see them conversing with each other on the bridge outside the house. The symptoms of arsenic poisoning would have been well known to many people: a burning in the throat, unquenchable thirst, vomiting brown liquid (or blood), clammy skin, difficulty breathing, black stools, black mucus. These were all things that Michael was experiencing, albeit over a long period of time.

Mrs Pettit stepped outside and asked Dr Marshall if there was anything she could do. He told her to remind Louisa to administer brandy for Michael's pain. He then pretended to be in a hurry — he said he wanted to make the last tram. In fact, as soon as Mrs Pettit went back inside, both doctors went to the Botany police station, where Constable Jeffes was on duty with his immediate superior, Senior Constable Abraham Robert Sherwood.

Shortly after eleven p.m. that day, these two police officers went to see Michael Collins.

'Has somebody made you ill?' Senior Constable Sherwood asked him.

Michael groaned, and murmured his usual answer: 'No, no. I'll be up and all right in a few days.'

Senior Constable Sherwood tried again. 'What have you taken that might make you sick?'

Louisa, hovering by the door, interrupted, saying: 'I know what he has taken! It was I who gave him his medicine.'

The policeman turned to Louisa, and regarded her with suspicion. Having spoken at some length to the two doctors, he already believed she was the likely culprit. To that end, both police officers stayed in the house for at least an hour that night, apparently waiting for Michael to die so they could arrange for an undertaker to immediately take his body to the morgue for an autopsy. When Michael still did not die, both officers decided to leave, but not before asking Louisa to send for them if her husband passed away.

Louisa watched them go. According to Mrs Pettit, she had been 'very much agitated' by their presence, and as soon as they were gone, she sat down on the side of the bed as if perplexed. 'Why do the police want me to let them know whether Mick dies for?' she wondered out loud.

'Don't be uneasy, Mrs Collins,' Mrs Pettit said. 'It may be best that they came.'

Louisa didn't agree. 'I can't understand them coming here at all,' she said, angrily. 'God knows I done my duty for him. They need not suspect me for giving him anything.'[26]

There is no easy way to describe the death of a man, especially a young man. Michael Collins fought until the end.

Sunday, 8 July 1888 was the last day of Michael's life. Both Dr Marshall and Dr Martin went to see him, arriving just three hours before he breathed his last.

'I could scarcely feel his pulse at all,' Dr Marshall would tell the coroner. The doctor asked Louisa if she'd been giving him the eggs and brandy, but she'd grown tired of the doctor's accusatory tone. She went up to Michael, put her arm around his neck, leaned over him, and twirled his moustache. 'Poor Mick!' she cried. 'Poor Mick!'

Was it a show? If so, Dr Martin wasn't convinced. He watched Louisa closely. She'd had a cup in her hand when they'd arrived and he made a note of that. A neighbour would later say that Louisa had used the liquid in the cup to try to wet Michael's lips with a quill. There being nothing else to do, the doctors then left the house, only to be replaced by the police, including Senior Constable Sherwood, who watched as Michael reached out to take a cup of brown fluid from the box by the bedside.

'What is in the cup?' the police officer said.

Michael, his voice raspy, replied: 'Cold tea.'

Really? Was Michael absolutely sure that nobody had given him anything? Did he have any suspicions at all? For at least the third time, Michael said no. Senior Constable

Sherwood nodded and retreated, noting as he did the presence of a large number of people all throughout the house: Mrs Pettit was still there, as was Mrs Collis, and at least three other women from the neighbourhood (they were Mrs Johanna Barlington, a Mrs Mudge, and Mrs Rosetta Mapstone). Louisa's daughter, May, was there, in the company of her little friend Florry, as was Arthur, his brother Frederick, and the youngest boys, Edwin and Charles.[27]

All knew when death finally came, for Louisa let out a terrible cry before breaking down over Michael corpse. It was three p.m., or shortly after. Then Louisa got up and began issuing orders: Arthur should take the next tram into the city to tell Dr Marshall that Michael was dead and to get a death certificate. May should run to Mrs Price and ask her to come and lay out Michael's body.

In her skirts and her boots, little May ran.

At 3.50 p.m., Constable Jeffes passed by the door and asked how Michael was getting on.

'He's dead,' Louisa wailed.

Constable Jeffes walked into the bedroom and saw Michael lying on the bed, his eyes vacant. Mrs Price had arrived, and together with Mrs Barlington had stripped Michael's body and begun to wash his corpse. Constable Jeffes told them to move the body to a table in the front room, and he told Louisa to place silver coins over Michael's eyes and cover his face with a sheet. The policeman then left the house to fetch Senior Constable Sherwood. They stayed only long enough to reaffirm that Michael was in fact dead, before heading back to the station to make their report. On their way, they ran into Arthur, who was already returning from town.

'My mother sent me for the death certificate,' Arthur told them, 'but the doctor said he won't give it.'

Alarmed, Constable Jeffes returned with Arthur to Pople's Terrace. He did not want Louisa to arrange to have the body buried. He wanted an inquest, and began collecting evidence, starting with the small teacup, half-full of brown liquid that had been by Michael's bed.

'It's brandy and water!' Louisa cried.

'I need to take it with me,' Constable Jeffes said before looking around for anything else that might have been used to disguise the poison given to Michael. He found a small box of white ointment and a bottle of hair dye, and tucked both of these away. Then he saw the small glass tumbler, that had been on the mantlepiece.

'That is the milk I was giving him,' Louisa said, but when Constable Jeffes tried to get hold of the little glass, she rose from her seat, took the policeman by the arm, and tried to shake him away.

'That is nothing!' she said.

'Stop!' Constable Jeffes said. He had to take 'everything in this place, all the medicine'.

Louisa said: 'There is no medicine here. Dr Marshall has taken it all away.'

Constable Jeffes kept his grip on the glass — Louisa had come close to knocking the contents onto the floor — and continued his search. He found a folded paper with powder inside under the looking glass on the dressing table. 'That is a powder I got for him,' Louisa said when he picked it up, but Constable Jeffes ignored her, and pocketed the powder.

Next, he discovered a small square bottle about three-quarters full of white liquid, with directions upon it. 'I thought the doctor had taken all the medicine away?' he said.

'What do you mean?' Louisa said.

Constable Jeffes showed her the bottle. 'It is medicine ordered by the doctor,' Louisa said. 'I got it from Mr Hamilton.' (Mr Hamilton was another local chemist.) By now, Louisa was hysterical and probably also drunk. She flung herself from the room and indeed tried to leave the house, stopping only when Charles's old friend Mr Sayers bumped into her coming the other way.

'Do not stop me, I want to leave!' Louisa cried. The body of her husband was still laid out on the table and was growing cold. 'I won't live after tomorrow. I'm tired of my life.'

Arthur just seemed confused.

'What are you talking about?' he said of Louisa's claim to not want to live anymore. 'What's going to become of the children?'

'I don't care about the children!' Louisa shouted back. 'I don't care what even becomes of them. My husband is dead! I don't want to live!'

Some who witnessed Louisa's outburst that night regarded her with sympathy: her baby had died not two months previously, and now her husband — her second — was dead, too. Others believed that Louisa was crying out because she could see her future: she had gotten away with the murder of Charles, but now that she had killed a second husband she'd pushed her luck too far.

Alarmed, Mrs Barlington ran to get Constable Jeffes, saying: 'You must come! Mrs Collins is threatening to harm herself!'

Constable Jeffes went to the door, where he found Louisa slumped against the door frame. 'Where do you think you are going?' he said.

The wretched, tear-streaked Louisa replied: 'For a walk to the beach. To the brickyards. I don't want live anymore.' (Besides being swampy, Botany was replete with good-quality shale that was quarried to turn into bricks.)

'You will keep quiet,' Constable Jeffes said, 'or I will take you to the police station.'

Louisa slumped down further, but only until Constable Jeffes' back was turned, when she again made a show of trying to get out of the front door and into the street.

'You will stay!' Constable Jeffes said.

Finally, Louisa nodded and eventually stopped sobbing, but, just as some semblance of calm had been established, she asked Arthur to get Michael's clothes and bring them to her. Arthur went into the bedroom and fetched the trousers and vest that Michael had been wearing before Mrs Price stripped him, and gave both items to his mother. Louisa quickly went through the pockets, taking out her husband's watch and chain, before throwing the clothes on the floor and again making for the door.

This time it was Arthur who managed to make her go back to her seat.

'I have sixty sovereigns in my pocket,' she cried. 'I won't pay the doctor until he gives the death certificate!'

'I said, you must be quiet!' Constable Jeffes said. 'You must not leave the house' — and then, to ensure that Louisa did not try to leave, he called for another officer to stand guard by the front door all night, until a cart came to take Michael's body away.

CHAPTER 4

Exhume the Bodies: The first inquest

10, 17 and 26 July 1888
The Coroner's Court at Chancery Square,
Hyde Park Barracks, Sydney
PRESIDING: Mr Henry Shiell JP

There was a time in New South Wales when both autopsy and inquest were done together. The body, presuming it was available, would be laid out on a plain, wooden table in the (barely ventilated) Dead Room at The Rocks. A jury would then assemble to watch while the corpse was opened up to see if the cause of death could be ascertained. (There were only two tables in the Dead Room, so in cases of mass death, such as in fires or shipwrecks, the bodies would be laid out in the hallway and opened there.)

When this arrangement became intolerable, especially to passers-by, who could clearly see the goings-on through the windows, new rooms were leased at the Observer

Hotel, which charged ten shillings for each autopsy carried out on the premises.

By the time of Michael Collins's death in July 1888, a proper morgue had been opened near what is now the Central Station terminus, to enable the autopsy to be carried out in relative privacy. That said, juries were still invited to view the body and whatever organs needed to be removed.

Three doctors were present at Michael Collins's autopsy: Dr Marshall, Dr Martin, and the kind-hearted Dr Frederick Milford, of St Vincent's Hospital. Dr Milford had been resident in New South Wales for thirty years, and had worked as a surgeon at St Vincent's for almost all of that time, including in the early days, when surgery was done in the bedroom of a house in Potts Point. His reputation was for the tender care of his patients and for his occasionally startling antics in court: he'd once held the skull of a murder victim aloft for the jury, while explaining how he'd come to his conclusions about the cause of death.[1]

Dr Milford began his examination of Michael Collins's corpse precisely twenty-eight hours after death, or at seven p.m. on 9 July 1888. As was the custom, the post-mortem began with a close survey of Michael's naked body on the plinth. It was, Dr Milford said, 'fairly nourished, muscular, but somewhat thin'. Rigor mortis was present. There was no obvious external injury, as would have been the case had Michael been shot, stabbed, or strangled, but Michael did have a six-inch long wound on his right leg midway between his knee and his ankle. The injury wasn't new, but Dr Milford could tell from the way it had healed that it had at some point been quite badly infected.[2]

With the external examination over, Dr Milford made a firm, clean slice down the centre of Michael's chest, to expose the organs. The three doctors leaned in, and then reeled back: Michael's stomach, intestines and bowel were tender and inflamed.

Using both hands Dr Milford reached inside, cut Michael's stomach free and placed it in a clean dish. Working quickly, he tied knots in both ends to stop the contents splashing out before turning it over so he could have a better look. The stomach was distended and covered in raw, circular patches, some of which were more than six centimetres across. When Dr Milford gently picked the stomach up and untied one end to let the liquid out, he noticed both a foul smell and a strange colour: instead of being pink and clear, the liquid was dark brown with a slight greenish tint.

Putting the stomach aside, Dr Milford turned to Michael's other organs. The liver, kidneys, and a portion of Michael's spleen were taken and put into sealed glass jars. The oesophagus was examined and found to have dark vertical marks on the surface. The spleen seemed quite swollen, the liver slightly enlarged, and the pericardium (the sac enclosing the heart) contained about four ounces of fluid.

Taken all together, these symptoms suggested to Dr Milford that the cause of Michael's death had been 'a fatal syncope' (or fatal collapse) probably caused by the 'presence of arsenic in the body'. On the other hand, death had been 'prolonged or protracted' (which probably meant that if Michael had been poisoned by arsenic, it must have been introduced to his system in small doses, over an extended period of time).[3]

More tests would have to be done, so Dr Milford took the jars with Michael's organs inside and stored them on a shelf, where they were supposed to stay until Constable Jeffes came to pick them up again.

The results of the initial post-mortem were then reported to the coroner, Mr Henry Shiell JP, who would conduct the formal inquest into the cause of Michael's death.

To be clear, an inquest is not a trial. The rules of evidence are quite different, in that evidence presented at an inquest may prove inadmissible at trial, on the grounds that it is only hearsay. Also, the aim of an inquest is not to find somebody guilty of a particular offence or to pass sentence upon them. The aim of an inquest is to ascertain the likely cause of death, and then, if suspicion falls upon somebody in particular, to refer the matter to the courts, where the stakes are much higher and the rules of evidence much stricter.

While it can today take months and even years for an inquest to be held into a suspicious death — to cite one example, the inquest into the likely death of the Queensland schoolboy Daniel Morcombe was held nine years after he disappeared — the inquest into the death of Michael Collins opened on 10 July 1888, just two days after he died.[4]

It was held at a place called Chancery Square,[5] which sounds posh but was really just the fancy name given to some rooms in the Hyde Park Barracks at the southern end of Macquarie Street.[6] (The building still stands: it was commissioned by Governor Lachlan Macquarie and designed by the convict architect Francis Greenway[7] as a place to house convicts, before becoming an immigration centre for destitute Irish girls; a vaccination centre; and later an asylum for women who were homeless, single and pregnant, or mentally ill.)

From the late 1880s, the city coroner, Mr Shiell JP, also worked from the barracks. His workload was enormous: more than 600 people died in suspicious circumstances in New South Wales in 1888. Many had been murdered, but some had died in fires or had drowned, and the coroner was responsible for the investigations into those deaths, too.

Of course Mr Shiell had no way of knowing this, but by the time the inquest into the death of Michael Collins came before him, he himself had less than a year to live. Born to British parents in the West Indies in 1826, Mr Shiell had endured the death of his father, an outbreak of smallpox, another of cholera and a major earthquake before moving to New South Wales in 1853. One of his first jobs was as a police magistrate at Lang's Crossing Place (now known as Hay) where he quickly developed a reputation for being too harsh on petty offenders.[8] Indeed, the local newspaper in Hay, the *Pastoral Times,* complained openly of Mr Shiell's 'cruelty on one occasion to a woman, and of his general inefficiency as a public officer' — and it wasn't as if his own record was unblemished. Upon leaving Hay, Mr Shiell had been forced to sell his buggy, his house and most of his possessions to make his way out of debt; upon his death, he would leave his young widow destitute.[9]

In any case, Mr Shiell empanelled a jury of twelve men to inspect the body of Michael Collins and assist him to find the cause of death.[10] Over the course of the inquest, he would take statements from Louisa, her neighbours, police and doctors; and he asked the New South Wales government analyst Mr William Mogford Hamlet to conduct the chemical analysis of the contents of Michael's stomach and other items taken from Louisa's home.[11]

Mr Hamlet was a short man with a tiny frame and a little pointed beard. He had arrived in New South Wales just five years previously, uncertain about what he might do, other than that which he always did, which was walk — but more about his walking in a moment. Even as a small boy, Mr Hamlet adored science. The beakers and the Bunsen burners had him in their thrall, but the school he attended in Bristol offered no science, or at least no chemistry classes. Much of Mr Hamlet's early learning therefore came from chemistry books he found in British libraries. As a young man, he attended evening classes before training more formally at the Royal College of Chemistry, London, where he obtained first-class honours and won the Queen's medal. Upon arrival in New South Wales, Mr Hamlet took a position as a chemistry lecturer.[12]

Besides being a passionate scientist, Mr Hamlet was also, for want of a better term, a health nut, obsessed with figuring out the relationship between food, exercise and general wellbeing. To that end, he conducted a range of walking experiments, usually on himself. For example, in 1919, Mr Hamlet and a similarly enthusiastic walking colleague from the Department of Health, Mr Henry J

Tompkins — author of the famous walking handbook *With Swag and Billy*[13] — walked from Sydney to Melbourne, a tramp during which Mr Hamlet wore out three pairs of boots.[14] He also walked from Sydney to Brisbane twice, the aim being not simply to get there but to conduct experiments upon the body along the way. Mr Hamlet placed strict limits on the weight of the load he could carry. He also had a number of rules about pace and stride, which was to be the military 30-inch step (and the speed strictly three miles an hour). He would weigh himself before each walk, and then after, and also all the food and water he consumed. He liked to keep his weight strictly to 59 kilograms. He would measure his blood pressure and take his own pulse, and write all of his findings down in meticulous handwriting in his journal, and then he would try to come to conclusions about the energy he had expended. Mr Hamlet was in every sense a pedant, and therefore the perfect person to become government analyst, responsible for such life-saving tasks in the new colony as testing meat and water for bacteria, and drugs for toxicity.

One can only imagine the frustration of a man as fastidious as Mr Hamlet with the way the samples from Louisa's house had been handled. The so-called 'chain of custody' — that is, the process by which items are seized and stored before being delivered to the laboratory — was not, in the context of a hanging case, ideal. Most of the items had been handled by several people, or moved from one container to the next. For example, Constable Jeffes would testify during one trial that he had poured the contents of the small teacup that Michael had been using into a brandy flask, assuring the coroner: 'It was clean. I washed it. I got it [the flask] for the purpose of carrying it.'[15] Constable Jeffes had also been responsible for handling the small glass of milk in a manner that astounded at least one correspondent to the *Evening News*:

> [That] glass of milk ... was in his possession for two days ... unsecured in an open cigar box, neither locked or sealed up. I respectfully submit that this glass ... should have been, without a moment's delay, sealed up in the presence of two responsible witnesses, and delivered so *sealed* to the Government analyst. It is obvious ... that this glass was not always under his observation. Such a statement is simply ridiculous.[16]

Still, Mr Hamlet got to work. According to his notes, he had received from Constable Jeffes a sealed glass jar containing a human stomach; a small brandy flask containing liquid; a chipped box containing ointment; a glass tumbler containing a liquid; a powder wrapped in paper; a square bottle containing medicine; a bottle containing hair dye; a bottled labelled urine; a bottle containing vomited matter; and an empty cup.[17] From Dr Marshall, Mr Hamlet received one bottle containing vomited matter, one bottle of medicine and one bottle of brandy, making up thirteen items in all.

On examining Michael's stomach, there was no question in Mr Hamlet's mind that something wicked — 'some powerful irritant' — had passed through it. Just by looking he could see that the stomach had a 'very discoloured appearance. There were yellow and greenish patches and extensive ecchymosis [an effusion of blood] pouring from it'.

Mr Hamlet unsealed the jar, subjected both stomach and its contents to chemical analysis, and immediately found 'between two- and three-quarter grains of arsenic'. There was a faint trace of arsenic in the urine sample, and in the vomit sample.[18] In short, there was no real doubt in Mr Hamlet's mind that Michael Collins had died of arsenic poisoning.

A lazy mind would leap from there to the idea that Louisa must have given the arsenic to Michael Collins, but Mr Hamlet did not have a lazy mind. The question for him now became: where had the arsenic come from? Mr Hamlet tested the liquid in the flask. It was brandy and water. One bottle of medicine contained a plain zinc ointment; the white powder that Frederick had purchased from the chemist was 'an ordinary gray [vomiting] powder'. The square bottle of medicine contained bismuth and peppermint, and the hair dye was just hair dye, containing nitrate of silver and water. Then he examined the small glass tumbler that Louisa had filled with what she said was milk. The result here was different: the glass was found to contain some milk and some thickening matter such as starch or arrowroot — and a tenth of a grain of arsenic.

Mr Hamlet packed his equipment away and reported his findings to the coroner. He was, he said, 'of the opinion that the cause of death of Michael Peter Collins was arsenical poisoning'.[19]

Dr Milford, who had assisted with the autopsy, agreed. He told the coroner that the inflamed nature of the stomach and the red-raw, weeping wounds on the other organs looked to him like they were caused by arsenical poisoning.

Mr Shiell wanted to know how arsenic might come to be found in the human body. 'Must it be introduced?' he said.

Dr Milford nodded: 'It must be introduced.'[20]

Michael's doctor, Dr Marshall, agreed, telling the coroner that Michael's symptoms — in particular the vomiting and the acute pain in his guts — 'together with the results of the autopsy, lead me to conclude that the patient died of arsenical poisoning'.[21]

Dr Martin, who had been Charles's doctor, thought so, too.

'I saw the deceased Michael Peter Collins in company with Doctor Marshall [when he was] in a very low condition, pulse being very weak, the extremities cold, the face sunken and the whole denoting a state bordering on collapse,' he said. '[He] complained principally of pain in his left shoulder. I saw that he was dying and after leaving the house, Doctor Marshall and I consulted together and we concluded to report the matter to the police.'[22]

Mr Shiell wanted to know: why was that?

'We thought the deceased was dying under very suspicious circumstances,' Dr Martin said.[23] Also, not much more than a year earlier, he had treated Louisa Collins's first husband, 'and the symptoms in both cases were remarkably similar'.[24] He'd also been on hand shortly after Louisa's tenth child, the baby John Collins, died at the age of four months.

This was enough for Mr Shiell, who ordered Louisa's arrest for the murder of Michael Collins — and the exhumation of the bodies of Charles and baby John from Rookwood Cemetery.[25]

The responsibility for taking Louisa into custody was granted to Senior Constable Sherwood. He arrived at her house on Pople's Terrace shortly before six p.m. on 12 July to find that Louisa had been drinking. Her hungry children — all of those who still lived at home — sat waiting at the kitchen table for their tea. Louisa's head was lolling on her shoulders and her mood was maudlin. 'Poor Mick,' she said, stumbling with her pot from the stove to the plates. 'Poor Mick.'[26]

Senior Constable Sherwood called her away from the little ones into the front room, and explained that she would have to go with him.

'But will I be coming back?' she said. Before Senior Constable Sherwood could answer, Louisa sat down quickly in one of the wooden chairs, put her hands over her face and said: 'I know I am not coming back again.'[27]

'We got her dressed and put her in the front room,' Senior Constable Sherwood told the coroner. (By dressed, he probably meant dressed for going out, which would have meant ensuring that she had her hat, cape and walking boots.) 'She was under the influence of drink at this time ... I then took her to Darlinghurst Police Station.' (Remarkably, it seems that they walked, the distance being at least six kilometres, and it would have been dark.) 'I charged her on suspicion with having caused the death of her husband Michael Peter Collins at Botany on or about the 8th day of July … She did not make any reply but answered some questions put to her by me … She said I gave my husband the medicine the doctor ordered. I asked her what medicine. She said the medicine in the bottle, some brandy and egg, some egg and milk.'

'I asked her if she had given him anything else,' Senior Constable Sherwood said. 'She said a man named Arthur Hamill prescribed some beer and egg for him, also a vomiting powder. The beer and egg did not seem to do him any good.'[28]

The accused has a right to remain silent. Anything they do or say can and will be used in court — or at an inquest — against them. That was as true in New South Wales in 1888 as it is today.

Louisa Collins was not required to give a statement in her own defence at the inquest into Michael's death, and yet she did give what was described as a 'long, rambling statement'[29] and then a second, follow-up statement to Mr Shiell — and the portrait she painted of having been without debts when Charles died and of being dragged back to desperate poverty by her new husband was indeed used against her in the later trials.

Louisa began by explaining that she was only just married to Michael, and that they had only recently moved from a house in Johnson's Lane back to Pople's Terrace.

Her family was then, she said, 'clear of debt … I had £25 in gold'.

Her new husband wasn't a hard worker the way Charles had been, but he had found 'two or three half days' work' in Botany before suddenly getting the sack, after which he was 'eight weeks idle'.

Money grew tight.

'One Saturday during that eight weeks, [Michael] said, "Louie, will you give me £1?"' Louisa said in her statement. '"I'll find a way of making money," naming a certain gambling house in George Street. I told him I had a great horror of gambling however I gave him the £1.

'He came home that night at half-past-eleven. He fetched me £4.10s. He was very pleased. He said it was better than hard work. He said: "If I had had £20 tonight I could have fetched you £100, just as easy as I did that."'

Louisa was apparently dazzled by this sudden bonus and yet — by her account — she remained cautious. 'He said, "Will you give me £20 next Saturday?" I told him it was a great risk. He said he felt sure he could get me £100 or more with it. I gave the £20 on the following Saturday. He did not come home till the last tram. I was in bed but not asleep. I said, "Mick, is that you?"

'He made me no answer, but struck a match and lit the candle. I never shall forget his look. He sat down on the side of the bed. He said, "Louie, I've lost all the money." He commenced to cry, and I did so too. I could not help it.

'He said, "I am out of work and lost all the money." I told him I would forgive him when I saw he was in such a terrible state of anxiety and misery. He said, "What shall I do at all to get work?"'[30]

Louisa had no idea: the boom that had accompanied the discovery of gold in both New South Wales and Victoria had long since burnt out, and the economy was sliding toward a serious depression that would see the closure of several banks, including the Federal Bank of Australia, when it simply ran out of money. Many pastoral families were ruined, and many industrialists, including wool merchants, shut up shop.

Restless and upset, Michael had climbed into the bed beside Louisa.

'He came to bed but could not sleep,' she said. 'He got up the next morning and only had a cup of tea. He said: "I wonder where I could go for work." He sat thinking for some time in the chair. At last he says, "I think I'll go up the Illawarra line"' (meaning on the train to Illawarra, where several coal mines had opened).

'I gave him £1. He said if he got work he would be away a week. He went up the Illawarra line and not knowing the stations, being a stranger on that line, I thought he would be away a week [but] he came back that night. I was surprised to see him. He was perfectly speechless. I asked him what was the matter. He says don't ask me. He says I have ruined myself and you to [sic]. I say tell me then what has happened.

'He said "I went six miles further than my ticket was for. The guard asked me for my ticket and when he saw the distance I was he caught hold of me and pulled me out of the carriage on to the platform and I struck him … When I got to the Railway Station in Sydney the guard said I'll let you off if you give me £3.10s. I had no money on me but the remainder of the £1 and said to the guard, 'I have no money on me if you wait till I pawn my watch, I'll give you the money.'"'

Louisa continued: 'He [Michael] said he pawned his watch and took the money back to the station and the guard let me [him] come home. He was thoroughly broken hearted. He said, "Louie I wish you had got someone else besides me. I have dragged you down to ruin." I told him not to mind, that I would put up with it.'

Louisa had by then had her pale and sickly baby, John, and was doubtless still nursing. Michael had promised to work harder at providing for his growing family, and in the days that followed, he did find work at Geddes and Sons but 'he just worked two weeks when the baby died. That sent us further into debt and trouble. I had no money. I borrowed £1.2s.6d from Mrs Bullock, Draper, Botany, to pay for the ground to bury the child. I have never been able to pay it back. I owe Doctor Martin £1.1s.0 for his visit. I have never been able to pay him.'

By Louisa's account, Michael's mood after his baby died was disconsolate. 'After the funeral of the child, [he] went to work,' she said, although he also said: 'There is no use of me working. My wages will never pay the … debts.'

Then, Louisa said, 'a month ago last Monday, I was brushing his overcoat and in the breast pocket I found a package in white paper. It had no writing on it. I opened it. There was a large tea spoonful of white stuff like salts only much finer. It had a bright and sparkling appearance. It had no smell and I put my tongue to it and it made my mouth hot and watery during the rest of the day. I could not help spitting.'

When Michael came home that evening to the empty cradle and the hungry children, Louisa asked him: 'Mick, what little package is that in your coat pocket?'

Michael, who had been a married man for less than a year, was indignant. He said: 'Have you been at my pockets?'

Louisa told him: 'I was brushing the coat and saw it there.'

'I'll search your pocket after tea, and see what's in it,' Michael said.

Louisa would not be deterred. 'I said, tell me what it is that's in your pocket?' she said, in her statement.

Michael was exasperated. 'I'm damned if I know what's the name of it. A man at Waterloo gave it to me to take in a little water for a lump I have in my groin.'[31]

Careful readers will understand what Louisa was getting at here: she was hinting at the idea that Michael — much like Mr Snelson — had grown so disconsolate over his debts and prospects that he'd decided to take some kind of poison, to end his life, or else she was suggesting that he'd unwittingly taken arsenic, in a powder prepared for his groin. This was not as fanciful as it may seem. Arsenic had for years been used to treat infections, although only in tiny doses. It could also be found in nineteenth-century fabric dyes and carpets, and in some cosmetics. Indeed, the term 'arsenic eater' comes from a late nineteenth-century fad for eating small amounts of arsenic to induce pallor in the skin.

Louisa told the coroner that Michael's groin affliction was something 'from which I know he suffered. I believed him'.

The couple had no further argument about the powder, but as Michael was removing his trousers to go to bed, Louisa asked him: 'Will you take some of that tonight then?'

'No, not tonight,' Michael said. 'It's too cold.'

Michael rose the next morning at around four a.m. He lit the candle, put on his hat and looked at Louisa, still lying in their bed, as if to bid her a gentle farewell.

'He put his hand up to the coat I spoke of before,' Louisa said, 'and took this package out, and put it into his trousers pocket. I said, "Will you take some of that now?" but Michael again said "No, I'll take it over at the stables."'

Michael was home again by seven a.m., and although Louisa had prepared 'meat he was always very fond of', he pushed the plate away.

'He said he wanted some sops,' Louisa said. 'I gave him a clean basin, and he made some sops himself.'

Then, just as suddenly as he'd sat down, Michael got up again and raced outside 'down to the yard, retching dreadful after eating the sops, the first time I had ever seen him retch. I said: "Whatever is the matter with you?" I said did you take some of that medicine?" meaning the stuff he took away. He said, "No. I did not."'

Louisa was alarmed. 'I said: Will you have some more breakfast? He said no, give me a sixpence. I hadn't a sixpence and gave him a shilling.'

'He was away all day as usual,' Louisa said, 'and came home to his supper.' He tried to force some food down, but had no appetite, and what he did get down soon came bubbling up again. Michael went to the bedroom and lay down on the bed, cramping and complaining. He had been there only a few minutes when he called out for Louisa to fetch him a small glass.

'I asked if a cup would not do,' Louisa said, but Michael wanted the glass.[32]

Louisa knew which glass he meant: it was the small glass, commonly known as a 'nobbler' (in court, this particular glass would sometimes be called the 'tumbler') from the Amos Pier Hotel. Such glasses were generally used to serve shots of hard liquor. They only had one like it, and such a glass wouldn't normally be used to serve milk or cold tea, because it's far too small. Then again, Michael was sick, and had been retching, and perhaps wanted only a sip of something for his dry mouth. In any case, Louisa found the nobbler and took it to their bedroom.

'I was surprised to see him sitting on the side of the bed with his new trousers on,' she said. 'I said, are you going out? He replied no you won't mind me sleeping in these trousers.'[33]

This mention of trousers — and of the fact that Michael had been sleeping in them — was an important element of Louisa's story that Michael, a man upset about his debts and the death of his son and perhaps overwhelmed by his new responsibility to Louisa's children, might have committed suicide. Perhaps, like Mr Snelson, he was keeping the arsenic in his trouser pocket. The fact that he was wearing trousers in bed was strange, but it would have allowed him to access the poison, even when barely able to rouse himself.

Louisa told the coroner that she did not object to Michael keeping his trousers on. 'I said no if you are comfortable I am satisfied. I said "whatever do you want this glass for?" He replied I want to rinse my mouth out with a little water that's all.'[34]

That, too, made some sense. Louisa had herself — or so she claimed — experienced an awful taste in her mouth after she had tasted a tiny amount of the powder she'd found in Michael's coat pocket.

'I believed him,' she said, earnestly, 'and went to bed.' But once again they got no rest: 'I was awake in the middle of the night by him retching dreadful,' Louisa said. 'I said there is something strange the matter with you. He said it is only the cold that I have.'

The retching did not stop all weekend, and by Monday, the glass was back on the mantlepiece, and poor Michael was flat on his back, pale and exhausted. Yet he still pulled on his work shirt and went to work, carting skins for Geddes. He retired only after his colleague saw him dash into the bushes to spurt out diarrhoea.

'I asked him to go with me to see the doctor,' Louisa said, 'and we went to Doctor Marshall [and] when we got home that night, he took a spoonful [of the medicine that Dr Marshall had prescribed] and said he was sure it would do him no good, it was throwing money away.' Michael then climbed back into bed, and passed the hours sweating and worrying about the debts that would accumulate while he was sick, saying at one point: 'The bailiffs will be in the house, there's nothing surer.' Every knock on the door during that week — the second week of his illness — 'he turned as pale as death and would say "Oh, Christ, I thought that was the Bailiffs."'[35] Michael's fear in this regard was perhaps well placed: one of the people who visited after he was laid out dead was Mr Edward William Pople of Waterloo, who owned Pople's Terrace, who would later tell the judge at Lousia's first trial that she still owed him 'about £4 or £5 for rent' and complained that she 'took some of the furniture away in a van ... I believe she had means to pay if she had wished.'[36]

Coming now to the end of her statement, Louisa beseeched the coroner to believe her version of events. She had no reason to kill Michael — 'I tended to him with great care' — and although she could see how it looked — one husband dead, and then another, and each suffering the same symptoms — she still hoped that the court would consider an explanation other than murder.

'There was two unfortunate things I done during his illness,' Louisa said. 'That was to take over that glass which he had used so often without having once washed it out, and to put the trousers in water which was taken off [him] after he was dead.'[37]

Also, it wasn't like she had anything to gain. 'His life was not insured,' Louisa said. 'He is in no lodge or any society ... he has left me penniless and in debt.'[38]

Mr Shiell delivered his summation of the evidence to the jury on 26 July 1888. He told the jury that all the evidence suggested that Michael had died of arsenical poisoning.[39] Traces of arsenic had been found in Michael's stomach and in the little nobbler glass from which he'd been drinking.

To his mind, this meant that Louisa must have poisoned Michael.

However, there was a flaw in this theory, and it was major: no one had yet been able to link Louisa to the purchase of any arsenic. In fact, when Senior Constable Sherwood had taken the stand at the coroner's inquest, he'd clearly explained how hard he'd looked for arsenic, and how none had been found.

'We looked for arsenic especially,' he'd said. 'There was not even a paper, nothing. I searched [Michael Collins's] pockets, the yard, under the beds, everything. There was no arsenic that I could find. I made searches at three chemists — Mr Thomas at Botany Road, Waterloo; Mr Hamilton in Regent Street, and Mr Osman in George Street. I found no trace in the last two places. I inquired if anyone [from] Botany had purchased arsenic … I could trace it to no one. There was no trace of it.'[40]

Mr Shiell acknowledged Louisa's statement in which she'd suggested that Michael may have poisoned himself, but he also made it very clear to the jury that he, for one, did not believe her.

'Gentlemen,' he said, 'do you think for one moment that [Michael Collins] administered the arsenic to himself … in small doses?' Mr Shiell couldn't accept that, saying: 'When arsenic [is] taken to procure death it [is] generally taken in large doses. This man died from small doses given to him from time to time … the question for [the jury] to consider was: Who gave him that poison, he himself or his wife?'

Mr Shiell acknowledged the fact that no arsenic (beyond that trace found in the tumber) had been discovered in Louisa's house, but told the jury that this was always part of the problem in a poisoning case. 'A woman that [is] poisoning anybody [does] not take anyone into her confidence,' he said. The use of poison was different from murder by shotgun or stabbing. The point of using poison was to cover up the murder and that, in Mr Shiell's opinion, was what Louisa had done. If the jury agreed, and wanted to see Louisa charged with murder, now, he said, was the time to say so.[41] (As previously mentioned, an inquest is not a trial. The point of an inquest is to ascertain the likely cause of death, as opposed to holding a particular individual to account.)

Still, the statement of the jury at the first inquest was both clear, and devastating. In short, it said:

> The deceased Michael Peter Collins met his
> death by arsenical poisoning, that poison being
> administered by his wife, Louisa Collins.[42]

Mr Shiell read the note and nodded. 'I entirely concur,' he said.

With that, Louisa was remanded into custody at the notorious Darlinghurst Gaol.[43]

CHAPTER 5

The Second Inquest: Four jars of human remains

14 July, 3 and 4 August 1888
The Coroner's Court at Chancery Square,
Hyde Park Barracks, Sydney
PRESIDING: Mr Henry Shiell JP

Louisa Collins had become the prime suspect in the murder of her husband Michael upon discovery of arsenic in his body, yet she maintained that Michael must have poisoned himself, either deliberately or by accident.

What, though, if arsenic were also found in the body of Louisa's first husband, or indeed in the body of her recently deceased son, John? Her fate would surely then be sealed, and so, on a cold, wet day late in July 1888, a deputy inspector from the water police, Solomon Hyam, trekked out to Rookwood Cemetery with the undertaker, Mr John Watters, to dig the bodies from the ground.[1]

Charles had been buried in grave 436 in the Church of England section, and his coffin was first to be taken from the cemetery aboard a cart to the South Sydney morgue, where Mr Watters was forced to watch while the lid was opened, so he could swear that the remains inside were those of the same man, Charles Andrews, that he had buried.

Baby John had been buried in grave 232 of the paupers' section at Rookwood. His little coffin was likewise taken to the morgue, where Mr Watters declared that yes, the remains were that of the child he had buried.

Next came the autopies, conducted this time by a man who was both a doctor and, of all things, a magician. His name was Dr Samuel Thomas Knaggs, and, in addition to saving lives, he liked to save gullible people. Proudly a man of science, Dr Knaggs was contemptuous of mind readers, palm readers, crystal-ball gazers, clairvoyants and, especially, phrenologists (people who claimed to be able to deduce a person's intelligence and other characteristics, such as their propensity for crime, from the size and shape of their skull). Dr Knaggs had trained as a magician specifically to expose the tricks behind such 'miracles' as levitation. (For the record, Dr Knaggs was not without strange beliefs of his own: in one of his several books, *Recreations of an Australian Surgeon*, published in 1888, the year of Louisa's trials, he claimed that tea — ordinary leaf tea — was harmful in the absence of food; dangerous if taken too long after a fast or if given to the poor and underfed; was terrible in low temperatures and worse in hot climates; and should under no circumstances be taken with a principal meal.[2])

Some thought Dr Knaggs a bit crazy, but the doctor took his responsibilities seriously, approaching the task of inquiring into the deaths of Charles and John with solemnity.

Charles's actual autopsy must have been ghastly to perform. His coffin lid had split, and muddy earth had poured inside. The corpse had been lying in filthy water for more than a year and was putrid. The slush had rotted the head and chest; the arms and legs had completely disintegrated. Earth from around the coffin was stirred in with the human remains.

Still, Dr Knaggs did what he could. He lifted Charles's corpse and placed it on the wooden table. Dr Marshall and Dr Martin were both present, and it was Dr Martin who reached into the stomach to scoop up what would later be described as an 'indistinguishable pasty mass'[3] for testing. He also removed two badly decomposed kidneys. These remains were sealed into three jars labelled 'Charles Andrews'.

Attention now turned to the tiny corpse of John. There hadn't been much to exhume. He'd lived for just four short months, and although he'd been in the ground only since April — it was by now the third week of July — there wasn't much left of him. Dr Knaggs removed about 10 ounces of a 'greyish-white matter' and sealed it into a fourth jar labelled 'John Collins'.

These four jars were delivered to Mr Hamlet, who conducted tests similar to those he'd conducted on Michael Collins. He would later tell the coroner that in the body of John, he'd found no arsenic, but in one of the three jars that contained the remains of Charles, he had detected 'a large quantity of ptomaine [bacteria caused by rotting flesh]; a considerable quantity of sulphur; a grain and a quarter of bismuth ... and a minute trace of arsenic'.[4]

A minute trace of arsenic.

On the face of it, such a finding was surely devastating for Louisa. But what did it really mean in New South Wales in 1888 to find a minute trace — estimated by Mr Hamlet to have been 1/500th of a part of a grain — in a corpse that had been in a sodden coffin for more than fourteen months? In 1888, the science surrounding arsenic and medicine was not what it is today. Still, most experts — Mr Hamlet included — did understand that it is not uncommon to find low levels of arsenic in soil and water. Arsenic is often present in fish, especially shellfish (which was a key part of the diet in Botany in 1888) and drinking water. A person might test positive for arsenic after breathing in sawdust or smoke from arsenic-treated wood, or if they lived in an area with elevated levels of arsenic thanks to nearby noxious industries (Botany was certainly such an area). Arsenic can be inhaled or ingested, but it can also enter the body through wounds in the skin.

Yet Mr Shiell did not spend much time asking Mr Hamlet about the ways in which arsenic might enter the body, nor about the ways in which arsenic might turn up in tests done on old, decayed bodies, exhumed from broken coffins. Instead, he asked Mr Hamlet whether the fact that no arsenic or, as in this case, only small amounts of arsenic meant that 'the deceased person *did not* die from arsenical poisoning?'[5]

At this distance, that seems like an odd question for the supposedly impartial coroner to be asking. Essentially, what Mr Shiell wanted to know was whether Louisa might still have killed her first husband with arsenic, despite the fact that only tiny amounts — nothing, really — had been found in his remains.

At least one of the twelve jurors sitting in on the second inquest seemed eager to offer an explanation as to why more arsenic hadn't been found. Unnamed, he called from his seat, saying: 'If water was to get into the coffin ... the water might dissolve the arsenic!'

True, but what of the fact that Charles's doctor, Dr Martin, had initially put Charles's death down to acute gastritis? Perhaps unsurprisingly, Dr Martin had changed his mind. He now believed that Charles had died of arsenical poisoning, so much so that 'even if arsenic had *not* been found in the remains, I would still have the same opinion. I am relying not only on the symptoms.'

No? Upon what then did he rely?

'I was struck with the idea that she [Louisa] had her eye on a second husband,' Dr Martin declared.

What on earth made him think so?

'It was her manner,' Dr Martin said. 'She seemed indifferent to [Charles's] fate.'

Two of Louisa's neighbours — Mrs Law and Mrs Collis — agreed, and lined up to tell the coroner how gleeful Louisa had appeared after Charles died. She'd held a party in the empty house on Pople's Terrace; she'd moved Michael into Charles's bed with haste; she'd refused to wear mourning clothes; and she had arranged for Charles to sign a new will under which she inherited everything.

Louisa called out from her seat, saying that the fact that Charles wanted to ensure that he could continue to provide for her and the children after his death merely 'showed that he was a sensible and sober man!'

Mr Shiell asked her to be quiet. He'd heard enough. He turned to the jury. In the matter of John's death, he was prepared to give Louisa the benefit of the doubt. No arsenic had been found in the body of little John, and while there were cases where arsenic had produced fatal results 'without leaving a trace behind', it was more than likely that John — a sickly baby born to a poor mother over the age of forty — had died of natural causes.

The case of Charles, though, was different. 'That Charles Andrews died from arsenical poisoning, very few could doubt,' Mr Shiell declared. 'The fact that [only] a small trace of arsenic was found in his remains *affords no evidence whatever* [my emphasis] that the deceased did not die from arsenical poisoning. The poison [arsenic] can be eliminated by vomiting and purging.'[6]

If the jury accepted the same — that Charles had died of arsenical poisoning — they should ask themselves 'by whom was the poison administered? Who had an interest in giving the drug to him?' Louisa had clearly fallen in love with another man. Charles had discovered the affair. He had thrown Michael from the house. Within a few days, 'he [Charles] became ill, the illness being a pain in the pit of the stomach. That continued up to his death; and very soon after his death a wedding feast followed. Was there no suspicion in all that?'[7]

In parlance, this was not so much leading the horse to water, as also making it drink. Just as at the first inquest, the jury returned quite quickly with a statement remarkably like the summation they had been given:

> We find that the child John Collins died from natural causes. We find that Charles Andrews met his death by arsenical poisoning, and further, that the poison was administered by his wife, then Louisa Andrews, now Louisa Collins.[8]

Mr Shiell committed Louisa back to Darlinghurst Gaol to await trial for the murder of Charles as well as that of Michael. Louisa's reaction to this decision was not recorded but she surely understood how perilous a situation she was now in: it may well have been many years since a woman had been executed in New South Wales, but murder was still a hanging offence there in 1888 and Louisa Collins now stood accused of not one, but two capital crimes.

CHAPTER 6

'A human ghoul, a fiend incarnate': The Hangman

The first person to be hanged in New South Wales was hanged less than a week after the arrival of the First Fleet, and hangings continued at roughly that pace — one a week, sometimes more — for more than 100 years.

Despite this, no hangman ever really got good at it.

One of the worst was also one of the first. Alexander Green was born in Holland in 1802, the son of a travelling circus performer. Green grew up a thief and by the age of twenty-two had been transported to Australia for the term of his natural life. His particulars document described him as being pale with a pitted complexion, blue eyes and flaxen hair.[1] By the time he reached his late twenties, he also had a hideous scar running the length of the left side of his face, where he'd once been hit with an axe.

Like most normal people, Green didn't set out to become a hangman: after receiving his pardon in May 1825, he worked for some years as a labourer, only later deciding to become both the colony's official flogger, and executioner.

From the day he was appointed until the day he finally went mad, Green hanged at least 490 people, including six women. The first of his executions were carried out from a platform behind the old gaol in Sydney's George Street; later ones took place at the gallows constructed outside the main gates of the new prison at Darlinghurst. Huge crowds would often gather: more than 10,000 people watched the execution of a Royal Navy captain, John Knatchbull, outside Darlinghurst Gaol in 1844, to cite just one example. Part of the thrill was surely in the expectation that Green would muck it up: on one occasion, he got the length of the drop so badly wrong that the man's feet hit the floor; on another, Green himself fell off the scaffold; on another, he pulled the lever before the gaol chaplain had finished saying the prayer.

Still, Green stayed in the job for twenty-seven years before being dragged off to a lunatic asylum. Into his shoes — not immediately, but soon after — stepped a new hangman, Mr Robert Rice Howard, known far and wide as 'Nosey Bob' because he did not have a nose. The story goes like this: Mr Howard had sailed to Australia in 1861 to take a position as a hansom cab driver. Being tall, blue-eyed, and handsome, he was also very successful: the delicate ladies of Darling Point loved to ride with him, as did Prince Alfred, who was ferried about Sydney by Mr Howard during his royal tour of Australia in 1868. (For the prince's trouble in becoming Australia's first truly royal visitor, somebody shot him. Happily, he did not die, and indeed, was so good about it that the Prince Alfred

Hospital was named in his honour.) Then, one day, one of Mr Howard's horses reared up and kicked him in the face. The hoof removed his nose, and although surgeons at the Sydney Hospital did their best, not much could really be done. Nosey Bob would forevermore breathe through two ghastly holes in the middle of his face.[2]

So disfigured was Bob's face that nobody wanted to ride in his hansom cab anymore. He looked around for other work before deciding, in 1872, to become the hangman. As strange as it may seem, Bob continued to take pride in his appearance, even on the gallows. His uniform for executions included a black frock coat, sometimes with a white neckpiece, and a scented handkerchief.[3] Given that there was no such thing in the nineteenth century as hangman etiquette, Nosey Bob developed his own. Early in his career, he composed a short speech to deliver to the prisoner on the scaffold: 'My poor man, no one regrets this more than I do,' he would say, with his back erect, or else: 'Now, don't be afraid, my poor man. It will soon all be over.'[4]

Some of the prisoners would nod and attempt to shake hands with Nosey Bob (which was difficult, since most were pinioned at the elbow before being led from their cells). Others would say they bore him no malice. He declined to meet any of them before the day of their execution, perhaps because he knew how hideous he looked. He claimed to always ask for their correct weight, so he could properly calculate the drop, and he also claimed to always grease the rope with animal fat, so it would slide more easily over the beam, ostensibly to allow for a nice, clean break.

(It's beside the point of this story, but one of the many famous men that Nosey Bob hanged in his career was the Aboriginal tracker Jimmy Governor, who had been sentenced to death for the mass slaughter of women and children from the family that employed him. Jimmy shuffled to the gallows, smoking a cigarette, in 1901. His life would later become the basis of Thomas Keneally's book *The Chant of Jimmy Blacksmith*.[5])

Like anyone, Nosey Bob was susceptible to flattery, and in the twilight of his career, he still enjoyed telling tales about men and women he had hanged. One reporter who tracked Bob down late in life recounted how a smile would spread over his face whenever he was reminded of a smooth 'job'. He couldn't understand why he was shunned on public transport; why innkeepers couldn't ever seem to find him a bed; why housewives threw out the cutlery after he'd been to eat; or why publicans smashed the glasses from which he drank. In Nosey's mind, he was a public servant, no better or worse than, say, Mr Hamlet, with a salary in the same order (around 300 pounds a year). On some level, he understood that the public could not accept this, which in turn prompted Nosey to seek solace in the bottle.[6] Nowhere was he more famous than the seaside town in which he lived, Bondi, where he was often seen clutching at lampposts at four o'clock in the morning.

All of this is necessary to know because if Louisa were to hang — at this early stage, with the inquests over but the trials yet to begin, that possibility wasn't yet the subject of public discussion — Nosey Bob would preside over her hanging.

The execution of a woman — the first in New South Wales for decades, and the first ever at the new Darlinghurst Gaol — would be controversial, but controversy was something that Nosey Bob didn't seem to mind. Less than a year earlier, in 1887, Nosey had been called upon to execute four men for a crime that had become known as the Mount Rennie Outrage. While these two cases may at first glance seem to be in no way linked, outrage over one influenced the other, as surely as night follows day.

The bare facts of the Mount Rennie case are these: late in the morning of Thursday, 9 September 1886, a former convent-school girl, Mary Jane Hicks, who was looking for work in Sydney, stopped to speak to a hansom cab driver in Sussex Street. The driver, Charles Sweetman, thirty-six, offered to take the girl to the employment exchange in Castlereagh Street. Instead, Sweetman drove his horse-drawn cab to a stinking tip that was then on the outskirts of Sydney (the site is now the Moore Park golf course, on the road out to Sydney airport).

What happened to Mary Jane at Mount Rennie has always been in dispute. She told police that the driver stopped his cab and groped at her. Her screams attracted the attention of other men, but instead of rescuing the girl, they pulled her away from the cab and pushed her into bushes. A passer-by, William Stanley, heard the commotion and tried to intervene but was chased away by men throwing bricks and bottles. Mr Stanley ran for the police but by the time they arrived, the damage was done. Mary Jane was found lying on the ground, exhausted and crying, with her drawers covered in blood and her blue dress torn.

Mary Jane would later say that she had been raped at least eight and perhaps as often as twelve times. Police were outraged, and the newspapers went wild. Here is a snippet from the *Evening News*, which printed the story under the headline 'A Horrible Outrage; A Girl Ravaged':

> A terrible story is to hand this morning of an
> outrage upon a girl ... Mary Jane Hicks was
> driven yesterday ... by a cabman to a spot known
> as the 'rubbish heap' [where] a terrible scene [was]
> subsequently enacted. From noon to six o'clock,
> when she was rescued by the police, the unfortunate
> girl was in the hands of the brutes, who, with
> no regard for her helplessness, her entreaties,
> her shrieks of pain, her lapses into insensibility,
> proceeded to gratify their carnal appetites.[7]

The *Globe* shared the outrage:

> Like wild beasts they tore her clothing from her
> body ... and it was only when a party of police was
> spied in the distance that the unfortunate victim
> was left, half dead.[8]

Twelve men were ultimately identified and arrested, all of whom professed their innocence, saying Mary Jane had gone willingly to Mount Rennie, and had willingly had sex with them. Three were reprieved before the trial but nine of the original twelve would eventually come before a judge known to some as a 'hanging judge' — Justice

William Charles Windeyer.[9] The hearing lasted just six days and on each of those days, the courthouse was packed with eager spectators.

All nine men were found guilty, and Justice Windeyer's denunciation of them, read even today, is utterly terrifying. He described the men as brutes and savages who had committed 'a most atrocious crime, a crime so horrible that every lover of his country must feel that it is a disgrace to our civilization'. To the surprise of almost everyone, he also sentenced them to hang.

'I warn you to prepare for death,' he said. 'No hope of mercy can I extend to you.'[10]

The sentence shocked many in the courthouse and the wider community. Although it could not be said that the tide had turned against hanging, it was generally accepted by 1887 that hanging was reserved for cases involving murder, and for those cases about which nobody really had any doubt. The Rennie case was a rape case — a brutal rape, to be sure — but it did not involve murder. Also, two of the boys were just seventeen. Everyone expected them to be severely punished — but hanged?

Adding to the sense of injustice Justice Windeyer had made it clear in his judgement that one of the reasons that he'd decided to have the men hanged was that he'd already let too many men off too lightly.

'I hold in my hand a list of crimes similar to this which have been perpetrated during the last few years,' Justice Windeyer said. 'The first is an outrage that was committed by a number of young men upon a girl in the neighbourhood of Parramatta-street ... this outrage was followed by an outrage upon a young woman at North Shore [and another] on an old woman in the neighbourhood of Ultimo … this was followed by another, where the wretched woman was done to death … this was followed up by another frightful outrage in Woolloomooloo, where the wretched creature was found lying dead, like a dog, naked in the street. Then last year I tried eight men … they all escaped the death penalty, too.

'The time has come when a terrible example must be made,' Justice Windeyer said. 'I warn you not to waste your time in idle protestations of your innocence. I advise you to prepare to meet your Maker.'[11]

The outrage over Justice Windeyer's sentence — and his remarks — was great. One of the most vocal critics was a man called JF Archibald. Journalists will know the name; so, too, will art lovers. JF Archibald was both the founder of the *Bulletin*, and the creator of Australia's richest prize for portraiture, which to this day bears his name.

Archibald is not an easy man to capture in a brief sketch: some say he was brilliant, others say he was crazy. Probably he was both, a brilliant, crazy man. Born with the plain old name of John in what is now the Victorian city of Geelong, he rather grandly decided to call himself Jules François because he adored everything French. Archibald was witty. He could cook (his signature dish was chicken simmered with lettuce). He wore wide-brimmed hats and carried a cane, and his coat always seemed too big. As founder and editor of the *Bulletin*, he had a large bullhorn to amplify his views.

One of the principles that Archibald held dearest was that hanging was a foul crime by the state against its citizens. This view he formed back in 1879, when he was still the thing he loved best: a humble reporter in search of the truth. An editor at the *Evening News* had sent Archibald out to cover one of Nosey Bob's hangings in Bathurst. The experience would change his life forever. As in so many of the cases already mentioned, the hanging was bungled, with the condemned, an Aboriginal man called Arthur, kicking wildly as he was slowly strangled to death. As one of the few witnesses, Archibald was horror-struck, and he wanted to make sure that everyone knew it. Instead of writing a straight story for the *Evening News*, he filed copy so extraordinary that his sub-editor actually copied it onto a giant blackboard and took it to the central Post Office for everyone to read. Archibald had described Nosey Bob as the most grotesque human being he had ever seen, and he described the way that Nosey carried off Arthur's body as being like a 'butcher would carry a slaughtered sheep'.[12]

Archibald's hatred of the gallows may have existed before he saw Arthur swing but his hatred of the hangman — and of Nosey Bob, in particular — was born that day, and he would work his whole life to bring others around to his point of view. The first issue of the *Bulletin* in January 1880 carried a story, written by Archibald, about the execution at Darlinghurst Gaol of two men known as the Wantabadgery Bushrangers, in which Nosey Bob was described as 'a human ghoul, a fiend incarnate. Were he to hang a million murderers no one from among them would or could compare with him in bodily hideousness.'[13]

When the young men of Mount Rennie were sentenced, it was Archibald who boldly stated what so many others were afraid to say: men should not be hanged for rape, he said, because it could only encourage other rapists toward murder (so they could not be identified by the victim). A former (and soon-to-be-again) premier of New South Wales, Sir Henry Parkes, agreed, saying that if the crime of rape was not punishable by death in England, then it surely shouldn't be punishable by death in one of the colonies.

Neither Sir Henry's considered plea, nor Archibald's rages, nor the many other arguments in favour of the commutation of the sentence came to much: four of the young men from the Mount Rennie Outrage were hanged.

The executions took place on Friday, 7 January 1887, on the scaffold at the Darlinghurst Gaol. As with the hanging of Arthur, and of poor Magee in South Australia half a century earlier, it was botched. More than 2000 people had lined up outside the gaol, hoping to be allowed to watch. Access was granted to only 140 of them, but that was still so many that witnesses had to sit in a specially constructed gallery that ran twice around the length of the room, which in turn resulted in pushing and shoving as people fought to get a better view, much like at a rock concert.

As in Adelaide, the executions had been scheduled, despite there being no suitable gallows. A special 'structure of death' had been hastily constructed, comprising a heavy cross-beam over which four ropes could be thrown. First onto the scaffold was George Martin, followed by Robert George Read, then George Duffy, and then William Boyce, who came with a Reverend Father from St Mary's Cathedral.

All four had their arms pinioned, or bound tightly down by their sides, but each had their hands loose. According to a report in the *Sydney Morning Herald*, Boyce was 'exceedingly pale throughout, and kept his eyes turned firmly upward; Duffy was flushed and his lips moved incessantly, as he repeated words of prayer; while Read stood with his eyes closed and face turned skyward'. There was a moment of 'painful suspense and solemn silence'[14] before the executioner — Nosey Bob — and his assistant produced the white caps for the prisoners' heads, and put the ropes in place. Then followed 'a most horrible scene'. The drop was at least half-a-metre too short, so instead of the youths being killed outright — surely the aim of a good hanging — by the breaking of their necks, they, like Magee, were slowly strangled. Boyce in particular gulped for breath as he dangled, clenching and unclenching his fists, until finally he breathed no more; for his part, Duffy managed to get a hand out to clutch at the rope, but after a 'few convulsive gasps and nervous twitches, all was over. At 9.20 am the men were dead.'[15]

That had been in 1887. Now it was 1888, and Louisa's trial was about to begin. The crime with which she was charged was more serious than rape: it was murder. Yet Louisa was a more sympathetic creature: she was a woman, and the mother of small children. Would she hang? It was far from certain. In decades past, the judiciary had shown no compunction about the execution of women: in 1855, for example, a 32-year-old mother of three named Mary Ann Brownlow, who had knifed her husband during a drunken domestic dispute, was hanged despite a spirited campaign by supporters in the town of Goulburn (Mary Ann had been pregnant during her trial; she was permitted to give birth to baby George before the hanging, and her last act on earth was to breastfeed the infant, who soon after died and is now said to haunt the Goulburn gaol).[16]

That said, because women did not kill as often as men, they were not hanged at anywhere near the same rate as men; the reprieve of female killers had also become more common (in the two years before Louisa's trial, at least two women sentenced to death for murder had their sentences commuted to life in prison).[17] Also, the campaign against capital punishment had grown in influence during the debate about Mount Rennie, and many Australian-born politicians, in particular, were determined to consign the stocks, the lash and the noose to history. What was it then about Louisa that made the Crown so determined not only to convict her — to try her, and then try her again, and again, and again — but to drag her to the scaffold, the last woman for all time?

CHAPTER 7

The First Trial: 'He was the apple of my eye'

6-9 August 1888

Central Criminal Court, Darlinghurst

PRESIDING: Justice William Foster

CROWN: Mr WH (William Henry) Coffey

DEFENCE: Mr HH (Hugh Hart) Lusk

JURY: Henry Short, John Killings, John McDonald, Tom Walter Cant, Ebert Cather, James Scott Leighton, William Fortier, Graham Cameron, Russell Burgess, David Davis, John Oldham, James Martin[1]

Charles Andrew had been the first of Louisa's husbands to die, yet it was for the murder of her second husband, Michael Collins, that Louisa now faced trial. Events got underway at the Central Criminal Court in Darlinghurst on Monday, 6 August 1888.[2]

Louisa had by this stage been held on remand at the Darlinghurst Gaol since her arrest. She was walked to court each day through an underground tunnel, with a female warden at each elbow. The two inquests had ensured that the case would attract a lot of attention, and hundreds of people turned up to watch.[3]

At least five reporters were in attendance, and each of them would at some point go to some trouble to describe Louisa's appearance. She was a relatively small woman (Louisa is described on her Darlinghurst Gaol particulars card as being five feet, three inches tall) with dark hair and dark eyes.[4] She wore a blue dress, a grey cape and a hat.[5] For reasons that are not entirely clear — was the courthouse smelly? Did Louisa wish to appear more sweet-natured and feminine than she might otherwise have looked? — she carried in her hands a small sprig of heliotrope.[6] Her expression was described by one pressman (we can call them that, because all were men) as 'cool, self-possessed … apparently indifferent'[7] and it seems that she maintained this calm demeanour throughout the months to come.

The most detailed description of Louisa's face, however, came not from a reporter, but from that species of quack that Dr Knaggs so despised: a phrenologist named Mr Pasquale Besomo, who believed that Louisa's guilt or innocence could be ascertained by an examination not of the evidence but of the shape of her head. To that end, Mr Besomo decided not only to sit in court every day, but to produce a finely worded pamphlet, complete with a sketch of Louisa's face, describing her features, and the characteristics he believed them to convey. At first glance, Louisa appeared to Mr Besomo not to 'portray any strong evil tendencies. She is rather good looking, medium size, and there is nothing very repulsive about her.' Her manner was likewise 'mild, even docile' but her thin lips suggested that she was crafty, and her long nose troubled him, too. Add to that the fact that her head shape was 'cattish' — widest between the ears, 'where the plotting and scheming went on', and narrowest toward the mouth, 'where sympathy should lie' — well, it all pointed to Louisa's guilt.[8]

Happily for Louisa, her first trial was to be decided not by Mr Besomo but by a jury. Today, they'd be described as her peers but in 1888, juries were comprised only of men, all of whom had either to be landholders, or living in Sydney and working in one of the acceptable professions (school teachers and chemists were acceptable; butchers generally were not).[9]

Presiding over the trial was a former Crown prosecutor (and former politician) Justice William John Foster, who had been appointed to the Supreme Court bench just four months earlier. Like most judges in New South Wales at that time (and probably now), Justice Foster had nothing at all in common with the working classes: born into a distinguished family in Ireland in 1831, his mother, Catherine, was a niece of the Duke of Wellington. Although well educated, Justice Foster sailed to Australia in 1851 to try his luck in the Victorian goldfields. When that didn't work out, he turned his hand to farming in Wollombi in New South Wales. Bored by country life, he soon turned to politics and the law. Foster was elected to the New South Wales Legislative Council in 1877 and then to the Legislative Assembly in 1880. He served as both attorney general and minister for justice before becoming a judge.[10]

As to the legal counsel, well, there can't be any doubt that the scales of justice were tipped toward the Crown, which had chosen Mr William Henry Coffey to be prosecutor.[11] Already a very experienced lawyer, Mr Coffey would go on to become a judge. By contrast, Louisa was to be represented by a barrister named Mr Hugh Hart (or HH) Lusk, who, at the direct request of Justice Foster, had agreed to work for her, pro bono (to his credit, Mr Lusk would stand by Louisa for all four trials, and the subsequent appeal; whether this would actually prove to her detriment is a question perhaps best left to history).[12] Unlike many of the bright legal minds working in the colony, Mr Lusk had not come up the ranks in the usual way. His qualifications were earned in New Zealand — nothing wrong with that — but his reputation had been ruined there after he was found to have taken bribes, which was why he'd moved to New South Wales. Also, by the time of Louisa's trial, Mr Lusk was well on the way to becoming the first barrister to be struck from the roll for dishonesty.[13]

In any case, Justice Foster banged his gavel and things got underway. Given that there was no direct evidence that Louisa had poisoned Michael — nobody had seen her do it, and there was no evidence that she had ever handled the murder weapon, meaning the arsenic — the Crown prosecutor would at some point have to establish a motive. This would prove difficult: several of Louisa's neighbours would testify as to her lust for her young husband. She had been married to Michael for little more than a year when he died and, if letters that she was writing to friends and to her own mother from gaol were a guide, Louisa was still in agony over Michael's death:

> He was tall and handsome ... he was good, loving,
> attentive, sober, honest ... respectable, fond of
> children ... He was very kind to my ... little
> children. The love he had for his own firstborn infant
> was beyond all I could describe ... This man was
> everything a woman could wish to have. He was the
> apple of my eye. His voice was music to my ear. He
> was all I wanted in this life. If I was between him and
> death, do you think I would let him go? Oh, no fear.[14]

The Crown would also have to convince the jury beyond reasonable doubt that no other theory as to Michael's death was plausible, including the suggestion, put forward in another of Louisa's letters, that poisoned berries might have made him sick:

> I don't know if you ever saw those berries: they
> are very plentiful in Botany, and they are very
> poisonous. ... There was spouting all round [the]
> house [and] of course these berries would lodge in
> the spout. [The] rain would come, and then wash
> them down into the tank and cask. This water we
> had to drink.[15]

Inexplicably, Louisa then said: 'Don't think I want to make you believe that he was poisoned by those berries, because he was not.' No, Louisa still believed — or said she believed — that Michael had been depressed by the death of his baby son and ashamed of his debts and his gambling habit, and that he had therefore committed suicide by deliberately taking small doses of arsenic slowly over a period of weeks so that nobody would know his despair (there was great shame attached to suicide in the nineteenth century, especially among Roman Catholics, of which Michael was one). 'He would not take a dose of poison all at once,' Louisa reasoned, because he did not want his family 'to hear that he committed suicide — it would be in the papers'.[16]

Would the jury accept Louisa's theory? She certainly didn't seem worried about the outcome of the first trial. At least according to the *Evening News*, she 'maintained a calm, indifferent demeanour while seated in the dock, and beyond an occasional glance at the witnesses giving evidence, took no apparent interest in the proceedings.'[17]

The first witness called was Dr Marshall, who repeated the evidence he had given at the inquest into Michael's death: 'On the first day, there was nothing alarming,' Dr Marshall said. 'I thought it was gastro-duodenal catarrh and the symptoms were consistent with that. I had no suspicion at that time of foul play … I noticed nothing to induce suspicion.'[18]

Dr Marshall did not deny that he had changed his mind only after his colleague Dr Martin had told him about Louisa's first husband suffering from a similar sickness shortly before he died. He also explained the results of the autopsy to the jury, saying the rawness and bleeding in Michael's stomach, intestines and rectum suggested to him that Michael had indeed been poisoned with arsenic, and suffered a slow, painful death.

Mr Lusk, for the defence, asked if that were all not a little bit convenient. Dr Marshall hadn't suspected poisoning when he first treated Michael. He'd come to the view after consulting with another doctor. Also, wasn't it true that death by arsenic was usually quick, as in days or hours? Yet Michael had lingered for more than two weeks.

Dr Marshall agreed that arsenic would normally kill a man rapidly, which was why he hadn't jumped to the conclusion that his patient was being poisoned in the first place. He was asked some specific questions about arsenic and, just as he had done at the inquest, he explained that it was easily dissolved in liquid, especially in hot water. As to how it might taste, Dr Marshall told the jury that he actually tried it — just a touch, on his tongue — and it was so bad he had to spit all day.

The jury heard next from Dr Martin, who explained that he had gone to see Michael in company with Dr Marshall, and after discussing their concerns, both doctors had agreed to report the matter to police.[19] This was obviously very damaging, as was the evidence from Mr Hamlet, who testified that arsenic was widely available in the form of rat poison. He mentioned Rough on Rats specifically, explaining as he had at the inquest that it was 'between 96 and 97 per cent pure white arsenic' with just a touch of charcoal to give it a little colour.[20]

Unlike today, jurors in the nineteenth century were allowed to ask questions during the trial, and it seems that one juror called out: 'Put into a tumbler of milk, would [it not] discolour the milk?'[21]

Mr Hamlet said no, it would not, provided the amount used was quite small. Another juror wanted to know whether arsenic would cling to the sides of a glass or sink to the bottom, or be completely dissolved. Mr Hamlet said arsenic would not sink if the substance was thick — like milk — because it would be 'suspended in the liquid'.[22]

Constable Jeffes was next to take the stand. He described the scene at Pople's Terrace: the bedroom in which Michael lay suffering was to the left as he entered the house from Botany Road. The bed was hard up against the wall. There was a 'sort of box, covered over with a print or something. It reached up to the level of the bed. It could be used as a seat or table. On it there was a watch chain, a small cup, a glass tumbler, and a book without a cover — a novel — the cup and the glass bottle.'[23]

Several of these items — the lemonade bottle that had contained brandy, and the glass tumbler, for example — were on display in court.

Constable Jeffes explained that there was 'nothing in the tumbler' on his first visit. There was, however, some whitish liquid in the cup, like 'tea with plenty of milk in it and creamy on the top'.[24]

A short time later, Michael was dead:

On the 7th of July at 11 o'clock p.m. [I went]
with Constable Sherwood [to the house in Pople's
Terrace]. We went into the bedroom [and] I saw
[Michael] Collins in the bed ... he was on his right

side facing me. He said I feel a pain in the left
shoulder and placed his right hand across to show
the spot. He said, well, I think I'll be up in a day or
two. [Then] on Sunday [8 July] at 3 o'clock p.m. I
went to the house, I saw Mrs Collins at the door. I
asked how Collins was? She said: 'he's dead!' I said
'is he?' and walked straight into the bedroom. He
was dead in bed. I asked Mrs Collins if she sent for
the doctor. She said: 'Yes! I've just sent my son by
this tram (one was just going) and my daughter for
Mrs Price.'

Constable Jeffes immediately began searching the bedroom,
and noticed that the tumbler now contained 'a quantity of
white liquid — she [Louisa] said that it was milk'.

Constable Jeffes explained that when he tried to seize
the small tumbler as evidence, Louisa had grown frantic.
'When I picked up that tumbler she rose off her seat and
caught hold of my right hand and said, "that is nothing". I
said I want everything and I must take it ... I had to tell
her to keep quiet. She nearly capsized the glass ... when
I found the powder she did not catch hold of me but got
up excited. She was excited all the night. She was under
the influence of drink.'[25] (While there is no suggestion
that Justice Foster was biased against Louisa, it should be
noted that somebody has underlined the fact that Louisa
was drunk in his notebook; and that he was a fiercely loyal
member of the temperance movement, so much so that his
nickname, bestowed upon him by the *Bulletin*'s editor, JF
Archibald, was Water Jug Foster.[26])

Constable Jeffes told the jury that he had taken the glass tumbler to Mr Hamlet, who had tested it for arsenic; Mr Hamlet explained to the court that a tiny trace of arsenic had indeed been found in that little tumbler. This left the Crown with a problem: where had that arsenic come from, and who had put it in Michael's milk? To that end, they had a very important, and very tiny witness waiting in the wings. Her name was May.

Louisa's only daughter, May Andrews, had not testified at either of the earlier inquests, but the Crown needed her evidence at the murder trial. Nobody else — not May's brothers, not the neighbours, nor the doctors, nor the police — could do what she could do: place the murder weapon — the arsenical poison — in the house. (If there were any kind of rule against placing a child of such tender years on the stand, or about calling a child to testify against her own mother, it appears not to have been raised by Louisa's counsel.)

May first testified against her mother at the Central Criminal Court in August 1888.[27] She was still only ten years old[28] and can't have stood much more than four feet tall. There is no way of knowing what she made of Justice Foster, an old man with a wooden gavel and a long curled wig; or of the black-robed Crown prosecutor, pointing his finger at Louisa; or the twelve men of the jury, each distinguished in some way by their professions, wearing heavy winter coats and hats; or even of her mother, now a prisoner in the Darlinghurst Gaol, standing there in her best dress with a small sprig of flowers in her hands.

What is known is that May impressed Justice Foster with her clear little voice, her honesty, and her intelligence.

May had been called to the stand because she had told one of her little friends, Florry Mapstone, that she had seen a funny-shaped box with such a strange picture — dead rats — on the lid. Florry had run home and told her mother who had told police. Police reported the matter to the Crown, which wanted the evidence — key evidence — put before the jury.

Did May understand that such evidence could be used to send her mother to the gallows? Once again, we don't know. All that is known is that May, described in newspaper reports as a fair-haired, tiny girl, took the stand as she was required to do and — with a Bible in her hands — swore to tell the truth.

The importance that Justice Foster placed on May's evidence is made plain in the notebook that he took into court. That notebook, with its hard cover and ink-smudged pages, is now in storage at State Records New South Wales. In it, he introduces May by saying she is 'May Andrews, 11 years old [who] was living with her mother and Mr Collins was married to her mother.'[29]

Mr Coffey, for the Crown, began gently. What was May's name?

'May Andrews,' she said.

And where do you live?

May looked confused. Her place of residence was at that point completely up in the air.

'I was living with my mother at Botany,' she said.

Did she know Michael Peter Collins?

'He was married to my mother.'

And did she see Michael when he was ill?

She did: 'I went into the room two or three times while he was ill.'

Was anyone else there?

No, May said. 'There was no one there.'

And did May give Michael Collins anything to eat or drink?

'I gave him some cold tea only out of a tea pot in the kitchen.'

Mr Coffey leaned forward. Did anyone else drink from that pot, May?

May nodded. 'We did take tea after dinner out of that tea pot,' she said.

Did she add anything to Michael's tea?

'I put milk and sugar into it.'

Did her mother tell her to do that?

'Mother was not there then. I did it two or three times.'

And what were you doing, May, the night that Michael Collins died?

'The night he died, I was doing something, dusting. She' — at this point, it seems that May pointed at her mother, in the dock — 'was in the kitchen.'

And did she remember seeing Michael Collins after he had died?

She did. 'I saw Collins's dead body on the table that night.'

All right, Mr Coffey said. And you have told police, haven't you, May, that you saw a little box in the house one night, and that you later noticed that it was missing?

'I missed that night off the shelf a little packet, a box,' May agreed. 'I saw it the Saturday before he [Michael] died, the week before he died. I had seen it in the kitchen.'

And what kind of box was it, exactly?

'It was a little round box. It had a lid.'

Was there anything on the outside of the box?

'There was nothing on the outside of the box.'

Nothing?

'There were pictures of rats on it. The picture was red, the rats were red, the rats were on their backs.'

All right. And what did you do with the box, May?

'I don't know what I did with it.'

Did you look inside? What did you see?

'I opened the lid. There was inside a dark blue powder. Some was taken out — about a teaspoonful. I put the lid on again.'

And did she show the box to her mother?

'I showed it to my mother. I said, "Look what I found on the shelf — Rough on Rats!"'

Mr Coffey went on: and did your mother say anything to you about the box, May?

'I don't know whether she said anything to me about it.'

Well then, did May remember what she did with the box? Did she put it back on the shelf?

'I don't know whether I put it back.'

Well, did she ever see it again? On the shelf, perhaps?

'I did not see it on the shelf again.'

Did your mother take it, May? Did your mother take it away?

'Mother did not take it,' May said. 'I forget what I did with it … I don't know what I did with it.'

Mr Coffey nodded. 'Would you know the box if you saw it again, May?' he asked.

'I would know a box like it,' May said. 'I had seen one like it once before when we lived in the paddock. The box was like that —' Here, it seems that she pointed at the box on display in the court. 'The powder was the same color as that there.'

The judge, Justice Foster, stepped in: when was that, May?

'It was before my own father took sick,' she said. 'I saw the box first on the very top shelf in the house, when we lived in the paddock about a year ago.' (These references to 'the paddock' would seem to refer to Berry's paddock where the family lived while Charles worked at Berry's bone dust factory.)

Mr Coffey nodded, but May's time in the witness box was not yet over. As incredible as it may now seem, the little girl was yet to be cross-examined by her own mother's counsel. Mr Lusk stepped up, wanting to know how long it was before Michael died that May had seen the box.

'It was about a week, on the Saturday before he died,' she said.

Mr Lusk said: And you're quite sure that you didn't give it to your mother, aren't you, May?

'I don't think I gave it to my mother,' May replied, uncertainly. 'I told mother first … I first spoke to Florry Mapstone about this box.'

All right, Mr Lusk said, but do you remember anything else about the box, May?

By this stage, it seems that May was upset. Her answer is recorded as: 'I have told all I know about that box.'

Mr Lusk turned to the matter of the glass tumbler, or nobbler, found by Michael's bed. Would May know such a tumbler if she saw it again?

'I would know them,' she said.

Mr Lusk picked up the nobbler from the court display. Was this it?

She nodded. 'That's one of them.'

The Crown prosecutor rose. That was one of them? How many such tumblers had been in the house?

'There was only one little one like that,' said May. 'The others were bigger than [that] on the table in the court.'

The Crown thanked May and for a moment it seemed like she was free to go but then one of the jurors piped up: how did May know that the box she'd seen in the kitchen was Rough on Rats?

'I read what was on the box,' she said, indignant. And then — to the sure dismay of her mother and the defence team — she proceeded to spell out the letters: R-O-U-G-H O-N R-A-T-S.[30]

May's evidence was devastating. Not only had she told the jury that she had seen an arsenic-based poison in the house in the week before Michael Collins had died, she'd also testified that the nobbler in which traces of arsenic had been found was the only one of its kind in the house.

Under these circumstances, Mr Lusk must have known that it would be pointless to argue that something other than arsenic had killed Michael. He concentrated instead on trying to prove that Michael had poisoned himself. He asked a number of witnesses — including Dr Marshall — about the fact that Michael had been wearing his trousers in bed (the idea being that he might have had a little packet of arsenical powder secreted away in one of the pockets). Mrs Ellen Price, who laid out Michael's body, testified that he had been 'partially clothed, in trousers, socks and shirt' when he died.[31] She did not claim to have seen any powder in Michael's pockets — nobody had seen that — but then, she hadn't checked the pockets, either.

Mr Coffey objected, saying: 'If there had been a small box or packet in the pocket of the trousers [the witness] would have known it.'[32]

But would she? In the hours after Michael's death, Louisa had asked Arthur to bring Michael's vest and trousers to her. She threw the clothes on the floor before washing them in a tub of water in the yard without, she said, checking any of the pockets.

Mr Lusk also called some of Michael's friends, including the grocer Mr Sayers, who told the jury that he had seen Louisa crying while tending to Michael on his sickbed. Another friend, Mr Walter Hayes, testified that Louisa had run through the streets of Botany late one night after Michael became ill, knocking on doors and begging people to help.

In his final address, Mr Lusk told the jury that these and other examples proved that Louisa had loved her husband. Throughout his illness, she had shown 'the greatest anxiety to assist him, she was attentive and kind to him, was repeatedly found to be affected to tears by his condition, and did all in her power to enforce the attendance of the doctor'. Michael himself 'appeared to have perfect confidence in his wife, and a great affection for her, and did not show that he in any way suspected her'.[33]

Also, Louisa had nothing to gain in financial terms from Michael's death. Unlike her first husband, Michael hadn't been insured. His behaviour in the days before his death had also been 'very peculiar'. When questioned by the doctor as to how he might have become ill, 'he was very reticent and never seemed disposed to volunteer any' information. He had insisted on keeping his trousers on, so it was 'quite possible for him to have had the arsenic in his trousers pocket'. He had 'monetary difficulties, was in debt, and not able to pay his rent'. In conclusion, Mr Lusk enjoined the jury to give Louisa the benefit of the doubt: 'Carefully consider these facts,' he said, for a woman's life was at stake.[34]

Now it was the Crown's turn. Mr Coffey would be brief. The idea of suicide was 'not consistent with the facts'. Michael had been in 'great pain for days, continually vomiting', and it would be absurd to suppose that he would submit himself to a week of torture, instead of killing himself quickly with one big dose. There was also the fact that two or three days before his death, Michael was unable, through weakness and exhaustion, to get out of bed, and it would have been practically impossible for him to have placed the arsenic, especially in such small quantities, in his own milk and yet two doctors had testified that the poison 'had been administered in small doses on different occasions'. In conclusion, the evidence pointed only in one direction — and that was to the guilt of the accused.[35]

With both sides now rested, Justice Foster would need to sum up the evidence. He warned the jury that it would take some time. What with all the witness statements and the forensic reports, there were more than eighty pages of testimony to consider. Rather than get started on it that afternoon, the judge sequestered the jury overnight, prompting reporters to rush from the courthouse to file their stories.

The next day, large crowds of 'sensation-loving people' braved inclement weather, and risked 'colds and discomfort' in order to get a seat in the courthouse on the final day of the first trial.[36] The *Evening News* reported that the doors opened at 9.20 a.m. and, less than three minutes later, there was not a vacant seat left in the public gallery. Louisa herself emerged from the underground tunnel 'in the sombre dress she has worn throughout the trial, namely, a crepe trimmed hat, dark grey cloak, and blue print dress'. Her face 'wore the same look of unruffled coolness which has been noticeable throughout the whole of the proceedings ... but she was undoubtedly paying much more earnest attention to the Judge than she had done to any part of the trial.'[37]

Undoubtedly.

Justice Foster had entered the courtroom to take his seat at precisely 9.30 a.m. He told the jury that his task was to sum up the evidence and to provide directions, as to relevant law. 'Gentlemen of the jury,' he began. 'The case which has occupied your attention during the past two days is one of very great importance, not only to the person who is charged here with the terrible crime of poisoning her own husband, but also to the public at large. You have heard all the evidence, and have paid considerable attention to it.'[38]

Justice Foster noted that most if not all of the evidence against Louisa was circumstantial 'with perhaps one exception which was the small glass which contained some whitish liquid' at the deceased's bedside. Even that didn't take the case 'out of the category of circumstantial' since nobody had seen Louisa put arsenic into the glass. But then, that was the problem with poisoning cases. As a rule, there would only ever be circumstantial evidence. Poisoners, by their nature, 'endeavoured to avoid detection and of course only secrecy could be expected'.[39]

Justice Foster then explained how circumstantial evidence could be used: in order to convict Louisa, the jury would have to find not only that the circumstances were consistent with her guilt, but also *inconsistent* with any other rational conclusion. It wasn't enough that the circumstances pointed to Louisa's guilt. The jury also had to be convinced that there was no other reasonable explanation for Michael's death. It couldn't be 'merely a case of suspicion — and no one could be convicted upon suspicion'. The stakes were too high. The Crown had shown that Louisa had the opportunity to kill Michael, for she lived with him, 'had the care of him, and admitted that she gave him the medicines which he had taken'. On the other hand, the defence was suggesting that Michael might have poisoned himself by secreting a small amount of arsenic in his trouser pocket and taking it gradually over a period of weeks or days. It was 'a remarkable fact that the deceased had his trousers on at the time of death and also the night before his death ... why did the deceased have his trousers on? Was it to keep himself warm, or was it to conceal poison which he might have been taking himself?'[40]

Justice Foster then turned his attention to evidence given by May. 'The Crown also relies on showing that there was a packet of Rough on Rats in the house,' he said. 'Rough on Rats is a compound of arsenic in the form in which it is allowed to be sold by law. Then there is the evidence of the poor little child, who was, it is sad to think, necessarily called to give evidence in a capital charge against her mother. The evidence seemed to be given with intelligence almost beyond her years ... but was given in such a manner as to show her thoroughly aware of what she was doing and saying.'[41]

Besides May's evidence, there was also 'direct evidence', Justice Foster said, that Louisa had given Michael a drink from the little tumbler in which grains of arsenic had been found. She had done so in full view of her neighbours (that Louisa would feed Michael arsenic in full view of witnesses seems bold, but this point was not raised by her defence counsel or by the judge). Justice Foster noted that 'this glass was found to contain one-tenth of a grain of arsenic to a half glass of milk, and therefore in ten glasses of milk there would have been enough to cause death'. On the other hand, if the glass was 'the only thing found in the house containing arsenic' why didn't Louisa get rid of it? It ran contrary to common sense to leave the glass there to be discovered by police, but Justice Foster said that he had known of other cases where murderers did not 'do away with the traces of their guilt ... some stupid thing left undone was often the thing which brought the crime home'.[42]

Justice Foster was prepared to concede that Louisa had 'carefully drawn the attention of the medical man to the condition of her husband'. While the Crown would argue that she had called the doctor 'to screen herself in case of discovery ... if the prisoner was committing a secret crime, why did she call in any medical man?' Justice Foster said. 'The fact that she did so must be considered in her favour.'[43]

On the other hand, Justice Foster asked the jury to consider the fact that Louisa herself had told Dr Marshall that she didn't think Michael would live through the night. Did that statement arise from the knowledge that the man had the poison in his system? He also noted that Louisa had given Michael a vomiting powder. 'It certainly seems strange that she should have done so if she was trying to poison her husband,' he said, but perhaps she was trying to get the arsenic out of Michael's system before he died.[44]

Justice Foster had by now been talking for more than three hours. The *Evening News* recounts him saying:

I have considered it necessary even at the risk of
being wearisome to put before you all the evidence,
in order to refresh your memories, and to draw your
attention again to the main points. In arriving at a
verdict you must be satisfied beyond all reasonable

doubt that the prisoner is guilty of the charge … On
the other hand, if you consider the evidence might
be consistent with the deceased having poisoned
himself, you must acquit her.

Of course, he recognised the enormity of the task,
adding: 'The responsibility rests on you and I do not
think I can help you very much'.[45]

At one p.m., the jury retired to consider its verdict.
The *Evening News* said the crowd in the court 'did not
diminish in the slightest degree' except during the interval
allowed for lunch and 'then they left the court only under
compulsion and passed [the] interval in the rain'. Returning
to their seats, they again waited:

> Two, half-past two, three, half-past three, went
> by, but still no word … The people kept their seats
> and waited wearily.[Finally,] at ten minutes past 4
> o'clock, the judge's associate, accompanied by the
> Crown prosecutor, entered the court, and at once
> there was solemn silence … Two minutes later, His
> Honour again took his seat on the bench and the
> jury were brought in once more.
>
> The prisoner was placed in the dock … eyeing
> the door at which her jurors entered with a look in
> no way different to that she had worn throughout
> the trial.[46]

The jury foreman, David Davis,[47] rose but did not announce
his verdict. Instead, he told the judge that the jury had paid

careful attention to the whole of the evidence, 'and one or two of them had even taken full notes throughout the trial, which were read over and fully considered by them', but they found it impossible to agree, and 'would not be likely to do so even if they were locked up for a week'.[48]

Justice Foster nodded. He understood the difficulties, but he had no choice other than to keep them at their deliberations. With that, he sequestered all twelve men for another long night, until Friday, 10 August 1888.

The following morning, Justice Foster again asked: 'Gentlemen, have you agreed on a verdict?'

Mr Davis rose again, saying, 'No, your Honour. It is impossible to agree.'

The jury had talked the matter through the night, and had remained hopelessly divided, so much so that the foreman now believed that they would never agree. He told the judge that, despite debating the case all night, they were not close to a unanimous decision: in fact, the division was nearly equal.[49]

Justice Foster seemed to empathise. 'I think the case is one upon which conscientious gentlemen might hold different opinions,' he said. He discharged the jury, and thanked Mr Lusk for taking the case at his request pro bono. As for Louisa, far from being set free, she was remanded into her former custody, pending a decision from the Crown as to whether a fresh trial should be held. There is some evidence that she felt confident about the road ahead: according to the *Evening News*, Louisa smiled on her way out of court.[50] Then again, the next day was her birthday.

CHAPTER 8

The Second Trial: 'She had no quarrel with her husband'

4–8 November 1888
Central Criminal Court, Darlinghurst
PRESIDING: Justice William Charles Windeyer
CROWN: Mr Henry Emmanuel (HE) Cohen
DEFENCE: Mr HH Lusk
JURY: Edward Davies, Alexander Geddes, Thomas Booth, Alexander Morton, Neil Sharkey, Arthur S Appleton, Joseph Hammond, Theodore J Eashleigh, Adam Sappan, Aaron Corderoy, Fred Bromerie, George Rutherford[1]

Some readers may think it unusual for the Crown to try a woman — indeed, to try anyone — a second time for the same offence, but in fact it is not so incredibly rare.

It can't happen in cases where somebody has been found not guilty. That's known as 'double jeopardy'. It can, and occasionally does, happen in cases like this one, where no verdict has been reached.

To pluck just one example at random, in 2013 the Crown kept open the option of re-trying an elderly man, Ronald Leslie Pennington, eighty-four, for manslaughter, after a jury in Western Australia failed to reach a verdict in his trial.[2] (Also at the time of writing, Bundaberg surgeon Dr Jayant Patel was waiting to hear whether he would face a re-trial after a jury failed to reach a verdict in a case in which he was accused of causing grievous bodily harm to a patient by removing his colon and rectum.[3])

That said, it is generally understood — a tradition, if you like — that if a jury can't reach a verdict the first time, the Crown will need to either abandon or strengthen its case, for there will be no third chances.

To that end, it's important to note that the second trial of Louisa Collins for Michael's murder was indeed delayed by the Crown, which wanted more time to make the case.[4]

Two more months was subsequently granted.[5]

Louisa spent those months remanded in her cell in the women's section at Darlinghurst Gaol. The youngest of her children, Edwin, eight, and Charles, five, had by then been taken into care at the Benevolent Asylum at Randwick (a letter on Water Police letterhead, dated 27 July 1888 and addressed to the Manager of the Government Asylums for the Infirm and Destitute, explains that the boys were taken into care between the first and second coronial inquests, because 'their mother, Louisa Collins, was yesterday committed for trial ... on the charge of poisoning her second husband ... There is nobody to take charge of them [and] the older children are barely able to support themselves'[6]).

By all accounts, Louisa caused no problems for her gaolers. Her prison record says no punishments were administered against her, but Louisa certainly wasn't happy to be confined, spending much of her time writing letters in which she either protested her treatment or declared her innocence, while hinting that a conspiracy involving the Catholic Church and police might be behind her arrest. In one such letter she wrote:

Sir,

Permit me most respectfully to address you. I wish to speak about my late husband, Michael Peter Collins. He was a Roman Catholic and then he took ill. I wanted to send for the priest. In fact, I begged of him to let me send for the priest. He said, 'no, my love. I will neither see a priest or a person. I only want you. I don't wish to see anybody' ... I could not in any way persuade him to see the priest when he was alive. So after his death I sent for the priest from Randwick as there was none living in Botany. The priest came in his buggy to my place. Two Botany police was stationed on my house all the morning. I certainly thought because they were friends but later on I discovered that Drs Marshall and Martin had ordered them to do so.

When the priest was about to come to my door the police detained him. I wondered at the delay. I sent someone to invite the priest in. He came in

and said prayers over the dead body of my husband
that was laying on the bed and then he left ... What
I want to find out is this — what was the police
saying to the priest?[7]

Some days later, Louisa made a second appeal to be allowed
to see the Catholic priest from Randwick:

> Sir,
>   I beg you grant me permission to see the Sisters
> of Mercy that visits this gaol. I am sure they would
> only be glad to take pity on me and see the priest in
> Randwick. I am sure it would throw some light on
> the subject of the death of my late husband Collins
> which is shrouded in mystery to present time. I asked
> Governor [of the gaol] for permission to see the
> Sisters and have made several other requests to him
> since I have been in gaol and he refuses me. In fact,
> he mostly insults me and speaks to me as though I
> was one void of feelings. He as a man ought to know
> better than how to speak to a woman in my position.[8]

Although it isn't clear whether Louisa did get to see the
Catholic priest, she was again hinting a few days later at
new evidence that would make her situation look very
different:

> Sir,
>   I have some awful disclosures to make before
> my trial comes of which will make things look

very different to what they do at the present time.
Praying that you may be pleased to grant my humble
requests, most humble and respectful, Louisa
Collins.[9]

Of course, Louisa wasn't the only one trying to find new
evidence for her re-trial. The Crown itself understood that
it would need to do more in the second trial than it had
done in the first in order to get a conviction. To that end,
police were sent back into the neighbourhood at Botany to
see if anyone could provide any further clues that might
point to Louisa's guilt.

Three women, concerned that Louisa had lied on the
stand, immediately came forward. The first of these, Mrs
Pettit, told Senior Constable Sherwood that she had been
reading about Louisa's trial in the newspaper and she felt
that some of Louisa's evidence had been false.[10] Mrs Pettit
was particularly concerned about a sworn statement to the
Coroner's Court in which Louisa had expressed regret
about re-filling Michael's nobbler with milk without
making sure that it was clean.

According to Mrs Pettit, this was simply not true. In a
sworn statement given to Senior Constable Sherwood, she
said that 'on the Saturday night before Collins died, Mrs
Collins asked her for a glass. She [Mrs Pettit] found this
small glass on the mantelpiece in the front room, bottom
up [and] she wiped it well with her apron both inside and
out, before giving it to Mrs Collins.' According to Mrs
Pettit, the glass was 'perfectly clean' when she handed it
to Louisa. In fact, she described it as 'shining'. She also

told police that Michael 'could not possibly put anything into the glass' himself because 'he was never on this night left a minute by himself as they were all watching for his death'.[11]

Mrs Collis agreed: 'I heard Mrs Collins ask Mrs Pettit for a glass ... I saw her get a small plain tumbler in the front room, wipe it well with her apron and then hand it to Mrs Collins ... The glass was perfectly clean.' Mrs Collis described how Louisa had gone into the kitchen and come back with the same little nobbler, filled with milk. '[She] put her hand under [Michael's] head, raised it up and gave him a drink,' Mrs Collis said, 'and after lying down he appeared to go off into a fit, struggling violently for about five minutes. I thought he was dying. Mrs Collins then asked us to leave the room for a few minutes. We did so, she then shut the door and was alone in the room with Collins for about five minutes.'[12]

Senior Constable Sherwood passed this new evidence to the chief inspector of police in Sydney. He also went back to the house at Botany to do another search, just in case there might have been another little nobbler-tumbler, similar to the one Mrs Pettit thought she had cleaned. But no: 'I took possession of all the glasses in the place (three in number) ... these I showed to the two women, but they state the one they refer to was a great deal smaller, and consequently, it must be the one produced at the trial,' he said.[13]

Also giving new evidence was Louisa's former friend Mrs Ellen Price, who had washed the bodies of Charles, Michael and baby John. She had been called as a witness at the first trial, not for the prosecution but for the defence.

Mr Lusk had needed her to tell the jury that Michael had died with his trousers on. According to Senior Constable Sherwood, Mrs Price now wanted to change sides and appear for the prosecution, so that she could tell the jury that while it was true that Michael had indeed had his trousers on, 'she is confident there was nothing in the pockets of them'.[14]

In a further effort to bolster the Crown case, Senior Constable Sherwood also took the opportunity to raise some of the rumours about Louisa that were flying around Botany. 'The prisoner's maiden name is Hall,' he said, in his new statement. 'She is a native of either Muswellbrook or Scone and is said to be either a daughter or a sister of a man named Hall, a notorious bushranger.'[15] He was talking about Ben Hall, and an extension of this rumour was that when Ben Hall found out that the beautiful young Louisa — the brown-eyed, black-haired 'pet of the village' — had married a middle-aged Merriwa butcher, he threatened to shoot Charles Andrews dead. It was all very romantic, except that Ben Hall was already ten years old when Louisa was born, and by the time she was married he was dead.

In any case, Louisa's second trial got underway at the Central Criminal Court in the first week of November 1888. She had, by this stage, been gaoled at Darlinghurst for more than four months.

The basic procedures were the same: Louisa was taken from her cell each day by two female wardens, who walked her through the underground tunnel to the courthouse. Some of the other, more important details were different: a new jury had been empanelled, for example, and a careful study of the names shows that one of the men chosen to sit in judgement of Louisa on this, the second go-around, was Alexander Geddes, of the Geddes wool family, which had employed both Michael and Charles, proving once again that the pool of people from which jurors could be drawn was very small.

Besides a new jury there was also a new judge, and it can't have given Louisa any comfort to know who it was: Justice William Charles Windeyer, of the Mount Rennie case. Then again, perhaps it was a mixed blessing: on the one hand, no other judge had such a fearsome reputation. On the other, no other judge was thought to have the same sense of compassion for poor women and their children.

Justice Windeyer was born at Westminster in September 1834 and had sailed to Sydney as an infant aboard the *Medway*. His father died when William was still a small boy and, according to the *Cyclopedia of NSW*, published in 1907, both 'widow and orphan were left badly off'. A family friend apparently offered to pay for some of the cost of William's boarding at the King's School in Parramatta, but the bulk of the cost of his education still had to be covered by his mother 'from the narrow income she derived from the farm and garden' at their property.[16]

William was not, at first, all that promising a student — a report card for 1846 commented that his Greek was 'humble' and his Latin 'improving'[17] — but he worked hard, and ultimately received a scholarship to the University of Sydney, becoming one of the first candidates to enter that institution and among the first to graduate.

Then, in 1862, the nation nearly lost him: William, along with 140 other people, was aboard the *City of Sydney* when it hit rocks off Green Cape and sank in a little over an hour.

William — and everyone else — was rescued, and it's perhaps just as well, for Sydney would not be the same city without him. Justice Windeyer was an early supporter of free education for all children and of tertiary education for women. He became a trustee of Sydney Grammar School and of the Free Public Library, and the founding chairman of the Women's College within the University of Sydney.

Having been raised by a single mother, he was widely believed to have a soft spot for women and children (some historians have argued that the reason Justice Windeyer was so hard on the young men of Mount Rennie was because he felt so keenly for the victim; and it seems that he could scarcely conceive of women as perpetrators). In the early 1870s, he had been asked to chair a Royal Commission into the treatment of the colony's many abandoned infants and neglected children, most of whom were being held in barrack-style accommodation in Randwick. He tackled the problem with zeal and in 1874 published what may well have been the first report anywhere in the world calling on such institutions to be shut down in favour of a system much like today's foster care.

So there was a new jury and a new judge. The Crown had also appointed a new prosecutor: Mr Henry Emmanuel (HE) Cohen. Like Justice Windeyer, Mr Cohen had a proud record of public service: he was for many years president of the St John Ambulance Association. Born on

1 December 1840 at Port Macquarie, he became a clerk at the age of sixteen and was called to the bar in Sydney in 1871. Old photographs show Mr Cohen as a completely bald man with an enormous dark beard concealing half his face. Besides being a barrister, he was a competent swimmer and 'an energetic walker' (did he walk with Mr Hamlet? — the record doesn't say). He was also a member of the board of the York Street Synagogue in Sydney.[18]

Given that Louisa was on trial for the same crime, much of the evidence at the second trial would be the same as at the first trial: Dr Marshall would be called, as would Dr Martin, Constable Jeffes and so on. It was what was different that was important. To that end, the Crown relied heavily on some of the inconsistencies in Louisa's evidence, in particular the inconsistency between the two statements she had given — one before Michael's autopsy and one after the arsenic had been found.

In her first statement, Louisa had said simply that Michael had been suffering from a cold. Only when the results of the autopsy came back did she begin to suggest suicide, which perhaps makes sense: why would Louisa bother to try to explain the arsenic before she knew it was there? Mr Cohen saw more sinister motives at play. He told the jury that Louisa had on three separate occasions told three different people that Michael had not taken anything that could disagree with him. She told police that he was not taking anything except the medicine that the doctor ordered; she told two doctors that he hadn't eaten any fish or taken anything that might upset his stomach. The idea that he'd had some powder in his pocket for a lump in his groin had come up only *after* the arsenic had been detected during the autopsy. Wasn't that a bit suspicious?

Perhaps it was, as was the fact that no folded paper of arsenic had been found in Michael's trousers after his death, or anywhere else — but a round box of Rough on Rats had been seen in Louisa's kitchen, by her own daughter, just before Michael died.

The fact that Justice Windeyer, like Justice Foster before him, regarded May's evidence about the poison as crucial is made plain by the notes he took during the trial.[19] He marked each page of her testimony with a long, black vertical line, as if to highlight its importance. Once again, it seems that she spoke clearly, repeating much of the evidence she had already given to police, which included this description of the days leading up to Michael's death:

> [He knocked] off work on a Saturday and on the
> following Monday my mother and him went to the
> [doctor] in the forenoon. They came home in the
> afternoon and had their tea and then Collins went
> to bed … Next morning Collins told my brother
> Fred to go to Mr Geddes and tell him he could not
> come to work as he was sick. He stopped in bed. I
> never went into the bedroom only when my mother
> was out. Mick called me in one day to empty the
> chamber. He always asked me to get him a drink of
> cold tea when my mother was out. She never let me
> into the room since my father died. My mother and

> Collins used to beat me and my little brothers with
> a walking stick and tell me I was like my bloody
> father.[20]

Given Justice Windeyer's well-known sympathy for small, neglected children, it's perhaps no surprise that these lines are heavily underlined in his notebook.

May also told the jury that she'd heard her mother, in the days before Michael's death, lamenting the state of the family's finances since Michael had moved in: 'She told me, money is no good while Mick is in the house, but she would get some more money when he died.'[21] (On the face of it, that seems an odd thing for May to have said, since Michael's life was not insured.)

As to the Rough on Rats, May said as she had said previously: she'd seen 'a little box on a shelf underneath a white basin'. It was 'a small round one' with a 'dark blue powder' inside, and the words Rough on Rats on it. Upon finding the box, she had said: 'Look Ma! What I've found — Rough on Rats' while holding up the box. Her mother had come into the kitchen to look, but more than that May could not remember, except that when she next went to clean the kitchen, the box was gone.[22]

This evidence was as devastating to Louisa's case as it had been the first time, and May's distress at having to tell the story again is captured in this paragraph from the *Evening News*:

> In giving evidence against her mother, Louisa
> Collins, at the Central Criminal Court today, a

pretty child, named May Andrews, 11½ years of
age, was much affected. The prisoner and several of
the jurors felt the situation keenly.[23]

What exactly this meant — that the prisoner and the
jurors felt the situation keenly — isn't made clear in the
newspaper report, but it seems that mother and child, and
others in the court, must have wept, and who could blame
them? The jurors in particular were in a terrible spot: to be
asked to find a woman guilty of her husband's murder — a
capital crime — was one thing. To be asked to do so on
the basis of evidence given by her own daughter would for
many people be impossible.

As it happened, help was on the way. It came on the
second day of the second trial. Evidence about Michael's
patchy employment history was being given when,
suddenly, one of the jurors piped up. Hadn't Michael been
employed as a carter for a wool merchant?

Yes, he had. He'd been employed by Geddes.

Well, then, didn't his job involve handling the skins?

The question seemed to startle the court. Why should
that matter? Because, the juror persisted, a lot of farmers
dip their sheep in arsenic baths before shearing or removing
the skins.[24] There was no better way to kill lice, ticks and
fleas, or to strip the wool of grease.

This was something that Louisa's defence counsel
should have known. The wool industry in New South
Wales in 1888 was massive. The removal of lice, ticks and
grease was essential to its success, and newspapers had for
years been full of advice for treating sheep without killing

them or ruining the wool, and the skins. Here is just one example, from the *Kerang Times and Swan Hill Gazette* in 1886:

> Lice and Ticks in Sheep?
> After shearing, try either of the following, both of which have been successfully used: 1. Take 70lb. of sulphur to 300 gal of water and 30lb. lime. To dissolve the sulphur, make it into a paste before putting it into the boiling water, as doing so all lumps will be the easier dissolved. Keep the mixture at blood heat when dipping. 2. *[Add] half an ounce of arsenic to the gallon of water* [my emphasis] ... do not let the animals remain in the water more than 60 sec.[25]

Recipes for arsenic dip were likewise easy to find:

> I read a paragraph in your paper about dipping sheep in arsenic. Half an ounce is too much, particularly at this time of year, when the wool is long on the sheep, as you run the risk of killing them. I dip my sheep in arsenic just after shearing, and they keep clear of ticks all the year. You cannot dissolve more than 5 oz. to the gallon, and you must not put it in till the water is boiling, and keep it boiling for half an hour, and stir it up occasionally. Many people make the mistake of not boiling it long enough to dissolve the arsenic.[26]

Despite this, it was again left to a juror, and not to Louisa's counsel, to point out that the arsenic in Michael's system might have come from the skins he handled on a daily basis. Why, the juror even knew a man who had suffered in such a way. As poisons went, arsenic was dangerous, and plenty of people knew it, so much so that by the late 1880s, ads for arsenic-free dip such as Little's had begun to appear in Sydney's newspapers:

> Last season I had 100 old ewes shorn and dipped
> during a cold wet afternoon to test the properties of
> it before putting through my stud sheep; and, to my
> surprise, next morning I found them all lively and
> well, and *I am sure had they been dipped with arsenic*
> [my emphasis], most of them would have died
> during the night. I dipped all my studs and 8,000
> other sheep last year with Little's Chemical Fluid,
> and intend using it for all this year.[27]

Here, then, was a real coup for the defence: Michael Collins had been riding around on a cart stacked with sheep skins for at least two weeks before he became sick, and had in fact been carting skins on the very day he got sick. Not only that, Louisa's first husband, Charles, had been a wool washer, meaning both men may have worked closely with the poison that cost them their lives.

Louisa's defence counsel, Mr Lusk, may not have come upon this evidence himself, but to his great credit he soon leapt upon it, grilling Dr Marshall about whether arsenic might have seeped into Michael's system through his hands or indeed through cuts on his body such as the wound on his leg.

Dr Marshall told the court that he wasn't even aware that 'squatters treated sheepskins with arsenic'. That said, yes, arsenic could enter the body and the bloodstream through a cut or a graze, so if Michael had cut his finger or, 'in working with arsenic, [he might] have placed his finger in his mouth … in this way [he] may have introduced the drug into his system'.

Mr Lusk then asked Dr Martin what he knew about the arsenic in skins. Like Dr Marshall, he didn't know a lot but agreed that small amounts — 'only a slight trace' — would be found in a person's body if the arsenic had entered that person's system through a cut as opposed to being ingested.[28]

Dr Milford, of the autopsy, said the same: he 'knew of cases in which the external application of arsenic had caused sore hands'. Better still — at least as far as Louisa was concerned — he said that he had himself suffered from sore fingernails through using arsenic in dealing with dead bodies, and he'd seen the same thing happen to a number of medical students.

Mr Lusk rose. Dr Milford had already told the court that he believed that Michael had died of arsenical poisoning, but was there anything in his post-mortem examination to show *how* arsenic had got into Michael's system?

Dr Milford said no, there was not.[29]

This was important evidence for the defence, and there was more to come: Louisa's neighbour James Law, who had spent some time working alongside Michael carting skins from Glebe Island to the sheds, agreed that it would not be unusual for a skin puller to get his hands poisoned. Another fellmonger, Alfred Ralph, who had also been employed at Geddes, testified that he had seen Michael driving a dray with green skins, which may well have been treated with arsenic before they reached Geddes and Walter Hayes told the jury that Michael had regularly handled 'skins both green and dry'. Moreover, Michael had a 'running sore on his leg at the time he was handling the skins' (this was the sore that Dr Milford had found during the autopsy).[30]

It came time to sum up. Mr Lusk began by thanking the jury. They had by this stage been listening to evidence for more than 72 hours, in 'what, on the face of it, appeared to be a very difficult case'. But was it really so difficult?

'Follow me through the facts of the case and consider … which are matters of opinion and not properly speaking part of the case itself,' Mr Lusk said. Because, when all was said and done, all the Crown had was circumstantial evidence. The prisoner, Louisa, 'had no quarrel with her husband … they lived amicably together [and] there was nothing in the shape of money to induce [her] to commit the crime'. With regard to the arsenic found in the nobbler, well, yes, Mr Lusk admitted that that 'played a very large part in the case', but who really knew what was in that glass? It had been taken away by Constable Jeffes before being delivered to Mr Hamlet, and by the time it arrived at the government laboratory some of it was missing. 'Was it not fair to assume that it had also been tampered with in other ways?' Mr Lusk said.[31]

Also, with regard to the box of Rough on Rats that May said she saw, Mr Lusk would ask the jury to consider whether Louisa would have been so stupid as to leave it on the shelf. If engaged in such a crime as poisoning her husband 'would she not have most carefully concealed the existence of the poison?' The same might also be said with regard to the liquid in the tumbler: if Louisa was using it as set forth by the Crown, 'there was nothing whatever to have prevented her from throwing the contents of the glass outside'.[32]

Then, too, came the problem of the skins. Michael had worked with skins both green and dried. He might have poisoned himself by accident — or, as had previously been argued, he might have committed suicide. Considering all this, how could the jury convict Louisa of murder? Surely there was too much doubt.

Of course, the Crown disagreed. Yes, the evidence was mainly circumstantial, but the idea that Michael had committed suicide was, in Mr Cohen's view, 'not feasible ... It is not reasonable to suppose that any man would submit to the torture that he underwent in order to destroy himself ... There is only one rational conclusion — the prisoner Louisa Collins is guilty of the crime of murder.'[33]

Now it was Justice Windeyer's turn. Those in the courthouse who remembered the blistering summation he had given in the Mount Rennie trial might have expected something similar, but a close reading of Justice Windeyer's summation reveals none of the fury he had displayed in that case. On the contrary, he seemed mindful of the terrible consequences if Louisa was found guilty, which is to say, she would very likely hang.

Justice Windeyer began by saying: 'Of all forms of murder, that by poisoning was the one that most shocks us' because of the 'treachery, the falsehood, and danger that necessarily surrounds it'.[34]

That said, he did not believe that Michael had committed suicide, and 'scarcely thought it necessary to dwell upon this portion of the case'. After all, Michael had been a young, healthy, temperate man. 'Was it feasible to suppose that he destroyed himself?' Justice Windeyer said. There was nothing to show that he had lost control of his reason. No, it seemed to Justice Windeyer that the theory of suicide was one that 'could not be entertained'. There were no grounds for it. As a rule, when a man commits suicide he did so as quickly as possible. Nobody had ever heard of a man 'destroying himself by inches' when he had decided to end his life.[35]

How then had Michael come to ingest arsenic? According to Justice Windeyer, there were four possibilities: Louisa had given it to him; somebody else had given it to him; he had taken it accidently; or he had absorbed the poison in the course of his work. Justice Windeyer noted that this last proposition had come from a juror, and not from Mr Lusk. He was not surprised by that. Indeed, he sounded impressed. It was important, he said, especially in a capital case, that jury members should 'peer into every possible hole for evidence'.[36]

But he still killed the idea dead — or, at least, he tried. 'The evidence on this point shows that the deceased had not suffered from anything of this kind,' Justice Windeyer said, 'as no arsenic had been used in the establishment where he had been working.'[37] (This evidence had been given by a representative of the Geddes family; it may well have been true, but there was nothing to say that the sheep skins hadn't been treated before they arrived at Geddes.)

On the other hand, there was May's evidence: she had found a box of arsenic, and then, when she showed it to Louisa, it disappeared. 'What had become of the box?' Justice Windeyer said. 'There was evidence that the little girl found it and showed it to her mother after which it was never seen again.'[38]

In short, there were, in Justice Windeyer's mind, compelling reasons to find Louisa guilty — but of course it was not up to him to decide. It was up to the jury, who should go now and come back with a decision.

The jury filed out of the court at four p.m. They debated the case for five and a half hours before returning at 9.30 p.m. to say they could not reach a decision.

Justice Windeyer urged them on, sequestering them for another night so they might continue their deliberations.

As at the first trial, when the court opened shortly after 9.30 a.m. the following day, all of the seats in the public gallery were filled 'with an expectant crowd of men, women, and children'. Only Louisa 'showed no traces of anxiety as to the result of the trial'. She took her seat in the dock 'with the same indifferent demeanour' (perhaps it was a quiet confidence?) that other reporters had noted during the first trial.[39]

The jurors filed in, and took their seats.

'Gentlemen of the jury,' the associate to Justice Windeyer said, 'are you agreed upon your verdict?'

'No,' the foreman replied. 'We are not agreed.' Furthermore, there was 'not the slightest probability of our agreeing, your Honour'.[40]

In fact, it turned out that ten of the jurors had voted for an acquittal; one juror could not make up his mind. Only one juror thought Louisa guilty.[41]

Justice Windeyer took up his ink pen and made a note in his notebook: 'NO VERDICT.'[42]

'Then, gentlemen, you are discharged,' he said.

Turning to the Crown, he added: 'Mr Cohen, what course do you propose to take?'[43]

It was a loaded question. Louisa had now been tried twice for the same crime and neither jury had been able to reach a verdict. By a long tradition, she should have gone free immediately. It was — and still is — extremely rare for any prisoner to be tried more than twice for the same offence, even in those cases where no verdict has been reached. The reason should be obvious: if a murder can't be proved beyond a reasonable doubt in the first instance — let alone in the second — how compelling can the evidence be? Also, by the time of a third trial — with the pool of jurors small and getting smaller, and all manner of wild rumours about Louisa's past circulating in the press — all hope of fairness would surely be lost.

While it's impossible to know for certain, Louisa herself seemed to think that she would soon be free. According to the *Evening News*, she again left the dock 'with a radiant smile upon her face'.[44]

*

One of the most unnerving aspects of this tale is the zeal with which the Crown went after Louisa Collins, especially because the Crown prosecutor himself was now saying that the case should be dropped.

If that sounds extraordinary, it is: rare is the case in which even the prosecution doesn't want to go ahead, and yet the fact that Mr Cohen didn't think that Louisa could ever fairly be convicted is revealed in a letter that he wrote to the attorney general, Sir George Bowen Simpson, to say that the case against Louisa should, after two trials, be dropped.

A copy of Mr Cohen's letter was kept, and can be found today, stored among the other papers from the trial at State Records New South Wales. It makes for remarkable reading. Dated 14 November 1888, less than a week after the end of Louisa's second trial, it says:

Sir,

I have the honour to report that in the case the jury disagreed and I have been informed that there were ten for an acquittal and one for a conviction and the 12th was undecided.

In my own opinion though the facts certainly point to the prisoner as having administered the poison which caused the death of her husband, there is evidence which certainly may in my judgment raise a doubt as to the guilt of the prisoner. I refer especially to her continually seeking the aid of doctors during the week or ten days previous to the death of the deceased; her allowing the small tumbler containing the milk in which arsenic was afterwards found upon analysis to remain untouched for some time after her husband's death when she might meanwhile have destroyed or done away with it and the contents; and to her having at all times after the death of Collins and even when under arrest asserted that she and she alone practically gave the deceased whatever he took in the shape of food or nourishment.

As I am asked whether she should be tried again for the offence of murdering the deceased Michael Peter Collins, I beg to state that in my opinion, she should not be put upon her trial again to answer this charge, two juries having now disagreed upon the question of her guilt in this case.

I have the honour to be Sir,
Your obedient servant
HE Cohen.[45]

The sentiment couldn't be clearer: '*She should not be put upon her trial again to answer this charge, two juries having now disagreed upon the question of her guilt in this case.*'

Just as clear is the fact that Louisa Collins would be tried again — and again. They — meaning someone, somewhere — were determined to get her. The question, of course, is who? And why? What was it about this case that made the Crown so determined to get a conviction? Some may say, well, that is the way the system works: a person is charged, and then tried; when the jury cannot reach a verdict, they must be tried again.

But then again? And again? In a case where all the evidence was circumstantial?

One thing is known for certain: many of the most senior judges in New South Wales in 1888 believed in Louisa's guilt. Also known for certain is that police — and others — were concerned by the idea that she had landed on arsenic as a murder weapon. Arsenic was cheap and easy to get from the local chemist. It was easily concealed in a glass of milk or brandy. Thousands of women in nineteenth-century New South Wales were trapped in miserable marriages, at the mercy of men who drank and then let their fists fly.

In all these circumstances, perhaps the Crown, and the government, and all those charged with keeping the peace in the colony, thought: Louisa Collins cannot be allowed to escape justice.

Louisa Collins must hang.

Louisa herself seemed oblivious to this. Some days after the second trial, she wrote a letter from prison to an acquaintance to whom she owed money:

> Sir — I hope you do not think of me as most people
> do as one of the deepest dye black. As soon as my
> trial is over I will call and pay you what I owe you.
> Hoping that your wife and dear children are quite
> well, I remain, yours truly, Louisa Collins[46]

As to whether Louisa would actually hang if ever convicted, well, all that can be said is that hangings had continued apace since the Rennie trial, with prisoners being taken from Darlinghurst Gaol to the gallows even while Louisa's trials were underway. Most of the hangings were in Nosey Bob's signature inept style, as a report from the *Balmain Observer and Western Suburbs Advertiser* in September 1888 attests:

> At 9.15 on Tuesday morning last, the man Robert
> Hewart, sentenced to death for committing
> a diabolical and fatal outrage upon a fellow
> prisoner ... was executed according to law in
> Darlinghurst Gaol.[47]

That suggests a reasonably well-ordered affair when, in fact, the hanging was at first 'considerably delayed by the non-appearance of the Sheriff' and then comprehensively bungled:

> After having stood in front of the culprit some
> time arranging his neck for the reception of the
> rope, the executioner [Nosey Bob] who throughout
> had proceeded in a very leisurely manner, as if
> he enjoyed his ghastly functions, beckoned to his
> assistant for a white linen cloth. Adjusting this so
> as to envelope the prisoner's whole head, [Nosey]
> next called for the rope, noose, which after some
> confusion his coadjutor handed to him. Having fixed
> it in proper position, the former then called out: 'Let
> go!' intending of course that his colleague should
> instantly draw the bolt and let the doomed man

drop. The assistant, however, became more confused than ever; not understanding what was required of him in the least but reaching for this, that and the other, instead of the fateful lever. While this was going on [Nosey] continued to call out in an excited manner: 'Let go! Let go! Let go, I tell you! Oh, C——, let go!!!'[48]

(For the record, the word Christ was often not spelled out in nineteenth-century newspaper reports, but recorded as 'C——'.)

Finally the bolt was drawn and the prisoner fell with 'a sickening thud'. The whole spectacle had taken a ghastly four minutes, leaving Nosey Bob to again try to explain his incompetence away. His excuse was that it was the assistant's first execution, but people were getting tired of excuses. As one editorial writer said: 'It is devoutly to be hoped that when next the services of a N.S.W. hangman are needed, the execution will not be characterised by such reprehensible delay and lack of efficiency.'[49]

No such luck.

CHAPTER 9

The Third Trial: 'The evidence here is very weak'

19–22 November 1888

Central Criminal Court, Darlinghurst

PRESIDING: Justice Joseph George Innes

CROWN: Mr Charles Gilbert (CG) Heydon and Mr WH Coffey

DEFENCE: Mr HH Lusk

JURY: Messrs George Hawksby Fielden, James Bolder, William Arthur Swan, George Hickman Robinson, Duncan Macpherson, Nathan John Preston, Alexander Smith, John William Eady, John McCarthy, William Henry Jones, Joseph Jonathan Dakin, Henry Prior Palser[1]

Louisa's third trial for murder began at the Central Criminal Court just ten days after the second trial had ended. Lest anyone think that they can skip this chapter, since this trial would surely be a repeat of the first two, it surely would not, and for one good reason: in addition to there being a new judge, a new jury and a new prosecutor, Louisa this time faced a whole new charge.[2]

In her first two trials, Louisa had been on trial for the murder of her second husband, Michael. In a clever twist, the Crown now decided to put her on trial for the murder of her *first* husband, Charles — but then, if the Crown had found it difficult to get a conviction on the first charge, this was going to be even tougher.

No autopsy had been done on Charles before he was buried and, by the time his body was dug up, he'd been in the ground more than fourteen months. A minute trace of arsenic had been found, but the cause of death was far from conclusive.

In an effort to overcome any doubts the jury might have had in that regard, the Crown had sent the doughty Mr Hamlet to Rookwood Cemetery to take samples of the earth for arsenical testing. If no arsenic was found in the soil around the grave, then the jury might be inclined to believe that the arsenic in Charles's body had been introduced to him by Louisa.

Mr Hamlet did his duty, returning to the gravesite with the police sub-inspector, Mr Hyam, and two gravediggers. With great solemnity, they took three samples of earth — one from the surface of the grave, one from a depth of six inches, and one from the soil about six feet away — and subjected all three samples to tests.

'No trace of arsenic could be discovered,' Mr Hamlet said, adding that the 'delicacy' of his test was such that 'the presence of one-five thousandths of a part of a grain can be observed with certainty ... I am therefore of the opinion that no arsenic compound exists in the soil of the cemetery.'[3]

In other words, what arsenic had been found may well have been given to Charles by Louisa. With this new evidence in hand, the trial got underway. The judge chosen to preside was the first to be Sydney-born: he was Joseph George Innes, whose father, Major Joseph Long Innes, had been superintendent of police (and whose son would become a Supreme Court judge). Besides being a lawyer, Justice Innes had also been a politician: in March 1872, he was elected to the Legislative Assembly, joining Sir Henry Parkes's first ministry as solicitor general.[4]

Given that the previous prosecutor, Mr Cohen, had expressed serious reservations about trying Louisa a third time, it perhaps makes sense that he'd either stepped aside or been replaced, by a Catholic lawyer, Charles G Heydon. Like all of the barristers on the Crown's side, Mr Heydon had already had a good, solid career — he'd been a banker and a journalist before becoming a widely admired lawyer — and he would go on to become a judge of the District Court.

By contrast, Louisa still had Mr Lusk, working pro bono.

Some readers may be wondering what had become of Louisa's older children after she went to gaol, and it's during this third trial that we find out: as noted previously, the two youngest had been taken into care at Randwick; the rest of them, including May, were allowed to scamper about the courtroom, prompting an exasperated Justice

Innes to ask if anyone was actually taking care of them, given the horrible circumstances.

Clearly, nobody was. Mr Heydon replied: 'I think one of the elder sons.'

Justice Innes was dismayed. 'It is most repugnant to my feelings of human nature to have the children about the court,' he said. 'I should have thought that some provision should be made for them.'

Mr Heydon was apologetic, saying that, as far as he understood, 'the police are to a certain extent looking after the little ones'.[5]

Of course, some of the children — especially May — had to be in court. The Crown still needed them to testify against their mother.

If May's testimony at previous trials had been harrowing, this would be more so. Charles Andrews wasn't only Louisa's husband. He was May's father and she had loved him, and now the Crown was determined to show that Louisa, by contrast, never had, and indeed had married him only because her mother made the match, back when she was barely sixteen years old.

One of the first witnesses to testify in this regard was Mrs Johanna Bartington, who told the court that she had been living at Pople's Terrace when Charles died, and she'd always remembered him as being besotted with his wife. 'I came to live in Botany in June 1886,' she said. 'I knew Mr Andrews because he was working at the Springvale Tannery under my husband, who was the manager. We lived in the same terrace — at No. 8. Andrews seemed fond of his wife, and very fond of his children.'

Louisa, by contrast, seemed frustrated and bored, and she would drink, and then Charles would get cross and they would squabble: 'Sometimes she would not take anything for a month and then she would drink late, perhaps for a week. Andrews used to quarrel about her drinking.'[6]

Mrs Collis also gave evidence, telling the jury that Louisa had not only told her that she'd never loved Charles, she didn't like any of the children either — a tough thing for May and the others to have to hear in court.

As in the first two trials, a key part of the Crown case was also Louisa's affair with Michael in the weeks before Charles died. Mr Law told the jury how he remembered Charles having a 'big row with [Michael] and turning him out of his house ... I asked what the row was about. He [Michael] said Andrews was jealous of him and cleared them all out. Shortly after this, Andrews took sick' and died. Less than three days later, Louisa and Michael were living together. And then came the big party:

> About a fortnight after Andrew's death, [there was]
> a dance in an empty house [on Pople's Terrace]
> ... Collins gave 2/6 and Mrs Collins 2/6 toward
> the spree and were both at the dance. I asked Mrs
> Collins to dance and Collins replied: 'My old
> woman does not dance.'[7]

All of this was damaging, as was the fact that May would again have to testify, not so much about having found Rough on Rats in the kitchen before Michael died, but about how she'd found a similar box — maybe even the same box — in the house at Berry's paddock, where she'd lived with her father. More emphasis would also be given to the fact that Louisa had sent May out for tram tickets not ten minutes after her father died, and then left May and the other little ones to sit with the corpse while she went to try to extract money from the insurance company.

The defence did not allow that to go unchallenged: of course Louisa had to go to town to get money. She was a mother of seven living children, five of whom were still at home. Her husband was now dead. She would need a coffin, a plot and an undertaker. She was merely being responsible.

As at the first two trials, May was preceded, or in some cases followed, to the stand by one of her brothers, including, in this instance, Reuben. Unlike May, it seems that he was willingly there for the Crown. In fact, he had written a letter to the No. 3 Police Station on 16 November, specifically making himself available for this trial to testify against his mother. The letter said:

> Reuben Andrews — son of the accused — residing
> with Mrs Elspeth Butcher of Adamstown,
> Newcastle, can give evidence on behalf of the
> Crown.

The letter went on:

> He [Reuben] was residing with his father and
> mother at Botany at the time of his father's death
> and continued to reside there until after his mother

got married to Collins in April 1887. Andrews is
over 19 years of age and [was] working with his
father at Geddes wool washing establishment at the
time of his father's death. Andrews is well known to
Constable Anderson of Adamstown.[8]

In court, Reuben described his father as a hard-working,
healthy, sober man. He could hardly believe it when he got
sick, and assumed that he'd soon get better. He recalled
his mother telling him that in fact his father was dead: the
shock was terrible, and rather than stay with his mother
after she remarried, he'd gone away to live near his brother,
Herbert, in Adamstown.

All of this was surely damaging, yet this particular
case would still prove an easy one for Mr Lusk to win.

The Crown had argued that traces of arsenic had been
found in Charles's remains, and Mr Hamlet's evidence
suggested that the arsenic hadn't come from the soil
around the coffin. However, Charles had worked as a
wool washer, and Mr Lusk had by now assembled a solid
argument that working with wool perhaps meant working
with arsenic. To this end, he called Alexander Geddes,
of Geddes and Son, to the stand to explain that Charles
had been in his employ for six years, and that part of his
job had been to wash the skins after the wool was pulled
off, and that it was possible that some of the skins that
Charles handled had been 'prepared or treated by the
squatters with arsenic before they reached his hands'.

Mr Geddes also agreed that 'some of the men had
suffered from sore hands through handling the skins',

although, as far as he knew, Charles had not suffered in this way.[9]

Mr Lusk also noted that Charles's own doctor, Dr Martin, hadn't put his death down to poisoning. In fact, he'd issued a death certificate that clearly said that Charles had died of acute gastritis. More than a year had gone by before any doubts had arisen in the doctor's mind, and only then because a colleague, Dr Marshall, had told him that Louisa's second husband was complaining of stomach pains that wouldn't ease.

'The case had passed entirely from the doctor's mind in the rush of other business,' Mr Lusk said. 'He must have entirely forgotten the circumstances.'[10]

Plus, 'it makes all the difference in the world through what medium a person looks at bygone events,' he said. 'The evidence here is very weak.' Yes, there was evidence that Charles's wife had a 'very strong liking' — as it were — for another man. However, it was not for the jury to judge Louisa on her 'social and moral character'. What they had to consider was not whether Louisa was playing around behind Charles's back but whether she had 'secretly murdered her husband'.[11]

Mr Heydon, for the Crown, tried to make a little more of his case by pointing out that Charles's life had been insured for the sum of 200 pounds, and that Louisa stood to inherit everything, but all that did was strengthen Mr Lusk's hand. Yes, Louisa stood to gain the 200 pounds of insurance money, but who really benefited from that?

Michael Collins.

It was Michael who got the new watch and chain and the new suit of clothes and all his debts paid off when Charles died. It was Michael who ended up in Charles's old house, with his lively, drunken widow on his arm. Michael had danced and sung — and laid claim to Louisa — at the party at the empty house at Pople's Terrace. In short, the jury should put aside their own high standards of 'morality or manners or social custom' and accept that there was at least one other person who 'had a stronger motive for removing the deceased'.[12]

'I do not wish to speak ill of the dead,' Mr Lusk said, 'but there was one other person who profited more by the death of the man than the accused did.'[13]

As in the previous two trials, the judge was required to sum up the evidence for the jury. He didn't feel the need to impress upon them the 'extreme gravity' of their duty. Everyone surely understood by now that this was a hanging case. It had been in the newspapers for months. The public gallery had been packed each and every day.

The main thing for the jury to remember, Justice Innes said, was the circumstantial nature of the evidence. The faint trace of arsenic found in Charles's body may have been introduced by accident. Charles's old boss, Mr Geddes, had been in the wool-washing business for nineteen years, and he had very clearly testified that 'some of the skins [at Geddes] were prepared or treated by the squatters with arsenic before they reached the wool sheds'.

This was such important evidence, yet Justice Innes qualified it, reminding the jury that Mr Geddes had 'never in the whole of that time known of a really serious case of illness through poisoning ... He had [only] known men to get sore or poisoned fingers through using the arsenic' — and he had never known anyone who had died from it.[14]

Would he have known?

Had he known, would Mr Geddes — would anyone involved in the wool trade at that time — have said so?

We will never know.

The jury retired to consider their verdict shortly before three p.m. A little under two hours later — the briefest possible time, really — they returned to say there was 'no chance' of them agreeing upon a verdict. Justice Innes urged them on, and so they went away again, but by nine p.m., they were still no closer, and by morning, this jury, too, had been discharged.

CHAPTER 10

The Fourth Trial: 'Is the prisoner guilty or not guilty?'

5–8 December 1888
Central Criminal Court, Darlinghurst
PRESIDING: Chief Justice of New South Wales,
Sir Frederick Darley
CROWN: Mr CG Heydon
DEFENCE: Mr HH Lusk
JURY: Edward Brett, Charles Frederick Lindeman,
Charles Ward, William Quintin, Samuel Simmons,
Albert Edward Dogging, John Simpson,
Christopher Lenehan, James William Lover, Charles
Barrow, James Joseph Waddell, William Hill[1]

Three trials. Three judges. Three juries. No verdict. Yet the Crown would not surrender. Just days after the third trial ended, the good men of New South Wales, going against all tradition and, it surely must be said, against all the rules of fairness, ordered a fourth trial (the charge this time would again be the murder of Michael Collins).

Far from backing away, the Crown had upped the stakes. The judge would be the Honourable Chief Justice Frederick Matthew Darley QC, holder of the highest legal office in the land. Not only that, the Crown objected to not one, but four of the prospective jurors, before the trial even began. But more about those objections in a moment: Chief Justice Darley was an Irishman who had sailed to Sydney in 1862 and pretty much immediately became an immensely successful barrister — so successful that he really didn't want to give the bar away to become Chief Justice. In fact, when first approached, despite it being a great honour, Sir Frederick turned the job down, telling friends the position paid only half the salary he was earning as a lawyer.[2]

Fate intervened when the second-choice candidate, Julian Salomons, quit the position just a few days after accepting it. Sir Frederick was again approached, with the then premier, Sir Patrick Jennings, saying: 'You must be aware that your consent to occupy the position would give, probably, almost universal satisfaction.'[3]

How could anyone say no?

By chance, the swearing in took place at the Banco Court on 18 December 1886 — about the time Louisa was engaged in her mad love affair with Michael. Now judge and prisoner were in court together. The fourth trial began on 5 December 1888, just twenty days before Christmas. According to the *Evening News*, Louisa 'appeared a trifle paler on the occasion of this, her fourth trial, and it would appear that the lengthened period of her incarceration in the gaol at Darlinghurst had to some extent militated against her health'. The courthouse 'was again crowded by the public ... the interest hitherto manifested in these now notorious trials seemed in no way unabated'.

Importantly, the newspaper also noted that while 'four challenges [to the jury] were issued by the Crown', Louisa's counsel objected to none.[4]

Chief Justice Darley began by opening his bound notebook (he would fill two of them before the trial was done). On the opening page, he wrote:

Wednesday 5 December 1888

The Queen

V

Louisa Collins

Next to that, he wrote: 'For the Murder of Michael Peter Collins.'[5]

With a bang of the gavel, the fourth of Louisa's trials was underway — and, once again, what was important was what was different. What, if any little extras, did the Crown have up its sleeve to secure a guilty verdict from a fourth jury when three had already raised their hands in surrender?

One of the first people called was Louisa's son Frederick. He had testified previously, but seems to have spent longer on the stand in the fourth trial, giving evidence that would damage his mother's case as badly as the evidence already given by May.

Mr Heydon, for the Crown, began by asking: What is your name?

'Frederick Andrews.'

And how old are you?

'I am now fourteen years old.'

And what is your relationship to the prisoner?

'I am her son.'

And did you know Michael Collins?

'I did.'

And were you living at home when Michael Collins died?

'I was not at home that day. About a week before he died on a Saturday I was at home as there was no work at the wool wash.'

And tell us, Fred, what happened when you went to get a drink of milk on the day that Michael died?

Frederick paused. 'I went into the kitchen,' he said. 'It was about 11 o'clock. I poured out some milk which was in a small jug on the side table. I was putting some tea into the cup and my mother came in and said where did you get the milk? I said, on the side table. She said, that is condensed milk. It is for Mick. Don't touch it!'

And did you drink it?

'I did not.'

What did you do with it?

'I left the cup on the table. I went outside to the pump and got a drink of water.'

And how much milk was in the jug, Frederick?

'Not much. It was a small jug. It would hold about as much as a tumbler.'

And did your mother use that jug for any other milk? For the milk from the milkman, for example?

Fred sounded perplexed. 'Sometimes,' he said. 'Sometimes the milk we got from the milkman was put in the large jug and sometimes in the small jug.'

And did your mother often have condensed milk?

'Sometimes. She would buy it from the grocer, Mr Sayers.'[6]

The Crown wanted to know if Frederick could remember any other occasion on which he'd had a glass of milk snatched out of his hand. He could not. This prompted the Chief Justice to make a note in his notebook: 'On Saturday the 7th the prisoner opened a tin of condensed milk ... a child got hold of it and [she] took it from him ...'[7]

Next came May, surely by now exhausted, having to repeat in her clear voice what she'd seen: a box of Rough on Rats on the shelf near the basin in the kitchen. Of course she knew what it was. There was a picture of rats on the box. Also, she could read.

The Crown prosecutor leaned in. Had May ever seen a box like that before?

Yes, she had, once before, back when she was living at Berry's paddock. She didn't know what had become of that box, either. She couldn't remember whether her mother had taken the box away, or whether she'd just put it down — all she knew was that next time she looked, it was gone.

Very good, Mr Heydon said, but had there been rats around the place? Botany was swampy, and Berry's paddock had been the site of a bone-dust factory with animal corpses everywhere. There were factories on the waterfront and slaughterhouses nearby, so the answer was surely yes.

But May said no. There had been no rats around.

Next came the questions about Louisa's relationship with the young and handsome wool washer or, if you prefer, the layabout gambler who had moved into their house. What did May know about it? They had gotten together so soon after her father died, but how did they get on? May didn't know, except to say that her mother had been worried about money, how there was never much with Michael in the house.

'We were going to move to Waterloo,' she said, 'where the food is cheap.'

As to her own relationship with her stepfather, May said that she did not love him. One day just before he died, Michael had tried to give her two pennies to go and get some beer for him but she had refused to go.

The Crown was intrigued. May had been sent to get alcohol for her stepfather, but what about her mother? Did Louisa drink, too?

Yes, she did, May said. She drank brandy. She even drank beer. It caused all kinds of fighting in the house, and the children would have to run and hide. She was drinking while Michael was sick and again after he died. May had seen her lolling on the bed, twirling his moustache and saying, 'Oh, poor Mick, poor Mick!' and everyone knew she was drunk.

May had been present when her father died, too. 'The day my father died, my mother sent me for some tram tickets ... my father was left lying on a stretcher in the front room.'

And had May already met Michael Collins by then?

'He did not live with us when my father died,' May said. 'He was at my father's funeral and he came to live at our house a couple of days after. Collins got married to my mother a couple of days after my father was buried.'

And hadn't there been a big party after Charles died? Did May remember anything about that?

'There was a dance in an empty house next to ours,' she agreed.

And her mother was there? What about Michael Collins?

'My mother and Collins were there,' she agreed, 'and a good many of the people living about the place.'

And what about later? Had her mother stayed on good terms with Michael? Did she care for him when he was sick?

'She tended to him,' May said. 'She prepared a jug of condensed milk for him.'

Of course, the Crown already knew this from Frederick — but here was confirmation from May that there had been milk in the house that nobody but Michael had been allowed to drink.

'The children weren't to touch it,' May agreed.[8]

Mr Lusk did his best to cast doubt upon this evidence, mainly by trying to again convince the jury that arsenic might have entered Michael's body by means of the wound on his leg. No one was sure how he'd gotten that wound but it had become infected, and one of the ways that people treated infections in those days was to smear a weak kind of arsenic paste on them. It was thought to prevent the 'bad smell' — gangrene — from rising. To that end, Mr Lusk called Dr Milford, who told the jury that while death 'might have resulted from arsenical poisoning', he did not believe that Michael had been given one large dose, but rather had been poisoned 'in a series of doses which were not immediately poisonous'.[9]

Mr Lusk pressed him further, saying: 'Arsenic might be taken into the body in various ways ... it might be inhaled through the lungs, and would enter the system still more easily if applied to a running sore.'

Dr Milford agreed, saying that 'if arsenic was absorbed by the body its action would be more retarded than it would be if taken in by the mouth'. Also, 'arsenic would prevent any bad smell arising from a wound ... the deceased must have known that, and he might have used arsenic on his leg'.

Mr Heydon objected. How on earth could Dr Milford know such a thing? How could anyone know whether Michael had been treating his leg wound with arsenic? The man was dead.

Dr Milford was adamant: 'I have given evidence in this case two or three times,' he said stubbornly. 'I have heard all that has been said about curing skins with arsenic and the deceased must have known that arsenic was used for curing skins.'[10]

Arsenic was used for curing skins. The use of arsenic by folk wanting to close reeking wounds was hardly unknown. It was the lesser of two evils — to get gangrene was worse.

Mr Lusk called Dr Martin and questioned him about the theory: was it possible that Michael had applied a kind of arsenic paste to his leg wound to control the infection, or to close up a weeping sore?

Dr Martin wasn't convinced. Of course it was possible — just not likely. Much more likely was the idea that he'd been poisoned, and deliberately.

Mr Lusk objected. The poisoning theory didn't make sense. Maybe it was true that Louisa had fallen out of love with Charles but she loved Michael. She couldn't bear to see him ill. She had run for the doctor. She had run back again. She had sent her children out to get the medicine. She fed him brandy from a spoon. Why would she kill him? Also, what had Michael thought? Lying there on his sickbed, coughing, rolling, spitting, vomiting, hurting and dying, and not once did he rise to whisper in the doctor's ear: 'I think my bride has done it.'

Next on the stand was Mr Hamlet, who testified to working closely with arsenic over the course of his life.

Had he ever suffered any ill-effects? Mr Lusk wanted to know.

No, never.

Pause. But what about on those occasions when Mr Hamlet might have had sores on his hands? He surely wouldn't handle arsenic then.

No, he wouldn't. That would be too dangerous.[11]

Poor old Michael Collins, though, he'd had no choice. He was a strong man but also a poor man, married to a woman with small children. He had lost all of Louisa's money at a gambling house and had been forced to go back to work, even though he had a wound on his leg, and even though it meant that he had to handle sheep skins.

The Crown prosecutor shook his head. This was getting too much. What was needed was an expert on the ways in which arsenic could enter the body, and so an expert — Dr Alexander M'Cormick, then a surgeon at the Prince Alfred Hospital, later a surgeon at the Australian Field Hospital in France — was called to explain to the jury that if Michael had applied an arsenical paste to the wound on his leg 'he would have died from poisoning before five grains of arsenic could have accumulated in the system'.[12]

This was not good for Louisa.

Also, if the paste was strong 'it would destroy the tissues'. Besides which, Dr M'Cormick had himself 'often worked with his hands in an arsenical solution for six hours a day; he had done so five days in a week for five or six months in the year during three years and had received no injury beyond a little soreness under the finger nails'.[13]

This was not good for Louisa, either.

Moreover, he had studied the case, and considered it 'impossible' for the arsenic to have been absorbed through the wound in Michael's leg.[14]

This was catastrophic.

Still, Mr Lusk did not surrender. It's a cruel irony, but his final, failed summation for the jury was probably the best he'd give in his life. As one of the only people who had taken part in all four trials, Mr Lusk knew the evidence better than anyone. He also understood the real problem with the Crown's case was not that it was so terribly weak, but that a successful prosecution would result in the hanging of a woman on the evidence of her small children.

To that end, he opened his summation by saying that this was a case 'involving the life of a human being' — not Michael's, but Louisa's. Yes, he understood that some of the jurors had their suspicions about what had gone on, but suspicions weren't enough: they were now dealing with a case 'in which a human being was placed upon her trial for the most terrible crime that any person could commit'. The jury needed to be careful before deciding that Louisa was guilty. In particular, they should be careful not to 'mix up matters in their minds, with regards to the death of another person' (Louisa's first husband, Charles). They should concentrate only on the case at hand.

'It was the accused who went for the doctor and she expressed the greatest anxiety that the doctor should attend,' Mr Lusk said. 'She was the most anxious that the deceased should be seen, examined and treated by a medical man.'

'From day to day, [she] urged the doctor to attend and laid all her own actions open to investigation. This she did from first to last ... her conduct was not the conduct of a woman engaged in the secret crime of poisoning her husband ... The Crown [has alleged] that the accused was the only person who had access to the deceased and that she alone could have poisoned him ... but on the contrary, the evidence showed that a large number of persons had easy access to the sick man's room.'

Louisa had readily admitted to being 'responsible for the medicine and drinks which the deceased received' as he lay dying but this, said Mr Lusk, was 'one of the strongest evidences of her innocence. She took the whole responsibility upon her own shoulders, even after she had been arrested by the police.' The Crown had relied on nothing but suspicion and yes, certainly, there were some parts of the case that were suspicious, but the jury could not convict the accused upon mere suspicion.

There were many ways by which the arsenic could have got into the body of the deceased. Michael might have taken it himself. It might have been taken into his system unconsciously. The Crown had suggested that the accused could have administered the poison — Louisa had handled the glass tumbler with the milky substance — but that was no reason to find her guilty of murder. The Crown had also to prove that no one else could have administered it, and yet the Crown had 'signally failed to prove anything of the kind'.

'The police visited the house and gave the accused every warning so that if she was guilty — and knew there was arsenic in the tumbler of milk — what would have been easier than for her to have disposed of the contents of the glass?

'The first instinct of a guilty person would be to destroy the traces of guilt and there was nothing ... to have hindered [her] from throwing the contents of the glass into the back yard.' No, if there was arsenic in that glass, 'it was there unknown to the accused'.

It was perhaps a touch audacious, but Mr Lusk then went even further: 'There was no arsenic in the glass at all. It had been clearly shown that the contents of the glass had been tampered with between the time that it was taken away by the police and its having been handed to the Government Analyst.'

In short, the Crown had failed to prove any motive on the part of the accused for committing the crime with which she was charged. It couldn't be money. By the death of her husband, 'she has been rendered destitute'.

Moreover, there had been no evidence to show 'that [her first husband] was poisoned at all', he said, and so the jury 'should discard all the evidence with regard to that case and ... deal with the present charge on its merits'. This, he said, was a case of doubts from beginning to end. Therefore, the duty of the jury was to 'give the accused the benefit of the doubt and acquit her'.[15]

Now it was Mr Heydon's turn. He got to his feet. The guilt of the accused had been conclusively proved, he said. Michael Collins had been poisoned by arsenic, and the accused was the only person who could have administered the arsenic. It was 'absurd to suppose that the deceased, if he had made up his mind to destroy himself, would have submitted himself to the torture which he had undergone'. Also, the theory that the arsenic had been absorbed through the wound in his leg 'had been entirely broken down by the Crown'. The symptoms were 'inconsistent with such a theory'. The whole of the evidence, he said, 'pointed to only one conclusion and that was that the accused was guilty of the murder of her husband'.[16]

It was by now 7.50 p.m. on the last day of the trial. The Chief Justice looked at his timepiece. He could hold the jury steady while he gave a summation of his own, or he could adjourn until morning. The wait, while he made his decision, must have been agonising. Louisa had now been tried four times. One thing everyone in the courtroom surely understood was that she could not be tried again. This was the Crown's last roll of the dice. If the Chief Justice wanted a conviction — and the evidence suggests that he badly wanted a conviction — he would need to give the best summation he had ever given. He would need some time, and so he adjourned the hearing.

Louisa Collins would not learn her fate until the next day — a Saturday.

It was by now 8 December 1888. Six months had passed since Michael had died. There were less than three weeks to go until Christmas and, if accounts in the colony's newspapers are a guide, Sydney had never looked lovelier. The windows of all the big department stores had been decorated, and the stores themselves were stuffed to the ceiling with gorgeous wares imported from England and all points in between. There were silks on display, and satins, and porcelain figurines; there were music stands and pearl treasures; tortoiseshell trinkets and toilet mirrors; feathered fans — and dolls! So many dolls. Dolls to inspire 'insatiable longing among all the little folks'. Dolls with hats. Dolls with petticoats. Dolls with fans and parasols. It was hard to move in the city streets for people jostling toward the shops, alive with the joy of Christmas.[17]

Outside the city, on the rise, there stood a place with no Christmas wreath and no Christmas bells. That place was the Central Criminal Court where the trial — the trials — of Louisa Collins were coming to an end.

The session opened with Chief Justice Darley reminding the jury that the decision they were being asked to make was one of the most important of their lives. They had to decide whether a woman on trial for the murder of her second husband was guilty or not guilty.

If she was guilty, she would hang.

That was an awful thing to have to consider, but they had to put it out of their minds. It was not for the jury to decide whether Louisa deserved the consequences of her actions. They needed only to decide whether or not she was guilty of murder.[18]

Chief Justice Darley said he had tried hard to ensure that the prisoner, Louisa Collins, received a fair trial. He had to ensure that all the relevant facts had been brought before the jury, facts in the prisoner's favour and those that went against her.

To that end, Chief Justice Darley had allowed the jury to hear the evidence about the love triangle between Charles, Louisa and Michael. The jury needed to understand that Louisa had, until December 1886, been living in a house with both her then husband, Charles Andrews, and the man she was now accused of murdering. A short time later, Michael Collins had been kicked out, and all the talk in the village of Botany had been of a scandalous affair. Some weeks later — in January 1887 — Louisa's first husband had taken ill, and in February, he died.

Louisa did not mourn. Instead, she danced. A short time later, she married Michael. Perhaps she had loved him then, but Michael was a gambler. The couple was in debt. Louisa had complained to her children that money was no good while Mick was in the house. He gambled everything away.

By June 1888, Michael had fallen ill, and by 8 July, he was dead. Perhaps it was a coincidence that he, like Charles, had suffered arsenical poisoning. Yet the jury should at least consider 'the improbability of an accident having taken place'.[19]

If Michael Collins alone had died from arsenical poisoning — well, that could have been an accident. The poison may well have been absorbed into his body through a cut on his leg while he worked with skins at the wool wash.

Perhaps he'd put some paste containing arsenic on his leg, to stop an infection.

But two husbands?

In Chief Justice Darley's mind, there was a 'strong presumption that the death of neither of [Louisa's husbands] was an accident'.[20] Here were two men — both healthy — dying within seventeen months of each other, and presenting with the same symptoms, too.

Besides that coincidence, there was the fact that Louisa stood to benefit financially from the death of Charles. This, coupled with the fact that she had fallen in love with Michael, might have meant that she wanted Charles out of the way.

In what can only be construed as an effort to drive home inconsistencies in Louisa's evidence, the Chief Justice took the time to read the statements she had given at the inquest. He 'pointed out certain discrepancies [when] compared or considered with the facts as disclosed by the evidence'.[21]

He also gave great weight to the evidence given by 'the little girl May Andrews'.[22] She had found a box of Rough on Rats in her kitchen. This was a very serious and important piece of evidence. It placed the poison in the house. The little girl wasn't a liar. Her evidence had been strong and true.

Chief Justice Darley did not accept a suggestion by Louisa's counsel, Mr Lusk, that the glass tumbler had been tampered with sometime between being taken from the house and being handed to the government analyst.

On the other hand, yes, of course, the jury would have to take into consideration the fact that Louisa had 'exhibited great anxiety as to the state of her husband's health, and had repeatedly called in the assistance of the doctor'.[23]

Also, as Mr Lusk had argued, there was no apparent motive for Louisa to take Michael's life — and yet, did it really matter, not to know the motive?

Chief Justice Darley did not think so. In fact, he said, it was often 'impossible for [anyone] to tell always what was in the mind of a person. It might be that the prisoner after having poisoned [her first husband] without being discovered took the same means of dealing with Collins after she had become tired of him.'[24]

She had the will and the opportunity, in other words.

In any case, the jury should go and consider their verdict. If they had any reasonable doubt, they should acquit — but the doubt should be a reasonable one. If, on other hand, they 'could come to no other conclusion but that this unfortunate man met his death by poison administered by his wife' — well, then they had no choice. They had to find Louisa Collins guilty.[25]

It was noon before Chief Justice Darley finished speaking. The court had opened at 9.30 a.m., and, because it was Saturday, the Chief Justice wanted to adjourn for the day at two p.m. — and so, shortly before two p.m., the jury came back. As soon as they had 'been placed in their proper positions' the associate and clerk of arraignments said: 'Gentlemen of the jury, have you agreed upon a verdict?'

The foreman replied: 'We have, sir.'

The clerk of arraignments said: 'How say you, gentlemen of the jury, is the prisoner, Louisa Collins, guilty of the charge … or not guilty?'

The foreman said: 'We find the prisoner guilty.'

The clerk of arraignments said: 'So say you all?'

The jurors as one replied: 'We do.'

There was pandemonium. Reporters rushed out to announce the verdict to their editors. It was big news: one, two, three juries, no verdict and now, on the fourth roll of the dice, Louisa was finally guilty. 'Verdict of GUILTY' the papers would say, in the crime of 'MURDER'.

Chief Justice Darley banged his gavel. Silence having been proclaimed, Louisa was called to her feet.[26]

The *Evening News* takes up the tale:

She was, perhaps, a shade paler than usual, but seemed otherwise quite unconcerned. She looked for a few seconds around the court, and for a very short time she trembled perceptibly. Clutching hold of the small desk in front of the dock, she looked the Clerk of Arraignments fully in the face, and he thus addressed her: 'Louisa Collins, you have pleaded not guilty to murder: the jury have found you guilty of murder; have you anything to say why the sentence of the court should not be passed upon you, according to law?'

Everyone leaned in, desperate to hear. But no, Louisa said. 'I have nothing to say.'[27]

CHAPTER 11

The Verdict:
'Be hanged by the neck
until you are dead'

The sentence would be death. Murder was a capital crime so it had to be death. Everyone knew that, before Chief Justice Darley even began to speak. Louisa would hang.

That was what the Crown wanted. That was what the Crown would get, and yet Chief Justice Darley's final address contained no ring of triumph.

Yes, Louisa had committed a wicked crime. She had taken the life of a man she had promised to love, but still, at least according to the *Evening News*, the Chief Justice was 'visibly affected' by his terrible responsibility and it seems that 'scarcely a dry eye was visible in the court' as he began to speak: 'Louisa Collins, after a most favourable and exhaustive trial, you have been found guilty of a most dreadful offence — the offence of murder.'[1]

Of course, the Chief Justice might have said 'you have *finally* been found guilty of murder', but he did not. He went on:

> No one who has heard this case throughout can
> have any doubt that this verdict which has been
> given is a true and honest verdict. In fact, no other
> verdict could be arrived at by a body of intelligent
> men such as those who have so carefully attended to
> this case throughout.[2]

In fact, three juries that comprised thirty-six men who had heard similar evidence over many months had been far from convinced of Louisa's guilt. But that was now irrelevant: the only verdict that counted was this final one.

> The murder you have committed is one of peculiar
> atrocity. You were day by day giving poison to the
> man whom above all others you were bound to
> cherish and attend. You watched his slow torture and
> painful death, and this apparently without a moment's
> remorse. You were indifferent to his pain, and gained
> his confidence by your simulated affection. There
> is too much reason to fear that your first husband
> Andrews also met his death at your hands; that he,
> too, you watched to the end — saw his torture day
> after day, and added to its horror this crime.[3]

Louisa had in fact never been found guilty of Charles's murder; this was pure suspicion on the Chief Justice's part.

He went on:

> I hold out no hope of mercy to you on earth. It
> would be wicked of me to do so. But I implore
> of you to seek forgiveness where it will assuredly
> be found. Seek the assistance of the clergyman to
> whose faith you belong. He will point out to you the
> way to gain such forgiveness.[4]

This was an appeal to Louisa to pray for God's forgiveness
or risk eternal damnation in hell.

> Your days are surely numbered, and it now remains
> for me only to pass the last dread sentence of
> the law upon you. The sentence of the Court is
> that you be taken to the place from whence you
> came, and on a day hereafter to be named by the
> Governor in Council, that you be taken to the
> place of execution, and there be hanged by the
> neck until you are dead; and may the Lord have
> mercy on your soul.[5]

Louisa rose from her seat in the dock. In the *Herald*'s re-
telling, she appeared 'quite unmoved by the result of the
trial' and remained 'perfectly calm and collected', even as
the sentence of death was passed.[6] She did not scream out,
or start to cry. According to the *Evening News*, Louisa —
now 'the wretched woman' — was 'at once removed from
the dock and taken into the gaol, where she was immediately
placed in one of the condemned cells'.[7] (This was in fact not

true, but more about the cell in which Louisa spent her last days later.)

As so many reporters had already said, Louisa remained calm: 'Throughout the whole of his Honour's remarks not a muscle of her face quivered, and she appeared as calm as it was possible for any person to be.'[8]

Why was Louisa so calm, where so many others in court were weeping? She certainly didn't want to die. In the weeks ahead she would beg for her life: '*Oh Lord, have mercy, I have seven children* ...'[9] Perhaps she understood what many in court that day did not: that while she had been sentenced to death, the fight to save Louisa's life was not in any sense over.

It had been almost thirty years since a woman had been hanged in New South Wales. That woman was Ellen Monks, who was executed in May 1860 for the murder of her husband, Thomas Monks, at Longnose Creek on Halloween 1859. One key difference between the cases was that Ellen had pleaded guilty.[10]

Conversely, just three years earlier, two women, Sarah Keep and her stepmother, Mary Ann Burton, who had been found guilty of the strychnine poisoning of Sarah's husband, had their death sentences commuted to life imprisonment after a sustained protest. Their supporters had argued that it would be barbaric to hang both a woman and her stepdaughter, especially since the daughter was just twenty-four years old and pregnant. (Only months after being granted a reprieve, Sarah died delivering her premature baby in prison.)[11]

Given this history, it's perhaps no wonder that Louisa felt confident that she would not be hanged, either. If all else failed — and pretty much all else now had — her gender would protect her.

One of the key features of a good democracy is the principle of the separation of powers: put plainly, it means that parliament shouldn't interfere with the business of the courts. Judges need to be independent — especially of politicians.

Despite this, debate about the fate of Louisa Collins moved from the courthouse to Parliament House in about the length of time it took to traverse the distance by foot. Well, not quite, but the point is made.

To be clear, parliament was not due to debate the case. In fact, when the by-now-premier-again, Sir Henry Parkes, and other members of the Legislative Assembly went into the bear pit — a ferocious debating chamber, ripe with insult and upset — six days before Christmas in 1888, the item of business was Estimates, and the topics at hand included the cost of running trams.

Nobody in the Parkes ministry expected Louisa's case to come up and almost as soon as it did, some members of parliament tried to shut it down, saying politicians had no business under the doctrine of the separation of powers debating whether a mother of seven should hang by her neck until she was dead. New South Wales was apparently too mature a democracy for that.

In any case, the Speaker took the chair at 4.30 p.m. and for at least two hours, debate was as scheduled — until

Sir Ninian Melville got to his feet. To sketch the scene, Melville was a former undertaker who liked to wear long black coats and puff on a grand, curled pipe, and although he was listed as a member of the temperance movement, he also liked to tell witty stories at his local public house. Now he wanted to talk about Louisa Collins.

The audacity of his move enraged Parkes. (For the sake of context, it's worth noting that Melville and Parkes loathed each other; at elections just a year earlier, Parkes had denounced Melville as 'the veriest charlatan that ever lived'.[12]) Melville didn't give a hoot. He was determined to have his say. Lest anyone in the House not be aware of the case, he gave a brief outline: Louisa Collins was, he said, a woman who had been tried twice already for the murder of her second husband. Both juries had failed to find her guilty but instead of setting her free, the Crown had tried her a third time, this time for the murder of her first husband. When that jury failed to reach a verdict, the Crown went back to the first charge, finally obtaining a conviction, but only after the Crown had objected to at least four of the potential jurors.[13]

This was not justice, Melville said. This was a travesty of justice. Was the parliament really going to sit back and let this woman hang?

'It has been years since New South Wales was disgraced by the execution of a woman,' he cried. The colony ought to be ashamed of its ongoing thirst for the blood of criminals. It was immature. New South Wales was surely no longer a penal colony. Wasn't there anyone who could see how poorly an execution would reflect upon the notion of New

South Wales as a fully grown democracy, striving to take a seat at the table of mature and dignified nations?

Also, it was the centennial year: one hundred years since the arrival of the First Fleet. Rather than remind the world of how far New South Wales had come, all the execution of a woman could do was demonstrate how far the colony still had to go.

Many in the chamber agreed. 'Hear, hear!' they cried.[14]

Unfortunately for Louisa, one man who did not agree was also one of the few men with the power to make a difference: Sir Henry Parkes.

To be clear, Sir Henry was in principle opposed to the death penalty. Just two years earlier, he had been part of the campaign to save the young men of Mount Rennie, writing personally to the New South Wales governor, Lord Carrington, to remind him that Britain didn't hang men for rape, and if New South Wales wanted to be seen as more than a penal colony where drunks were sent to dry out in the stocks and men were flogged with the cat-o'-nine-tails, then it probably shouldn't hang men for the crime of rape, either.

Of course, Sir Henry hadn't then been premier. Now that he did hold that office — and could make a difference — he was on the side of death.

Sir Henry's lack of support for Louisa cannot have been for lack of empathy. Unlike many of the men who occupied positions of power in New South Wales at that time, men who came from aristocratic British families, Sir Henry actually knew something of grinding poverty (and of grand love affairs, although you'll have to go to the epilogue to read about those). He also understood power, having either hungered for, or exercised, it all his adult life.

Born in Britain in 1815, Sir Henry was already in his seventies by the time Louisa's case came to trial. He had a great, flowing white beard and unusually long white hair: 'leonine' was the word most commonly used to describe him. Although by most accounts a magnificent orator, Sir Henry had received only a few years of formal education.[15] As a boy, Henry did his best to scratch out a living in a brick pit before taking an apprenticeship with an ivory turner, opening a store and marrying a butcher's daughter called Clarinda.

By 1838, Henry's business had failed, and although Clarinda had twice given birth, both children had died. Henry pawned his tools and the couple sailed for Sydney in 1839, arriving two days after the birth of Clarinda's third — but only living — child with only a few shillings to the family's name and no letter of introduction. Henry looked for work but there was none to be found. He sold his possessions to survive, before finally taking labouring work at the estate of grazier Sir John Jamison near Richmond in New South Wales. Six months later, the family returned to Sydney, where Henry worked at a foundry and a brassworks before opening an ivory and luxury goods store in Hunter Street. That business also failed but, never mind, it wasn't business that Henry wanted to be in. It was politics.

Parkes won the seat of Wentworth in 1854. One of the first committees he chaired as a parliamentarian examined the conditions of the working classes. He wrote critically of people living in hovels, alongside rats and disease, and of the more than 1000 vagrant children who roamed Sydney's streets barefoot, hungry and illiterate. A man of action as well as words, Parkes created a school — a magnificent little school — for orphan boys on a hulk in Sydney Harbour. Later still, he took steps to ensure that primary education in New South Wales would be compulsory, secular and free.

Sir Henry became premier (then called prime minister) in 1872, but his first term came to an end in 1875. And therein lay Louisa's problem: Parkes's reign had ended, at least in part, because Sir Henry had expressed sympathy in parliament for a notorious bushranger, Frank Gardiner, who had been on the run from police for at least a year before being recaptured, during which time he'd displayed exemplary behaviour (in fact, he'd been busy running a little shop). Sir Henry believed that Gardiner could be rehabilitated; others were thirsting for a sentence of least thirty years' hard labour, and while that debate alone would not cost Sir Henry the premiership, it would not assist him.[16]

It is entirely possible that the debate about Louisa's sentence took Sir Henry by surprise, and he would certainly have been offended by the idea that New South Wales was not a mature democracy. Sir Henry was by then on the verge of planting in Lord Carrington's mind the audacious idea that he could federate the colonies to create the nation that is now the Commonwealth of Australia in less than six months. (It would in fact take ten years and Sir Henry would not live to see it, but he is today regarded as the man with the greatest claim to the title of the Father of Federation.)

Few had done more to prove that Australia was ready to stand on its own, and here was his arch-enemy arguing that the execution of Louisa Collins would somehow prove that the colony was still a penal outpost.

Parkes got to his feet, took up a position next to the dispatch box and he gave a mighty speech, condemning Louisa to her fate.

This woman — Louisa Collins — had had as fair and patient a trial as any person ever had, Sir Henry said, his voice booming across the bear pit. Moreover, she had been convicted of 'one of the most cruel, inexcusable, and frightful murders ever perpetrated in the world's history'.

Energised, Sir Henry's supporters began to cheer: 'Hear, hear!'

If the taking of a life could ever be justified, then Louisa's life could justly be taken, Sir Henry said. If it were ever sound to inflict the punishment of death, this was the case in which that punishment was sound.

Hear, hear, his supporters cried.

Louisa Collins had been ably defended. What's more, Sir Henry said, he had already put these very questions — whether the trial was fair and the punishment just — directly to the Chief Justice, and the Chief Justice had assured him in the 'most exhaustive and complete report ever conducted' that this woman had indeed received a fair trial. Moreover, the Chief Justice had given him no reason to believe that mercy could or should be extended to Louisa. In fact, when Sir Henry had asked whether the Chief Justice would consider mercy, the answer he had received had been a 'most decided negative'. Louisa

Collins was guilty. The Chief Justice was in no doubt about that. Who could disagree?

As for Melville's argument that Louisa could not be hanged because she was a woman, and therefore somehow precious and delicate, Sir Henry knew better: when women gave into a life of crime, he said, they soon became more evil and unpredictable than even the worst men. 'The worst of crimes have been committed by women,' Sir Henry said. In fact, 'in the fearful period when France ran riot in blood, those who were the most guilty of the most ferocious delight in blood were women — young women and tender girls!' Rising to the occasion, he went on, saying women had 'hoisted the heads of their fellow creatures on pikes!'

Hear, hear!

Further, once a woman forgot the character of her sex, 'there was no barrier to the lengths which she would go in crime!'

Now Sir Henry's voice dropped. Let his fellow politicians understand: he did not himself believe in capital punishment, certainly not as having a deterrent effect.

'Hear, hear,' mumbled others in the chamber, less agitated now.[17]

Capital punishment was, however, the law — and the parliament was bound to uphold the law. The sentence of death had been carried out on women whose cases were far less compelling than that of Louisa Collins. Did nobody in the chamber remember the case of Mary Ann Brownlow from Goulburn? Sir Henry did, and for the benefit of those who didn't, he was prepared to revisit the case.

Mary Ann had been 'young and married, and a mother', Sir Henry said. 'She had killed her husband with a knife in a fit of temper. She was found guilty of murder, and sentenced to death. Efforts were made to secure her reprieve, but [all was in] vain ... The unfortunate woman [had] a young child at breast and just before ascending the scaffold steps' she paused to feed the baby, who nuzzled at her breast, before being taken from Mary Ann so she could hang.

At this, 'a howl of indignation shot up from all sides of the House' and cries of 'Shame, shame!' and 'Outrage, outrage!' and 'Disgrace to civilization!' rang out — but Sir Henry pushed on.

The execution of Mary Ann was, in his opinion, 'an inhuman thing' and yet it had been carried out, because murder was a capital crime and the law was the law, and if Mary Ann could not be reprieved for an 'impulsive murder', how on earth could the conniving Louisa Collins be reprieved for a poison murder involving vastly more scheming and plotting?

Also, if the death sentence was wrong, there was an easy way to remedy it: those who thought so should move to abolish it. If such a bill were to come before the Assembly he — Sir Henry — would support it, for he did not believe in death as punishment. But there was no such bill before the House.

Furthermore, the idea that he, as premier, or any other member of the parliament, could interfere with matters of justice was dangerous for democracy. The courts were independent and had to remain so. Any member of the

House that desired to take action should do so as a private citizen — and not as members of parliament. This was not the forum. This was not the place.

'Hear, hear!' his supporters cried.

Sir Henry sat down. His speech had been loud and passionate, and wild debate now ensued. The member for Northumberland, Mr Thomas Walker, shouted that the state was 'on the eve of committing … murder'. Imprisonment for life was surely enough for the interests of justice to be served. Member for Monaro, Mr Thomas O'Mara, agreed, saying no woman should be placed upon the scaffold. 'There was a distinction made between man and woman,' he cried. 'Women were not flogged in this country' — and if they couldn't be flogged, surely they couldn't be executed.

The member for Paddington, Mr John Neild, was next to his feet. In terms of extraordinary appearance, Neild gave even Sir Henry a run for his money: he had a pure-white, twirled moustache and his outfits included shirts with upturned collars and dinky neckties. In years to come, he would form his own militia and join the Senate. On this day, he argued for Louisa's life on the grounds that her children — especially May — had probably been coaxed or even forced into giving evidence against her. These were little children, he said, who were brought to the court time after time after time, until they became educated as to what to say.

Some members were outraged by this accusation, and cried out: 'Shame! Shame!' Sir Henry, in particular, was livid, saying: 'That remark should not be made in a place like this!'

But Mr Neild stood firm. He hadn't meant to suggest the Crown had coached the children but 'these little children could not be brought so often into court without the matter being impressed on their minds … repeating a lie often [would eventually make any person] believe it!'[18] (There is some evidence for this: in one of his earliest statements, Louisa's sixteen-year-old son, Arthur, told police that he couldn't remember any squabbles between his mother and Michael Collins; by the time of the final trial, he was saying that they squabbled often, and usually about how much she drank.[19])

The member for Gundagai, Mr John Henry Want, was astonished. The children had not been coached, he said. The children were merely witnesses. It was very bad form to raise such allegations in parliament. A terrible precedent was being set, one that the House might soon regret.

Now Sir Henry rose again. He, too, was appalled by the debate — not the way it had roiled out of control on the floor of the House but by the gall of those who argued for Louisa's life while keeping capital punishment in place.

'There is nothing more abominable to my sense of feeling than the strangling of a woman,' he said. 'A woman! From whose breast the nurture of life is drawn by the human family! A woman! Who presides over the paths of our little children. A woman! Who is the very centre of everything that is gentle and lovable in social life!'

Those who considered him bloodthirsty were wrong. He had spoken out in the Mount Rennie case because he didn't believe that young men should die for the crime of rape. He had genuinely believed that a mass hanging would scandalise the colony throughout the civilised world.

But that case and this one were different. Britain did not hang for rape. Britain *did* hang for murder.

'It would be a most dangerous practice to interfere here,' he said, because Louisa was guilty of murder, and if murderers could escape with their lives, a precedent would be set.

'Hear, hear!' his supporters shouted, but they were soon drowned out by those on the other side, arguing for Louisa's life. Mr Thomas Henry Hassall, for example, cried out that the death sentence should be done away with, adding that it was a disgrace to the 'manhood' of any nation when a woman was hanged.

By now Sir Henry was furious. Who said it was only men that wanted to see Louisa hang? 'I believe that the women of the country would vote for Mrs Collins being hanged!' he cried.

It was an audacious thing to say. Sir Henry knew as well as anyone that the women in New South Wales in 1888 could not vote on anything.

Mr Hassall got to his feet. 'Slander!' he said. 'That is slander upon the women of New South Wales … The women of Australia were not so depraved as to desire anything of the sort. I am astonished at a man like the premier uttering such a slander on the women of Australia!'

Sir Henry was unrepentant. No, he said, the women of Australia would not support Louisa Collins. The women of Australia would be appalled by what she had done. The women of Australia 'do not approve of wives poisoning their husbands!'[20]

CHAPTER 12

The Women's Petition

Would the women of nineteenth-century New South Wales have voted to hang Louisa Collins? We will never know, for they were never asked. What is known is that many women stepped up when Louisa was sentenced to death, taking the fight for her life right to — and then right through — the door of Government House.

It cannot have been easy, even to simply speak up. Women in nineteenth-century New South Wales were actively discouraged from playing any kind of role in public life. They were not permitted to run for office let alone hold it. There were no women in parliament, and no women in the court system.

The first indication that significant numbers of women were concerned about Louisa's plight — mainly that she had been sentenced to hang, but also that she had been tried four times in front of forty-eight men before a guilty verdict could be secured — came in December 1888, when the following advertisement appeared in the *Evening News*:

> Sentence of Death on Louisa Collins — A petition
> that the criminal's life may be spared (to be signed
> by females only) lies for signature at Mr PALSER'S,
> 141 York and Market Streets.[1]

The advertisement is intriguing: who was Mr Palser? And why was the petition to be signed by females only?

First, to Mr Palser: the record suggests that a young boy called Henry Palser sailed to Australia with his parents at the age of three. He would live in New South Wales for more than eighty years, working as both a grocer and, for a brief time, as a milliner. Like many in New South Wales at that time, Mr Palser was also a temperance advocate. He believed that alcohol was the devil's brew, and that control of alcohol was necessary to curb violence against women and the neglect of children, especially in homes where the menfolk took their wages and spent them at the public house.

Mr Palser and his wife, Mrs HP Palser (as was the custom, she went by his initials), were early campaigners on behalf of the poor and destitute. They ran a soup kitchen and helped establish the Sydney Night Refuge, to help get poor and abandoned women off the streets after dark. Mr Palser was also a founding member of the Society for the Abolition of Capital Punishment, which believed that 'men had no right to take the life of a fellow creature' and that the time would come when capital punishment 'would be regarded as one of the foulest blots upon the history of the world'.[2]

With that in mind, it's worth going back to examine the list of jurors from Louisa's third trial. The last name on the list is Mr Henry Prior Palser. Mr Palser had been a juror at Louisa's trial for the murder of Charles Andrews. No wonder the Crown couldn't get a conviction: Mr Palser was opposed to seeing *anyone* hang. This may explain why the Crown objected to not one but four potential jurors at Louisa's fourth trial. Conceivably, they were screening out capital punishment abolitionists and other conscientious objectors.

Now Mr Palser was encouraging women to get behind a campaign to save Louisa's life by signing a petition in his store — but was it really Mr Palser? The text of the advertisement — 'to be signed by females only' — suggests that *Mrs* Palser was the driving force in this campaign.

In any case, the Women's Petition, as it would soon be known, attracted more than 600 signatures in just a few days, before being delivered to the offices of the *Sydney Morning Herald*. Apparently unsure what else to do with it, the *Herald* published the document in full on 27 December, along with these words: 'The following petition to his Excellency the Governor in favour of the condemned prisoner Louisa Collins has been handed to us for publication.'[3]

The Women's Petition said:

> To his Excellency.
> The petition of the undersigned female inhabitants of Sydney and its suburbs [concerns] Louisa Collins [who is] now a prisoner under sentence of death in Darlinghurst Gaol for the murder of her husband, Michael Peter Collins.

Your petitioners pray that mercy may be
extended to the prisoner on the following grounds:

1. That it is abhorrent to every feeling of humanity
   and a shock to the sentiments in this 19th
   century, both here and in other English speaking
   communities, that a woman should suffer death
   at the hands of a hangman, and at the hands of
   one of the opposite sex, so long as imprisonment
   can be substituted;

2. That the prisoner having been tried three times
   for the same offence, but practically four times,
   is (your petitioners are informed) contrary to the
   practice in the mother-country;

3. That there is no positive proof of the prisoner's
   guilt — it has rather been assumed upon suspicion
   only, supported by circumstantial evidence;

4. That the fact that three juries, consisting of 36
   men of intelligence, were each in deliberation
   many hours and during one night, and were
   unable to agree as to the prisoner's guilt, your
   petitioners consider is strong and convincing
   proof that the case is not free from doubt and
   your petitioners conceive [this] to be good
   grounds for not inflicting the extreme penalty;

5. That innocent individuals have frequently
   been executed on circumstantial evidence, and
   your petitioners entertain a just horror at the
   possibility of a mistake occurring;

6. That in the case of two women condemned to
   death at West Maitland for not alone having

deliberately conspired to murder, but having actually murdered by poison the younger prisoner's husband — a much more heinous case than that of Louisa Collins, and one in which their guilt was proved beyond doubt, yet these two prisoners had mercy extended to them. [This was a reference to the case of Sarah Keep and her stepmother, Mary Ann Burton,[4] who in 1884 had been found guilty of the strychnine poisoning of Sarah's husband, Henry Keep. Both were sentenced to death; and both reprieved.]

7. That no execution of a woman has taken place in New South Wales for the last 28 years;[5] and your petitioners believe that the substitution of imprisonment would act as a greater deterrent.

Your petitioners, therefore, pray that your Excellency will exercise your Royal prerogative of mercy in favour of Louisa Collins — a prerogative which is a sacred trust solely in your Excellency's hands, and which your petitioners pray you will graciously be pleased to exercise. And your petitioners will ever pray.[6]

The petition was dated 22 December 1888. The women who wrote it, and presumably at least some of those who signed it, had a very good grasp of Louisa's case and of the law. The text makes important points about the evidence, and about precedents the governor might want to consider. The language is authoritative and firm.

How did the *Herald*'s readers — and readers of other newspapers, which also published the document — react? Sadly, many greeted the Women's Petition with scorn. One correspondent — like letter writers, they did not always give their names — who authored the column known as 'As You Like It' castigated the 'female inhabitants of Sydney' for daring to interfere in the matter. 'The petition [is] a document to which most women ought to be ashamed to append their names,' the column said, mainly because 'the fairness of the trial is attempted to be questioned'. The women who signed the petition had complained that Louisa had been found guilty 'on suspicion only, supported by circumstantial evidence'. Did they not understand that it was quite common for a jury to convict a person based only on circumstantial evidence? Why, it happened all the time — but of course women, with their limited knowledge of important things, could hardly be expected to know that![7]

Letters flooded into the newspaper, including one which complained that the women behind the petition had stepped out of line — beyond their station, perhaps — in daring to criticise a decision made by the Chief Justice. 'When our Chief Justice sees not the slightest reason for varying in his judgment, ought we to give way to mawkish cant and drivelling sentimentalism?' this letter said. 'Can they [the women] have read and realised the fact that this woman had daily watched the slow torture of a dying man who ought to be most near and dear?

'As to circumstantial evidence, anyone who has looked into the matter knows that all such cases depend upon it … [and] as to a woman suffering the [same] penalty [as a man] … Why not a woman as well as a man reap the result of her own acts?'[8]

Why not?

Why should a woman *not* be given the same punishment as a man? Because women could not vote. Because they could not sit in parliament. Because they had nothing whatever to do with the making of the laws by which they were bound, and because they — unlike the men in the colony — had never been given an opportunity to vote on capital punishment. Because women in New South Wales in the nineteenth century had barely more rights than children, yet when it came to crime, they would be hanged as if they were adults.

Still, day after day, scorn was poured upon women who had dared to complain. Louisa Collins was, in the words of one unnamed *Sydney Morning Herald* columnist, no different from a man-eating tiger or a shark and 'other enemies of the human race'[9] — and, like such pests, she clearly needed to be put down. 'Unless we are to believe that trial by jury is a farce, we must confess that Louisa Collins has been guilty of one of the most cold-blooded and deliberate crimes on record,' this writer said. What if the tables were turned? What if Michael had murdered Louisa? Would there be 'a single person in this colony who would have stirred a finger to prevent the ordinary operation of the law?'[10]

It wasn't only men who disagreed with the women behind the Women's Petition. At least one 'female inhabitant of one of the suburbs' wrote to say she could not 'let [the petition] pass unnoticed'. In the first place, the petition claimed that it was 'abhorrent to every feeling of humanity ... that a woman should suffer death at the hands of a hangman', this woman complained. 'No doubt it is abhorrent, but no more horrible than the cruel, cold-blooded murder which she committed.'

This woman was not speaking from a position of ignorance. She had clearly read the judgement. She quoted what Chief Justice Darley had said when sentencing Louisa: specifically, that Louisa, above all others, was bound to love and cherish her husband, and had instead slowly tortured him to death. 'I say such a creature is a disgrace to the very name of woman,' she said, and as for the argument that all the evidence had been circumstantial, she didn't know 'what more convincing proof is required, unless they [the female petitioners] actually wanted to see the deed committed'.[11]

Other women pleaded for Louisa's life not on the grounds that she was innocent, necessarily, but because she was both a woman and a mother. One example: a woman describing herself as 'An Anxious Mother' told the *Evening News* that 'pity should arise' for Louisa's 'poor innocent children':

> For their sake I think the extreme penalty of the law should be reduced to a lesser punishment ... Let her innocents appeal in her behalf. Do not break their already saddened, sorrow-stricken hearts by such a death for the mother they still love so dearly. If the first, kind, good, loving husband and father's voice [that is, Charles's voice] could be heard from beyond

the grave, I feel sure his words would be, 'spare her
for the sake of our loved innocent children … pity
her children, broken-hearted, cowering 'neath the
brand of shame; For their innocent lives, O, spare
their mother.'[12]

To this, a man calling himself 'An Anxious Husband'
argued that no mercy ought be extended to Louisa on the
grounds that she had little children, saying: 'If people are
to be spared death penalties because they have children, it
will be very rough on the community, as almost all married
people have them.'[13]

On the other hand, a number of men, including one
of the colony's leading veterinarians, John Pottie, wrote to
support the women, saying:

Had I been on the jury, the scientific evidence
would certainly never have made me bring in a
verdict of guilty … I can understand any person
administering a dose of arsenic sufficiently large to
poison at once, but I cannot understand an ordinary
mortal suddenly becoming able to use arsenic in
such small and well-regulated doses as to bring
about a class of symptoms at once so mysterious and
so misleading. Possibly this woman may have learnt
this, but this has never been shown, and completes
the weak link in the chain.[14]

Another man pointed out the unfairness of the four trials,
saying:

I would beg to point out that a criminal being
tried, owing to a disagreement of jurors, practically
four times for the same offence is a course of
procedure ... unknown in the mother country. I
believe there is no record in England of a criminal
under such circumstances being placed on trial more
than twice. Where is the limit to be? If four times,
why not eight times?[15]

Debate was robust. It was also spreading from Sydney
to neighbouring colonies, with one correspondent to the
Sydney Morning Herald compelled to write despite being 'a
Melbourne resident'.

'I deeply feel that in [Louisa's] just punishment the
safety of society from ... cold-blooded criminal women
will be ensured,' this correspondent, Mr Frederick Tayler,
said. 'If, through the idiotic, absurd folly of humanitarians
(so called), she escapes the right award of the law, not
only Sydney but all Australian society will be rendered
unsafe from the like heartless dealings of unscrupulous,
wicked women.' (For the record, Mr Tayler also compared
Louisa's crimes to those of Jack the Ripper, who was
murdering women in London's Whitechapel at around
the same time, saying: 'Is not the crime of Louisa Collins
still more heinous? A crime, not the butchering of the
few horrible minutes, but the torturing, hour by hour,
day by day, of those who depended on her for loving
sustenance? Women who commit such enormity as this
unsex themselves ... and deserve the same treatment as
bad men.'[16])

The only known portrait of Louisa Collins and her second husband, Michael Collins, appeared in the *Australian Town and Country Journal* on 11 August 1888. The accompanying article described Louisa as a 'tolerably good-looking woman' who had been accused of Michael's murder, and noted: 'The couple appeared to live happily together until lately, when Collins began to complain of excessive vomiting and pains in the stomach, and he died on 8 July.'

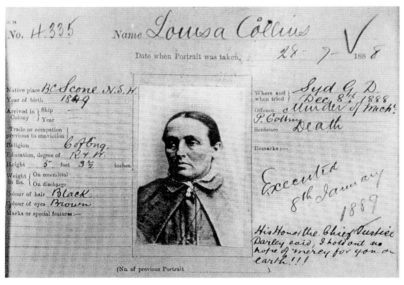

Louisa's prison card from the Darlinghurst Gaol lists her date of birth as 1849, but Louisa had a terrible habit of lying about her age. She was in fact born on the Belltrees estate, near Scone, in 1847. Possibly she lied because her husband Michael was so much younger.

The Central Criminal Court in Sydney's Darlinghurst, where Louisa was put on trial, was built in the 1840s, and still stands near Oxford Street. Louisa was walked to court each day by two female wardens, via an underground tunnel from the Darlinghurst Gaol.

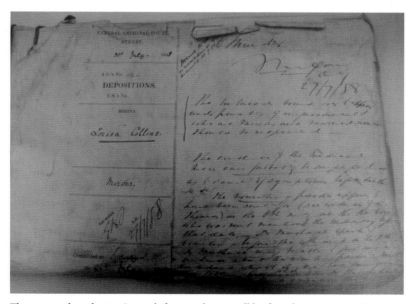

The notes taken during Louisa's four trials can still be found in storage at State Records New South Wales. The four judges filled six notebooks; there are also letters from Louisa, and from many of the women who tried to save her, stored in various files and boxes.

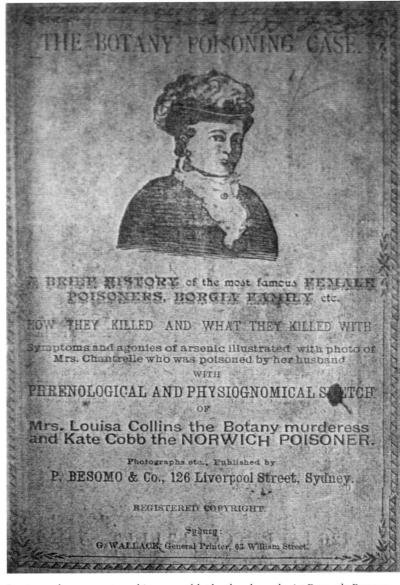

Louisa as she was portrayed in a pamphlet by the phrenologist Pasquale Besomo who, like many people at that time, believed that a person's criminal tendencies could be ascertained by studying the shape of their skull. Mr Besomo told his readers that Louisa's thin lips suggested she was crafty.

This sketch of the Geddes wool sheds in Botany appeared in the *Australian Town and Country Journal* on 3 December 1881. Both of Louisa's husbands worked at Geddes; both handled sheep skins, which were regularly treated with arsenic, the poison that killed them.

Rough on Rats was a potent rat killer, consisting largely of arsenic, imported to Sydney from the United States. Louisa's little girl, May, told the court that she had seen a box of Rough on Rats on a shelf in the kitchen, and that a teaspoonful was missing.

Louisa Collins' signature on a letter from Darlinghurst Gaol. Several of her letters have survived, including one in which she begs the governor, Lord Carrington, to show mercy, and save her life.

left: Premier Sir Henry Parkes (pictured here with his third wife, Julia) refused to intervene to save Louisa's life, telling parliament in a fiery speech that the women of New South Wales did not approve of wives who poisoned their husbands, and would surely vote to see Louisa hanged — but, of course, no woman was ever given a say, in any part of Louisa's many trials.

below: Landscape artist Elizabeth Parsons led the fight for Louisa from Victoria, collecting hundreds of signatures from women on a petition that said, in part: 'While loathing the crime for which this woman has been condemned we regarded the punishment of death as a barbarous method of executing justice.'

left: One of few surviving photographs of the remarkable Eliza Pottie, who also campaigned to save Louisa's life. Mrs Pottie went on to join the suffrage movement, which achieved the vote for Australian women less than fifteen years after Louisa was hanged.

Louisa after her hair was cropped in readiness for her execution. Several pressmen noted that Louisa's beauty had faded during her time in prison.

Louisa was a pretty child who grew into a desirable woman. Here, she has become a vamp. Louisa as portrayed in *People* magazine in 1984, as part of a summer supplement on Australia's most notorious female killers.

above: Louisa's eldest son, Herbert Andrews, with his loving wife, Annie (far right), and his two daughters, Pearl and Mabel. Herbert's girls went on to marry and have families of their own. Many of Louisa's descendants, including some who grew up in the house that Herbert built, still live around Newcastle, in New South Wales.

left: Thelma Cairney was the granddaughter Louisa never knew. She grew up, got married and had five children, who remember her as sweet, kind and loving. This adorable photograph is courtesy of the Thompson family of Lambton, New South Wales.

Sydney letter writers agreed, saying:

Louisa Collins has been tried by the open and fair
trial of a jury of intelligent men for a crime of the
most revolting nature, the slow poisoning of the one
whom she had promised to love and honour, and
there is but little doubt that the first husband shared
the same fate. Is any punishment too harsh for such
a creature? No.[17]

Was Louisa herself aware of the growing debate regarding
her sentence? It seems very likely. Although she was being
held in a cell at the Darlinghurst Gaol, she was receiving
regular visits from the gaol chaplain, the Reverend Canon
Charles Rich, a well-educated man who would later join
the campaign to try to save Louisa's life.[18]

As had been the case before her sentencing Louisa wasn't
a difficult prisoner. She ate well and slept easily and never
had to be punished. She was sometimes maudlin, sitting in
her cell saying things like 'poor Mick, poor Mick' but she
rarely expressed any self-pity. At some point, a rumour went
around that she might be pregnant (or 'enciente' or 'with
child', to quote the words so quaintly used in newspapers of
the day) and it seems that Louisa herself did little to dismiss
the notion, for a physician was sent to investigate.[19]

Sir Henry Parkes was also told and reportedly said that
if the rumour was true, 'the condemned woman will have
to be withheld from execution'.[20]

The rumour was not true. How could it be true? Louisa
had been arrested in July 1888 and had been in prison for

six months. True, she had worn a cape to court each day, but her female wardens would surely have noticed a great swelling under her plain, wincey prison dress.

Still, a doctor was summoned to conduct an examination. Louisa was judged not to be pregnant, and the execution was on again.

Or was it? Even to a laywoman, there would seem to have been at least half a dozen grounds on which Mr Lusk could have launched an appeal. Both of Louisa's husbands had worked at Geddes woolsheds. Both had handled skins. While it's true that a Geddes representative had testified at her trial that the company did not use arsenic in its tanks, there was no way for anyone to guarantee that none of the sheep from which the skins and wool had been sourced hadn't, at some point, been dipped in arsenic.

The wool industry was immensely important to the New South Wales economy. The rights of workers to a safe place of employment was an extremely low priority, particularly compared to the merchant's right to a quick profit. There were plenty of reasons why the risks to workers from arsenic might have been ignored, hidden or downplayed, yet this suggestion had never been put to a jury.

If that avenue of appeal failed, there was also the fact that both of Louisa's husbands had lived at Pople's Terrace in Botany, which, in turn, was a heavily polluted industrial site brimming with noxious chemicals. The water in the pump behind Louisa's house was never tested. The dirt around the house was never tested.

Then, too, was the fact that Louisa had never been convicted of Charles's murder, yet his sickness and death were repeatedly raised at her trial for the murder of Michael, to lend weight to the theory that she might have killed both of them. This, in particular, troubled many of the colony's finest legal minds. How could Louisa possibly have received a fair trial when the jury was being told that she had probably killed her first husband as well as the one she stood accused of murdering?

CHAPTER 13

The Appeal

Friday 28 December 1888
Central Criminal Court, Darlinghurst
PRESIDING: Chief Justice Sir Frederick Darley,
Justice Windeyer and Justice Foster
CROWN: Attorney General George Bowen
Simpson, Mr Charles G Heydon
DEFENCE: Mr Francis E Rogers QC with
Mr T Slattery and Mr HH Lusk assisting

Shortly after Louisa's fourth trial ended with her conviction, she requested a meeting with her little daughter, May. The child was dutifully brought into the Darlinghurst Gaol in December 1888 in the company of a warden. At no point were the two left alone, and this is perhaps just as well, for it was not a tender visit. Some reports would later suggest that Louisa spat in her child's face.[1] What is certain is that Louisa chastised the little girl for what she had said in court. How could May have seen the box of Rough on Rats on the shelf, she said, when it was up so high?

'I saw it,' May said, so clearly that everyone, including her guardian, could hear, 'when I stepped up on the chair.'

But was she really sure? Because Louisa remembered things differently — and if May did not change her testimony, Louisa would hang by her neck until she was dead. Some of Louisa's supporters would later insist that mother did not pressure child at this visit but it seems that May did come around, because almost as soon as the visit was over, Louisa wrote directly to Lord Carrington, pleading with him to allow her daughter to return to the stand during an appeal, to be re-examined by Mr Lusk.

In her letter, Louisa made plain that she wanted May to be allowed to give new evidence about the small glass tumbler — to say that it wasn't really one of theirs at all — and about the milk (how it wasn't true that the children had been scolded for drinking the condensed milk that had been put aside for Michael; in fact, Michael only ever drank fresh cow's milk).[2]

At roughly the same time — December 1888 — the *Evening News* published a letter from one of Louisa's supporters, Mr Frederick Lee, alerting readers (and Lord Carrington) to what May might say if she was allowed to return to the stand:

> May Collins, I am informed, has said, in the
> presence of a warder and the prisoner since the
> conviction, that the glass produced in Court was
> never in the house of the prisoner (and as she used
> to wash up the glasses, she had the best opportunity
> of knowing) and that she [May] never saw it before.

May Collins has further stated that 'the prisoner never gave yellow [condensed] milk to Collins; he always had the usual cow's milk from the milkman.' [But] the milkman was not called [to testify] although I am informed he could have proved that large quantities of milk were daily taken from him.

The evidence of May Collins, who was a witness for the Crown, was, I am informed, thoroughly relied on by the Crown, who believed her testimony as a witness of truth and that she is peculiarly intelligent for a child of her tender years.

Another important point ought not to escape your notice. No evidence was produced by the Crown as to the purchase of poison by the prisoner or by anyone on her behalf, although I learn inquiries by the police through the city and suburbs have been made from all vendors of poison with no result.

I would respectfully beg to point out that the Crown has signally failed in proving or suggesting any motive for the murder of Collins by the prisoner.

The case after all rests solely on circumstantial evidence, a species of evidence upon which many innocent individuals have been found guilty and executed … Imprisonment for life would leave the case open for reinvestigation should anything interesting turn up … and the community would not be shocked by the execution of a woman, and

everyone not possessing savage instincts would be
satisfied.

I have now the honor [to] respectfully ask you,
in the interests of justice, that the child May Collins
be examined, on oath, as to these alleged facts.[3]

Louisa's and her supporters' campaign for an appeal did
not go unanswered. The premier, Sir Henry Parkes, had
already told parliament that the state would cover the cost,
and that he was willing to hear any evidence that would
place Louisa in 'a better light'. And so, three days after
Christmas 1888, an appeal was heard.

It would be the first time that Louisa had been given the
benefit of having a Queen's Counsel. Mr Francis Rogers QC
had agreed to take the case. On the face of it, Mr Rogers was
a good choice for her (not that Louisa was given a choice, of
course; he was assigned to her). Born in 1841 — the year
that Nosey Bob had sailed to Australia — Mr Rogers had
graduated from the University of Sydney not only in law,
but with a gold medal in chemistry, and chemistry was key
to the case. Mr Rogers also had more than twenty years'
experience, having been admitted to the New South Wales
bar in March 1864 (he took silk in December 1887).[4]

Mr Rogers' main problem — and it was a big one — was
that he was having to follow in the footsteps of Mr Lusk.
The rules regarding appeals to the Full Bench were then as
they are now: it wasn't enough to simply front up and ask
for the case to be heard again (and then try to introduce
new evidence). Mr Rogers would have to demonstrate the
ways in which the fourth trial had been unfair to Louisa,

but Mr Lusk hadn't really flagged any problems with any of the procedures.

Also — and this would never happen today — while the appeal would be heard by not one but three judges on the Full Bench, they were three of the same judges that had already presided over Louisa's earlier trials. (To put that another way, Chief Justice Darley, Justice Windeyer and Justice Foster were in effect sitting in judgement of themselves.)

If that were not enough, the Crown was to be represented by the attorney general, George Bowen Simpson; and by Mr Charles G Heydon, who would later become attorney general himself.

Still, Mr Rogers agreed to have a go. As to the grounds for the appeal, he intended to raise two:

1. That evidence about the death of Charles Andrews should have been inadmissible at Louisa's trial for the murder of Michael Collins; and

2. that one of the jurymen had received and read a telegram in the middle of the trial.

Without getting too technical, neither of these grounds were in the scope of what's known as a 'writ of error' — meaning, neither of them had been flagged as a problem for the defence during Louisa's trial — but, perhaps in an effort to prove to the public that Louisa was getting a fair go, the attorney general told the court that he was prepared to let them through.

'On behalf of the Crown, I am perfectly willing that any points which could be raised in favour of the prisoner might be raised,' Mr Simpson said. 'I will put no obstacle in the way.'

The Chief Justice, however, was dubious. 'Can we legally take that course?'[5]

The attorney general insisted: a woman's life was at stake. Neither the Crown nor the Parkes ministry wanted to find themselves accused of not doing all in their power to at least have an appeal heard.

That said, Mr Rogers didn't get far. His first point was that the jury in the fourth trial had been allowed to hear prejudicial evidence about the death of Louisa's first husband, Charles Andrews. Naturally, when the jury heard that Louisa was also accused of the death of her first husband, they were more inclined to believe that she had killed her second husband, too. The introduction of such evidence about Charles's death — especially the doctor's suspicion that he, too, had died from arsenical poisoning — would today be regarded as highly irregular. As a general rule, such evidence — known as propensity evidence, in that it suggests that somebody has done something similar before, and may therefore have the propensity to do something like it again — is regarded as highly prejudicial and is therefore mostly inadmissible. However, the system in 1888 was different. Evidence about Charles's death — including the inference that he'd died from arsenical poisoning, which hadn't been proved in any court of law — was introduced at all four of Louisa's trials, without much objection from Mr Lusk.

Unfortunately for Louisa, all three judges of the appeal court agreed (with each other and with themselves) that such evidence ought to have been admissible because it was so important for the jury to hear it.

'If a person poisoned half a dozen people, and they all died in the same manner,' Justice Windeyer said, well, that would have to be put before the jury, and it was absurd to suggest otherwise.[6]

Justice Foster agreed, and so did Chief Justice Darley, and why wouldn't they? Each had made the decision to allow the evidence in the first place.

Perhaps realising that he was flogging a dead horse, Mr Rogers moved quickly to his second point: the fact that one of the jurors had received and read a telegram during the trial. This was obviously outrageous. It is absolutely and completely out of bounds for a juror to receive a letter, a telegram, or any kind of communication from the world outside the courtroom while a trial is underway. It's why jurors don't get access to newspapers (and, in modern times, to the internet) and it's why they get sequestered of an evening, lest anyone try to influence them with evidence not before the court.

Unfortunately, although Mr Lusk had clearly seen the telegram being delivered, he hadn't complained about it at the time.

Mr Rogers' hope was the Full Bench might let him complain about the telegram anyway, since so many people had seen it delivered and it was so obviously outside the rules. Chief Justice Darley seemed unconvinced, saying: 'I have no recollection of any telegram whatever being received in court.' However, the Crown prosecutor, Mr Heydon, was on side: 'Towards the close of the trial, a telegram came in for one of the jurymen, who on reading it gave as an answer, "That is all right".'[7]

Mr Lusk agreed. 'The occurrence took place at the last trial. There was a telegram passed to a juryman. It was just as the court was about to adjourn for lunch on the third day of the trial.'

Justice Windeyer was amazed: 'Why did you not object to it then?' he said.

Mr Lusk replied: 'It was not until the prisoner asked me afterwards what the meaning of it was that I thought it of much importance.'

Louisa herself, in other words, had been forced to draw it to her own counsel's attention.

Mr Rogers tried his luck: 'If it could be proven that a telegram came into the court, could the record be altered, so I might move a writ of error? I can think of nothing more dangerous than an unopened telegram getting into the hands of a juryman during a trial ... an unopened telegram might be extremely dangerous.'[8]

This was certainly true, and every eminent juror on the bench must have known it. Alas for Louisa, Chief Justice Darley had an idea: the telegram should be found. Then everyone could see what it said, and if it was nothing, well, then they would see.

The hearing was adjourned. Two hours later, they all traipsed back. The telegram had been found, as had the juror who received it.

In its entirety, the telegram said:

> In the event of further detention, anything you
> require?[9]

That was it, a simple question from one Mr Donald Hill to his brother in the jury, who had already been sequestered for two nights, asking if he needed anything.

To Mr Rogers' great credit, he didn't immediately surrender. So long as Louisa's life was at stake he would keep fighting for her. A telegram had entered the courtroom without the Chief Justice even noticing, and that was out of order.

Chief Justice Darley agreed: 'As far as that is concerned, I must blame myself ... if my attention had been called to it I should not have allowed the telegram to go to the juryman without opening it. No doubt my mind was at the time fixed upon the evidence.'

Mr Rogers rushed to mollify him, saying: 'We are not complaining of that ...'

No, no, Chief Justice Darley understood, nobody was criticising him personally, but it was 'clearly an irregularity'. Nevertheless, he still thought it would be 'very improper' to call off the whole conviction on the basis of such a telegram. 'It could not possibly have had any influence upon the jury at all,' he said.

Justice Windeyer agreed. 'Justice could never be carried out efficiently if such a thing were allowed to affect a trial.'

The Chief Justice nodded. 'I am very glad this matter has been cleared up,' he said. 'However, this matter could have had no effect upon the verdict in the case ... it could have had no possible effect upon the result.' Then he went further — quite a lot further, actually — saying that, in his opinion, there was not a 'shadow of a doubt' that Louisa was guilty 'not only of the murder of which she now stands convicted' but of the murder of her first husband, too. 'She was, in my opinion, guilty of both murders,' Chief Justice Darley said.

Justice Windeyer agreed, saying: 'I tried the prisoner once [before] ... and the case is now stronger than when it came before me, but, even without that evidence, I considered it one of the clearest cases that ever came before a jury.'

Justice Foster nodded: 'I also think the case is one of such a nature that it would be a flagrant wrong to public morals if a mere technical objection should be allowed to prevail. I had occasion to try the case in its earliest stage, and at that time much of the important evidence — much of the most telling evidence — was not then called, and yet I had no doubt that the case was proved.'[10]

And so it was revealed: all three judges believed in Louisa's guilt. None thought the appeal should be upheld. The conviction should stand. Louisa should hang.

CHAPTER 14

A Wife and Mother

With the appeal to the Full Bench over, very little stood between Louisa Collins and the gallows, and the public — as well as Louisa — now seemed to understand that.

From the end of December 1888 into January 1889, letters about the trial — and specifically about the planned execution — began pouring into local newspapers and, as noted earlier, many were again from women.

Not all were in favour of mercy. In fact, one woman calling herself 'A Wife and Mother' thought hanging too good for Louisa: 'Like many thousands of my own sex,' this 'Wife and Mother' had 'pursued the correspondence ... and, with your permission, I would like to give my opinion. I think the unfortunate creature ... is guilty of the crime [and] any person who doubts this must be entirely devoid of what is usually called common sense.'[1]

Fair enough, that was her opinion. The woman went on:

Here is a cold-blooded woman ... a mother, and therefore capable of the highest emotions, who

deliberately [commits] one of the most diabolical
crimes which our history can record ... If I desired
to put one of my cats to death by a process of
slow poisoning, do you think I could witness the
sufferings of the poor beast day after day? Would
not her groans and moans have the effect of
compelling me to at once put her out of her misery?
I think hanging is too good for the creature and if a
petition in favour of the sentence being carried out
is got up I would willingly canvass for signatures —
I am A WIFE AND MOTHER [capitals in
original].[2]

The response to this letter was immediate. A correspondent
calling herself 'A True Woman' quickly wrote back to the
Herald letters page, saying: 'I refuse to agree with "A Wife
and Mother". She does not know women. I know my sex
better.'

This 'True Woman' criticised the 'Wife and Mother' for
being 'gloriously inconsistent ... while deploring the fact that
a human being has taken the life of another human being,
she urges the state to commit the same crime.' Moreover,
she would be 'ashamed' to think that other women 'could
join in the cry to hunt a fellow creature to death, for I am
A TRUE WOMAN [capitals in original]'.[3]

Then, too, came this, a letter from a woman who had
been holding her tongue, despite 'feeling deeply' about the
case. 'But today, having seen a letter from "A Wife and
Mother" I can hold on no longer,' she said, 'and I trust
you will therefore publish the opinions of another Wife

and Mother. I have gone carefully and attentively, I think, over all the evidence against the wretched prisoner … and, at the risk of being considered devoid of common sense, I have most grave doubts, which I share with thousands of my sex, of her guilt as a murderess.'

Moreover, she said, she could not understand how the other 'wife and mother' could gloat about Louisa — a 'wretched creature now lying in a miserable cell'. 'For a woman to denounce another in such pitiless strains is unseemly and horrible in the extreme,' the woman wrote. 'Apart from this, is it not monstrous that a mother should be hanged on the evidence of her own little child?' To hang Louisa would be a triumph of 'vindictiveness and bloodthirsty revenge' and she prayed for a day when 'capital punishment will no longer stain this world of ours'.[4]

Another representative of the 'softer sex' felt bound to protest not so much in favour of Louisa but against the 'barbarous tone' adopted by 'A Wife and Mother'. 'To say that hanging is too good for such a creature is almost incredible,' she said. 'I think of what Louisa Collins must have already suffered in going through four terrible trials on such a charge.' She was also dismayed by the 'miserable bequest [Louisa] will leave her innocent family'. Curiously — or perhaps typically, given that women were not generally canvassed as to their opinions on matters of law — this correspondent believed that 'to go into the question of her guilt or innocence is not a woman's province'. However, she reminded all and sundry about 'dangerous and irremediable mistakes made through relying on circumstantial evidence only. Why can we not think the best of each other? Suppose Louisa Collins is not guilty?' She went on: 'The crime is shrouded in mystery. What if Collins was responsible for both Andrews' death and his own? Many people talk of her cold-blooded guilt as if they had been eye-witnesses of crime.' She also refused to believe that one who had fallen 'morally and socially for love of a man could possibly bear to take that man's life by inches, and gloat over the torture he endured'.[5]

Another correspondent pleaded for mercy on the grounds that it was gruesome to deliver a woman over to the 'cruel hands of the executioner ... The policy (to use the coldest word) of deliberately putting any woman to a death [is a crime of] violence in a Christian land [and] I am firmly persuaded that such a horrid spectacle is essentially brutal and demoralising. [It] must do much harm generally, and can do no possible good.'[6]

Men — who would make the decision, after all — were urged to 'think of [their] mother: any man who has a wife, a sister, or a daughter, think how abhorrent is the thought that any of that sex ... should come to such a shameful death'.

'Men are different from women,' the writer continued. 'They naturally realise more directly the results of all offences, especially those of violence.' As such, when men were found guilty, they should 'pay the full penalty'. Women, on the other hand, should be sentenced only to 'civil death, to hopeless imprisonment, for life'.[7]

On the other hand, a different correspondent said: 'Why should those seeking her reprieve plead sex? ... When a woman sinks to such a state of iniquity that she will poison her husband, I say that woman has lost all the noble, gentle characteristics that are natural to her sex.'[8]

Energised by the debate, the *Herald* itself decided to intervene (this should not be so surprising; the then editor had a feisty wife, who would later join the campaign for women's right to vote). In an editorial published on Friday, 4 January 1889, just five days before the date of the scheduled execution, the newspaper published a 'leader', or opinion piece, praising both male and female correspondents for speaking up. 'It is only right that the opinions of the community generally should be heard,' the newspaper said.

However, it disagreed with the idea that Louisa should not be hanged on the grounds that she was a woman:

> It would appear that people consider it chivalrous to ask that the law be set aside for a woman, as though she should not be held responsible for her acts. But it is a false chivalry ... If women hold the same rights and privileges as men, and share the advantages of law and society alike with them, they should also share the responsibility that their citizenship places upon them.
>
> There is no equality between men and women if there is not an equality of responsibility ... The question we must face is this: if a woman is not to be hanged, is a man to be hanged for a crime similar to that the woman has committed? Let us reverse the circumstances. Had Peter Collins [sic] poisoned his wife in the same manner that she

poisoned him, would there have been memorials for the commutation of his sentence? A more horrible and cold-blooded atrocity than that which this wife committed can scarcely be conceived. Why, then, should a plea for mercy be raised for a woman whose criminal hardihood betokens a nature as flinty and as cruel as that of any man could be? It is all very well to talk of mercy but there is such a thing as justice as well ... If Louisa Collins is not hanged, then we can hang no woman ... for none could commit a worse crime. That being so, we are taking away the deterrent effect which keeps crime in check ... If we are to have capital punishment at all we must have it irrespective of sex.[9]

The flaws in this argument are obvious, and were immediately pounced upon. 'I contend that women have NOT the same rights and privileges as men and as citizens,' cried one letter writer, in response. 'They are not citizens; they have no voice in enacting the laws of the country; they have to obey [but] they have no share, nor are they consulted, in electing the lawmakers; they have no representation in the Parliament of the country, although taxed as if they were citizens. That is taxation without representation — the worst of tyrannies! I say Louisa Collins ought not to be hung.'[10]

Taxation without representation. That's exactly what it was, but worse. Louisa's position was at least as bad as that of the colony's Aborigines: she was to be tried — and hanged — by a system in which she had no say.

*

It would be entirely wrong — and unfair — to suggest that no men in power anywhere moved to try to save Louisa. There were in fact many men — including those quite certain of her guilt — working hard to save her life. A key player in that respect was Sir George Richard Dibbs, who served as premier of New South Wales more than once in the decade before Federation, just never at the right time to commute Louisa's sentence.

Matching Sir George — still Mr Dibbs, in those days — for passion was Mr Frederick Lee.

First, to Mr Dibbs. On Thursday, 3 January 1889 — shortly after the appeal, and less than a week before Louisa was due to be hanged — he chaired a public meeting at Sydney's brand new Town Hall. The meeting was designed to put as much pressure as possible on Sir Henry Parkes and Lord Carrington.

Of course Mr Dibbs had never met — nor would he ever meet — Louisa Collins, but he was exactly the kind of person anyone would want in their corner. He was not only an experienced politician, but was among the first politicians to be Sydney-born. (George's father, John Dibbs, a ship's captain, had arrived in the colony in 1820.) Mr Dibbs had already been premier once before (briefly, in 1885) and would soon be premier again (sadly, his elevation would come ten days too late for Louisa). He was a passionate supporter of free education, saying it was the 'absolute duty of the state to educate every child'. He had been raised by a single mother (his father was lost at sea when George was still a boy). He was also fiery or, as one biographer put it, 'courageous but not disciplined'. He had once been arrested — the matter in question was complicated, involving another man's adultery with his brother's wife — and when the bailiff came to take him away, Dibbs calmly took off all his clothes and challenged them to physically remove his naked bulk. He ended up spending a year in gaol, later describing the experience as a 'pleasant retreat' from political life. He had in the past gotten along with Sir Henry Parkes, but right at the moment of Louisa's trial they were at war. ('He is a mean, despicable, dastardly man,' Sir Henry had declared during a debate over Chinese immigration in 1888, '[with a] genius for destruction, for degradation and for confusion.')[11]

Sharing the platform with Mr Dibbs at the Town Hall meeting were others on the side of mercy: Mr Melville, he of the curled pipe and undertaker's clothes, was there, as were fellow members of parliament Mr Walker and Mr Edward O'Sullivan, and one Mr William Ellard, whose role in New South Wales politics is somewhat difficult to ascertain. Mr Ellard was not a member of parliament nor a member of the judiciary. A search of his name turns up few facts, other than when he died in 1902, his family asked that no announcement appear in the obituary columns for fear that the crowd of mourners would be too big for the house to handle.[12]

The crowd that gathered at the Town Hall that evening was likewise large: no precise figure was given, but one newspaper said the Town Hall was 'crowded to excess'[13] and the *Herald*, which had a man there, noted with apparent astonishment that even 'a few ladies' turned up (it seems that none spoke, or else nobody bothered to record their contribution).[14]

A consummate politician, Mr Dibbs opened by saying he had no lengthy speech to give: 'We are here to save a woman from the humiliating punishment of death by hanging,' he said, 'and to let every speaker be heard.'

Mr Ellard was one of the first to his feet, explaining that he, like many, would be perfectly happy to see Louisa 'suffer any punishment short of death' (women were not being flogged in New South Wales in 1888, so he must have meant life imprisonment). 'Every right-minded man should see that even if the woman is guilty, it would be better that she be allowed time to repent,' Mr Ellard said. 'I would be ashamed to be here, thirsting for her blood.'[15]

Mr O'Sullivan (a former journalist and compositor — sketches show him with a thick moustache that made him look more like a policeman than a parliamentarian) made plain that those on the side of mercy had 'no sympathy for the crime' and would never suggest that Louisa go unpunished. 'I stand on behalf of mercy,' he said, and then added: 'This has been an extraordinary case. This woman had been tried by 48 jurymen — and 36 of them were unable to find her guilty.'[16]

'The fourth verdict is now said to be more over-powering than the three other verdicts,' he said. But 'from that standpoint alone, better there be a mistake on the side of mercy, than to hang a woman with such doubt hanging over her case.' Also, anyone who looked at the evidence — and this was to say nothing about the judges who had tried the various cases — would agree that it had started weak, and then appeared to grow stronger as the trials continued. Worse — much worse — was the fact that so much of the most compelling evidence had been given 'mostly by the unfortunate children of the unfortunate woman'.

Surely, for the children's sake, the penalty of death could be waived? What would their legacy be? What was to be gained by executing this woman?

Here, a voice cried out: Nothing!

'It is repugnant to our humanity to hang a woman,' Mr O'Sullivan continued. Sir Henry Parkes said in parliament that he would not flog a woman. 'And if it was repugnant to flog a woman how much worse was it to hang one?'

Others in the crowd rose to speak. Some argued that it was a travesty of justice to hang a woman who was friendless and penniless and probably insane. The language was often emotive, and always fantastic: if they dragged Louisa onto the scaffold and placed the rope around her neck, every one of them would be engaged in the horrible task of shooting the bolt which dropped her and hurled her into eternity. Also, it was simply wrong to say that the law must apply to women as it applied to men: where was the man coward enough to say that any woman should feel the lash upon her back?

To this, Mr Walker added that the law readily recognised differences between the sexes. Had women the same privileges and equalities with man as a lawmaker? he said.

No! the crowd cried.

Had she the same advantages as a property owner?
No!

Had she the same liberties in the various walks of life?
No, no!

Well, then, if women were disqualified in many walks of life, it was because it was felt that there was something in her that required the greatest sympathy … here was a woman of the same sex as our wives, sisters, mothers, daughters! What would be the good of carrying out the sentence? It could only mean adding another victim to those already in the grave.

Hear, hear!

Also — without the voice of those children, the mother never could have been brought in guilty!

The crowd cried: Shame, shame!

Let them think of these children. The source of their lives the court sought to remove. Let us think of these children who knew not what they were doing, who were coached by police …

Here, there was more wild applause.

… and who were told perhaps what to say …

Cheers and more cheers.

'Think of it that these children would have the stigma resting on their character for the rest of their lives that their mother's death was due to them at a time when responsibility had not formed in their minds, and when they knew not what they did!'

Thunderous applause!

Now it was Mr Melville's turn to speak. He could not agree with Mr Walker about the children being coached.

Where he could agree was that the main evidence against her was that of her own little girl. And the child, having told the truth … would the punishment of imprisonment for life not be enough? Or did the child now need to see her mother hang?

Mr Melville agreed that everything might point to Louisa's guilt, but it was just as possible — and it is always just as possible — that in the future, it might turn out that she was not so guilty as she appeared to be. If the hangman was permitted to perform his work, they would not be able to reopen the grave. There were doubts in this case. Circumstantial evidence was right and good but there was not a man living who could put his finger on a particle of evidence that perfectly and absolutely proved Louisa's guilt. 'We could base mercy on the fact that we are not certain of her guilt,' Mr Melville said, but the public should also remember this — yes, remember this: according to Christian teaching, the very first thing Louisa would receive after death would be the greatest mercy of all. Shouldn't the good folk of New South Wales not heed that example?[17]

After several hours of this kind of debate, the meeting resolved to send a deputation to see Lord Carrington. Mr Dibbs would lead the group, accompanied by Mr Melville, Mr O'Sullivan and Mr Ellard, among others.

Why did the group decide to petition the governor and not, say, the premier? This was, after all, the year 1888 — the centenary year in New South Wales, one hundred years since the First Fleet landed at Botany Bay. It wasn't as if the colony didn't have its own parliament, and its own premier in the form of Sir Henry Parkes.

One reason was obviously that half the group were from parliament, and already knew that parliament did not wish to get involved.

Another was the fact that the governor of New South Wales still had an important role to play as the Queen's representative in the colony, and as a member of the Executive Council, and so, when Louisa was first sentenced to hang, many people looked to him to save her.

His Excellency, Lord Charles Robert Carrington had arrived in New South Wales just three years earlier, and in terms of life experience, he had nothing whatsoever in common with either Louisa, her husbands, or their poor children.

Lord Carrington was a member of the British aristocracy. Born in Middlesex, England in 1843, he was the first-born son and heir of Robert John Smith and his wife, Charlotte Augusta Annabella. He was educated at Eton and Trinity and, when he married, in 1868, no fewer than ten member of the British royal family attended the ceremony.[18]

Although committed for life to service of the Crown, it is very likely that Lord Carrington was less than thrilled to be appointed governor of New South Wales, which was, after all, a former penal colony about as far from London society as it was possible to get. Still, he sailed to Sydney — and ports in between — aboard the *Carthage* in 1885, accompanied by Lady Carrington and their three children, the Honourable Miss Harbour (Lady Carrington's sister), and their servants, who included aides-de-camp, two nurses, two lady's maids, and one valet (these staff were in addition to the servants already awaiting the family's arrival at Government House). By most accounts — and there were dozens — His Excellency's voyage from England was comfortable and both lord and lady 'made themselves exceedingly popular on board' by handing the 'captain of the *Carthage* a cheque for £50, to be distributed among the crew of the vessel'.[19]

Upon their arrival at Port Jackson on 11 December 1885, the family was met by a cheering crowd and by the then premier, George Dibbs, who led His Excellency on a private tour of the romantic sandstone mansion known as Government House. Replete with turrets, it sat in a beautiful setting on Sydney Harbour and had a five-hectare garden overlooking Farm Cove. Besides being Lord and Lady Carrington's new home, Government House would also be his office, and official reception space.

Life at Government House was a whirl of banquets, balls and political meetings held in magnificent reception halls with open fires, cigar boxes and oil paintings on the walls. Lady Carrington busied herself with good works: she established the Jubilee Fund to relieve poor women and, in 1887, she hosted a banquet for 1000 poor boys to mark Queen Victoria's jubilee (all the boys were given medals struck for the occasion, and heard grand tales of the Carrington family's humble origins in England).[20]

Such acts of grace were not uncommon, and there seems little doubt that the people of New South Wales loved Lord and Lady Carrington. As to whether the lord and lady loved New South Wales, well, all that can be said is that when Lord Carrington travelled home to England in 1888 — no small journey — a rumour surfaced that he did not want to return to Australia.

The *Evening News* reported this gossip under the headline 'An Extraordinary Rumor'. In part, the text read: 'Lord and Lady Carrington will probably return from Sydney early next year, as I hear that he is sick to death of Australia, and intends to resign his office as Governor of New South Wales.'[21] Other newspapers carried much the same report: 'A rumour is current here that Lord Carrington, Governor of New South Wales, has resigned his position, being, it is alleged, tired of life in Sydney and anxious to return to the fashionable circles of the old country.'[22]

Part of the problem, or so it seemed, was that Lord Carrington simply could not live on his salary of around 8000 pounds a year. In any case, the rumours came to naught: Lord Carrington returned to New South Wales, and was soon publicly joking about the gossip, telling the crowd at one banquet that he had 'scarcely read a paper during the past week without seeing a telegram from England that it was his intention to return to his native shores'. He couldn't imagine how this particular rumour got started (this, despite the fact that some newspapers had already named his replacement, a fellow called Wolff) but it was his 'fixed determination to stop here until the end of his term of office … and do whatever he could to keep the wolf [Wolff] from the door!'[23]

The crowd laughed and cheered.

Given the esteem in which he was held, it's no surprise that when something as momentous and ghastly as the execution of a mother of young children stormed into the public's consciousness in December of that same year, many in the community believed that the governor could, well, *do something*.

Just what he could do wasn't clear.

Lord Carrington was a member of the Executive Council, comprising the premier and his senior ministers (including the justice minister and the attorney general), and he had been part of the discussion when the young men from the Mount Rennie case sought mercy. Many in the community therefore believed that Lord Carrington could now grant mercy to Louisa Collins.

But could he? A close reading of the rules suggests that Lord Carrington could show mercy only after consulting with the Executive Council — which would in turn take advice from the Chief Justice — and even then, there were some parliamentarians and judges who believed that Lord Carrington had not the power to commute the sentence without their explicit approval. Lord Carrington, on the other hand, had made plain in speeches that he *did* have such power, saying:

> As the law stands now, under our Constitution, the Governor, much as he may desire it, can in no way relieve himself of the responsibility of saying whether the prerogative of mercy may be exercised. Should the Governor have fair and reasonable grounds for believing that the extreme sentence of the law should not be carried out, notwithstanding the strongly expressed opinion of the Court, notwithstanding the advice given him by the

Executive Council, it would be beyond all doubt his
duty to interfere ... [and] save the prisoner's life.[24]

Ministers could resign over it, and that would be fine, 'but
one thing is certain, the prisoner's life would be spared'.[25]

Certainly the deputation that made its way from the
Town Hall on the Friday morning before the scheduled
execution of Louisa Collins believed that Lord Carrington
was in a position to act. Why else would they have trekked
out to Government House, on Sydney Harbour, to see
him? The reception room was then — and is now — on
the ground floor. The deputation waited upon him there.
Unbeknownst to them, Lord Carrington was at that very
moment hosting a meeting of the Executive Council in
which the fate of Louisa was being discussed.

The clock ticked. Finally, at around three o'clock, the
deputation was asked to move into Lord Carrington's
rooms. The grand double doors were flung open. There
was the usual bowing and scraping. Mr Dibbs read aloud
the petition, asking the governor to exercise his royal
prerogative, and save Louisa's life. He then explained
that the meeting at the Town Hall had been large, and
yet more respectable and orderly than he had ever seen. It
seemed to him that most people were in favour of mercy.
He understood the painful position that Lord Carrington
found himself in, having to make such a decision, when
the Full Bench of the Supreme Court — and the premier,
Sir Henry Parkes — had already declared that the sentence
should stand. It was not Mr Dibb's intention to doubt the
wisdom of the jury or the judge.

However, Louisa Collins had been convicted 'entirely on circumstantial evidence, and the most serious evidence against her was that of her own child', Mr Dibbs said. May was only eleven years old but one day she would be twelve and then fifteen and then eighteen and then she would know what she had done, and it would be agonising for her. Pray the governor think of May ...

Also: hanging was barbaric. It would disgrace a colony that was desirous of being taken seriously in the world.

Mr Dibbs agreed that Louisa had 'degraded her sex', but the degradation of all the women of the colony was at risk if she were to hang. His Excellency had the 'terrible power' of life and death in his hands, and 'we ask you to extend your mercy'.

Mr O'Sullivan argued that Louisa had been convicted on 'the purest circumstantial evidence', and while there was the slightest doubt that she could be innocent, the sentence should be commuted: 'Better that one guilty woman escape than that an innocent one should suffer,' he said.[26]

Lord Carrington sat and listened, and from the words he used, it's impossible not to sense the sorrow he felt at not being able to do as these men wanted and save Louisa's life. 'I do not for a moment wish to shrink from the responsibility placed upon me,' he said, and yet he was bound to confess 'that had I had the smallest idea previous to my leaving England that such a duty would have been imposed upon me as Governor ... proud as I was to have been sent out [to] ... this great colony — *no power on earth would have induced me to come* [my emphasis].'[27]

On the face of it, that was an extraordinary statement. Lord Carrington obviously knew, well before he set sail, that the power of mercy would extend if not wholly, then at least partly, to him as governor. What he had not expected, it seems, was when the moment came, the prisoner would be a woman.

(In the days after Louisa was hanged, the *Bulletin* would provide its own translation of those words: '*I had no idea I should ever be called upon to do anything responsible. I thought the position was to be purely ornamental ...*'[28])

'All these occasions on which the Governor is asked to exercise the Royal prerogative of mercy are painful enough,' he said, 'but in this individual instance the painful circumstances are ten thousand times intensified by the unhappy circumstance that the criminal is a woman.' Yet the duty was his, as he said himself:

I am responsible for it. I have listened attentively to the speeches that you have made, and I read most attentively the reports in the daily papers of the meeting held last night. Mr. Dibbs, who has held the position of Prime Minister of the Crown, knows how thoroughly and anxiously the Executive Council on all these painful occasions go into the details of the case and how anxious they are to avail themselves of every possible loophole by which mercy can be extended.

In this case the Executive paid the most close and minute attention ... in fact, just before the deputation came in, the members of the Executive

Council met in this room and looked over the
petitions received during the last few days ... [and]
I am bound to say ... that the advice that has been
given me is that the sentence of the Court should
not be interfered with.

I have given this case the most anxious and
careful consideration. If it had been possible to
see any reason for interference on my part I would
gladly have availed myself of it. No such reason
however presents itself. It is therefore, my duty to
accept the advice tendered to me by the Ministers of
the Crown, and I with deep sorrow have to refuse to
interfere with the sentence of the Court.[29]

In short, if left to the governor, Louisa Collins would hang.

Almost as soon as the deputation withdrew, Lord
Carrington wrote to the premier:

My Dear Sir Henry,
A deputation from the Town Hall has just left.
Dibbs, Walker, Melville, O'Sullivan, Bennett and
two others.
They all spoke very swell.
Dibbs particularly so.
I told them that it was impossible to interfere.
They seemed disappointed.
These cases are simply awful.
Yours,
Carrington.[30]

CHAPTER 15

The Women Roar

In order to understand the role that women played in trying to save Louisa's life, it's important to reiterate the position of women generally in nineteenth-century Sydney. It won't take long to describe: as has previously been touched on in these pages, most women — rich or poor —were pretty much powerless.

To expand on that a little, Sydney in the 1880s was a thriving commercial centre with three distinct classes. The poor lived in crowded conditions around Surry Hills, Redfern and out toward Botany, where there was work for men in the woolsheds, brickworks, and slaughter yards. Poor girls tended to work as domestics, often for no more than food and board; poor married women carried the burden of child-rearing (some also took in sewing and laundry, to make ends meet).

The middle class in Sydney was fairly new, but it was growing fast. It comprised men with clerical jobs, and of course their wives and children. The ruling class, from the governor down, controlled most of the money and all of the power. This group included the British aristocrats, the big pastoralists (also called the squattocracy) plus all of the men in serious professions — judges, doctors and so on — and their wives, who also had children, but whose burdens were eased by the presence of nannies and maids.

No women could vote, not even if they were property owners or, indeed, if they paid taxes. The idea that a woman's place was in the home was firmly entrenched. A man could not be found guilty of raping his wife, and a woman's children could be taken from her after divorce.

The idea that women might deserve the same rights as men was still considered radical. The suffrage movement only really came to Australia in the late 1880s — which just happens to be around the same time as Louisa's four trials got underway.

Here, then, was a perfect example of the inequality under which women lived: Louisa had no right to vote, and no women could have a say in whether capital punishment should be abolished. Louisa had also been tried by four juries comprising forty-eight men, none of whom could easily be described as her peers. (Imagine the opposite scenario: a man sentenced to death after four trials before forty-eight women, whose fate was then debated by an all-female parliament.)

Now she was to be hanged.

Women had taken tentative steps into the debate when Louisa was first sentenced, with more than 600 of them signing the petition at Mr Palser's shop, and by writing letters to the colony's newspapers. Now that Louisa's appeal had been rejected — and now that the premier and,

it seems, the governor had ruled out any further appeals —
more forceful action was called for.

And so, in January 1889, a small group of women
formed to fight for Louisa's life. One of the fiercest warriors
in the battle was once described in one of the colony's
newspapers as 'a dainty, pink-cheeked, blue-eyed, silver-
locked Quaker lady',[1] but don't let that fool you: Mrs Eliza
Pottie was one of the most compassionate and remarkable
women ever to call Australia home. Picture her if you can,
at the time of Louisa's trial: a fifty-year-old mother of ten
who always dressed in the high-neck style of the Quakers.
Her husband, John, was a leading veterinarian, tasked with
keeping sheep — and New South Wales' police horses —
free of disease. The couple lived in a number of different
houses, all of them enormous, but Eliza still liked to get
about Sydney on the tram, usually while scribbling poetry
into a pretty little notebook she kept in her purse.

Mrs Pottie's labours on behalf of the women of New
South Wales were extraordinary: for more than twenty-
seven years she was president of the Mission Home for
Women at Glebe, which tried to help unmarried mothers;
she was also a member of the Ladies Sanitary Association,
which provided poor women with good advice on how to
care for and nourish their infants; and she was active in
trying to place widowed, deserted, and single mothers in
employment 'to enable her to try to keep her child with
her'.[2]

First and foremost, however, Mrs Pottie was a
committed member of the Women's Christian Temperance
Union. By way of background: the temperance movement

came to Australia from the United States in the late 1870s, and the reason that so many temperance union members later became suffragettes is that their principles were similar. Temperance advocates believed in controlling the supply of alcohol to protect women from violence at the hands of drunken husbands. They also believed that too many women and children were starving in homes where men spent all the money on liquor. Over time, those arguments evolved: why not grant women freedom from poverty and violence by enabling them to earn wages of their own? And then of course if women were going to work, they would also have to vote, for — as the old saying goes — there shouldn't be taxation without representation.

To all these causes, Mrs Pottie was committed. Perhaps politics was in the blood: Mrs Pottie had been born Eliza Allen in Ireland in 1837, the daughter of a soap and candle manufacturer who came to Sydney in 1841 (the same year, again, as Nosey Bob). Both her father, William Allen, and her brother, Alfred Allen, would become members of the New South Wales parliament, and neither was shy about pushing their views (William was an avowed protectionist, while Alfred was a free-trader. Family dinners must have been interesting).[3]

At age twenty-five — quite late, for the era — Eliza married John Pottie. The first of their brood was born the following year, and there followed twenty years of pregnancy, birth — and grieving. Only six of the children survived infancy, which perhaps explains Mrs Pottie's commitment to the cause of poor and neglected children.

Lest there be any doubt about her commitment to temperance, it's said that Mrs Pottie's zeal for the cause extended to ensuring that unfermented wine was used in the sacraments at her local church. She was also committed in ways that beggar belief to the cause of social justice. At the time of her death in 1907 — more of which later — Mrs Pottie was a member of at least seventeen organisations serving children, women and the poor. Besides being a founder of the Mission Home for unmarried mothers, she was a regular visitor to homes for abandoned children, where she would receive her meal on a tin plate at the long table with the orphans crouched around, listening to her stories about the loving Jesus.

Her charity extended to her own home: Mrs Pottie was very often so taken by a child she met at an orphanage she would invite him or her to have a little holiday at her house. She also established a tradition of opening her home on the Monday prior to Christmas to poor and widowed mothers, who would come with their children to have a hot meal and to receive a package of flour, tea, and a toy.

Besides her acts of charity, Mrs Pottie was one of the few women prepared to speak up on political matters. Key to her appeal, in fact, was her absolute determination to have a say on policy at a time when women were actively discouraged from so doing. She was clearly intelligent — both Sir Henry Parkes and Sir George Dibbs would, from time to time, seek her advice on how to best assist the poor — and she was not at all shy about giving new ideas a go.

Among other things, Mrs Pottie campaigned for the aged pension. As difficult as it now is to understand, there was in the nineteenth century a great deal of opposition to the idea that the elderly deserved a pension, on the grounds that the state should not interfere with the duties of children toward their parents. To this, Mrs Pottie said: 'The state doesn't do anything of the kind. The state helps the old people in the closing days of tired lives. It is a truly noble act, and money well spent ... Let us not hamper the effort in any way, seeing that it brings great joy.'[4]

Another of the causes in which Mrs Pottie ultimately triumphed was in removing irons from prisoners sentenced to hard labour at the Darlinghurst Gaol. 'It seems to me that the spirit of revenge is too much mixed up' with this, she said, while campaigning on this issue. 'Let us look at a case. A man commits a crime, a dreadful crime ... for this he loses his home and all therein — his liberty, his means of livelihood, his character — all are gone, and rightly gone ... but that he should [be] loaded with irons and chains around wrists and feet seems to me like oppression.'[5]

She concluded: 'I know that this is not a popular subject ...' but, as ever, Mrs Pottie could not be silenced in the face of suffering, including the plight of people then known as 'the blacks of La Perouse'.

'Some two or three years ago I drew your attention to the state of the blacks at La Perouse and I would again ask for space to bring their condition and that of the other aboriginals under the notice of Australians,' Mrs Pottie said, in one of several letters on this subject, addressed to the *Sydney Morning Herald*, in the early 1890s.

> To 'jump' as it were [onto] the land and native home
> of these people, to deprive them of their rights
> and heritage, to plough up their hunting grounds,
> and cause their game to become almost extinct,
> is bad enough, but to see them year after year in
> those wretched little houses, without schools or any
> kind of comfort or religious instruction ... is too
> reprehensible altogether.[6]

Mrs Pottie spoke not only from the heart but from experience: for several years, she organised what she called 'surprise party' visits to La Perouse, taking 'plenty of provisions, and receiv[ing] a warm welcome' from the Aboriginal people who lived there. Upon her return, she would take a seat at her writing desk, and compose letters to the *Herald* in which she described the way the Indigenous people lived in small, corrugated-iron houses with no glass windows and no privacy from the outside world.

In one such house, she found 'an old black man' and a woman who had been bitten by rats. There were seven or eight children 'who ought to be at school, but there is no school nearer than Botany, and if there were one, they have no clothes or boots suitable for school'. In a second house she found a crippled, widowed woman and her son, sharing with others who had no place else to go. They had no bread, and were in mourning for one of their children who had recently died 'from the bite of a tick which had fastened to its neck'. While many in the community favoured a policy of assimilation, Mrs Pottie did not, saying: 'They are by nature a wild, free people. Why should we force them to live any particular life?'[7]

Mrs Pottie followed closely the details of Louisa's trial and it was she who decided, in January 1889, to organise a women's meeting in aid of Louisa Collins, ironically, at the headquarters of the Temperance Union, in Sydney's Phillip Street.

Only a handful of people turned up — maybe twelve in total — and the names of most of them are lost to history. One who is known to have been in attendance was a woman who was in every sense as remarkable as Mrs Pottie: her Christian name was Caroline, but she signed in that day as Mrs FB Boyce, and she was the wife of the temperance advocate, social reformer and Anglican priest, Reverend Francis Bertie Boyce, of St Paul's, Redfern.

Mrs Boyce — like Mrs Pottie — was a compassionate woman, always on the side of the down-and-out. For example, when city leaders were trying to kick poor-as-church-mice flower sellers out of Martin Place, Mrs Boyce wrote to the *Herald* to plead their case, saying they were, in the main, respectable people 'doing their best to maintain themselves and families in the absence of other employment'.[8] They were allowed to stay.

As astonishing as it may seem, given how unrecognised she is, Mrs Boyce was also a founder of one of the organisations that grew into the program now known as the Royal District Nursing Service. Working alongside her husband in the late 1880s, she identified more than 400 families living in deplorable poverty around their church and, with the support of benevolent friends, employed a nurse to visit them.

According to press reports, this nurse carried bandages, warm wraps, soft cushions and dainty cakes as she went from house to house, providing treatment and succour. Her patients were people rejected by the hospitals as incurable: some had consumption and others were in crippling pain with cancer or else suffering 'helpless old age'.[9]

There would hardly be an Australian family today that has not used a similar visiting nurse service.

Caroline Boyce doesn't get to have her portrait on a banknote. As far as can be judged, no portrait of her hangs in any gallery anywhere in Australia, and yet she helped found one of the proudest institutions in the world. Remarkable.

In any case, Mrs Boyce, Mrs Pottie, and perhaps ten others held their meeting for Louisa on Friday, 4 January 1888. Not everyone agreed on the way forward, but at the end of it, the following resolution had been passed:

We have the honour to form a deputation from a meeting of women held in Sydney to intercede for the commutation of the death sentence passed on the woman Louisa Collins.

1. The law of the land has judged the woman guilty of the awful crime of murder by poison.
2. In accordance with that law, the highest and most extreme penalty that the law can inflict has been pronounced. This is justice.

3. We plead for mercy [and we believe] that by so
   doing we are fulfilling the teaching of Him who
   said: 'Blessed are the merciful, for they shall
   obtain mercy.'[10]

The resolution also argued that it was abhorrent that a 'woman and mother, comparatively young in years' should be 'hung till she is dead' — especially with 'her little children being cognisant of the fact'.

Having passed the resolution, a deputation from the meeting comprising Mrs Boyce, Mrs Pottie and a woman named Mrs Lee — who may or may not have been the wife of a local justice of the peace, Mr Frederick Lee (her initials weren't given) — made its way to Government House to plead with the governor (to be clear, this group was quite separate from the group being led by Mr Dibbs). This was a time, as the novelist William Faulkner once said, women did not walk but seemed to float. Skirts and petticoats were worn to the ground. Boots were buckled up the ankle. Throats were coated in lace. Women rarely spoke in public, and yet, there they were, ready to plead with one of the most distinguished and powerful men in the colony, Lord Carrington, to take a merciful view of Louisa's plight, and commute her sentence to life imprisonment.

And they were not alone.

At around the same time, a number of women in the neighbouring colony of Victoria were busy doing what they could to save Louisa's life. Of course, word did not travel in the nineteenth century the way word travels today. News — even terrible news — took some time to move even from one colony to the next. Still, within two weeks of Louisa being sentenced to hang, her case had energised the women of Victoria.

The champion in Louisa's corner in Melbourne was not a parliamentarian, or a charity worker, but a warm-hearted water-colourist whose name was Elizabeth Parsons. Lest anyone get the idea that Mrs Parsons was sitting pretty with her easel and not much else on her mind, know this: she was a coffee-drinking bohemian in the city that would eventually be famous for them. Born Elizabeth Warren in England in September 1831, she was thirty-five years old before she married, not because she was ugly, stupid or poor, or any of the other reasons that were once given when women delayed marriage, but because she was busy, independent and free.

The young Elizabeth studied drawing and painting in London and Paris in the 1850s and, in her early twenties, joined a now-famous colony of artists near the village of Barbizon in France that included Théodore Rousseau, Jean-François Millet and Camille Corot. Although only four hours by carriage from Paris, this was truly a bucolic experience: artists from the Barbizon colony would venture out into the forest of Fontainebleau in their smocks and berets to paint gentle landscapes in a new realist style that eventually gave birth to impressionism. Local innkeepers made them welcome. Some stayed in the ruins of Norman castles.

Upon her return to England in the mid 1860s, Elizabeth met her husband, Mr George Parsons, who was the manager of a marble mine called the Serpentine.

George had already been married and widowed, and he had two boys: George and Cecil. In 1870, this newly blended family departed England aboard the SS *Great Britain*, bound for Australia. Also in the travelling party was Elizabeth's seven-month-old daughter, Adeline, and Elizabeth was pregnant with her first son, Henry.[11]

Just six months later, Elizabeth had exhibited new works. Neither Elizabeth's creative output nor her bohemian soul were tamed by marriage and motherhood. Shortly after arriving in Melbourne, she joined the now-defunct Buonarotti Club. Established by Cyrus Mason, it was named in honour of the great Italian painter, architect, poet and sculptor Michelangelo, and its headquarters, at least for a time, was the Prince's Bridge Hotel (now Young and Jackson's, where the lovely nude, Chloe, hangs). The club's membership consisted mainly of those who aspired to be professional painters, and they included Frederick McCubbin. Women were made welcome — this could not be said for every Melbourne club, not even today — and indeed the club encouraged their membership by hosting 'Ladies' Nights' at the Melbourne Coffee Palace, where everyone was invited to sing, play music, dress up in costumes, smoke tobacco, and display new works.

Photographs from this time show how happy these endeavours made Elizabeth: unlike so many women, shy about having their picture taken, this curly-haired woman looks straight at the camera and gives a cheeky grin. This was surely because, besides being fun, Elizabeth was good. Not as in a good citizen and a good person, although all the evidence suggests that she was both of those things, but as in a good artist at a time when it was wonderful to be an artist: Henry Lawson, the writer and poet, was working in the 1880s; so, too, was Banjo Paterson. Melbourne had a Shelley Club, a Burns Club, and a Shakespeare Club. Besides the Coffee Palace, there were musical salons, poetry nights and heaven knows what else.

Upon settling in Melbourne, Elizabeth also had three more children: sons Warren, born 30 July 1872; Noel, born 6 January 1875; and Jonathon, born on 18 August 1876. Yet she also managed to travel widely and exhibit her paintings. In 1875, the year of Noel's birth, Elizabeth was elected as the first woman council member to the Victorian Academy of Arts.[12]

Unlike many artists who sat in Melbourne and painted as if they were in Europe, Elizabeth painted the hot, dry Australian landscape, including the curious flora, and she painted it lovingly. She travelled all over Victoria, even to Tasmania, in search of landscapes, often setting up an easel in areas so remote that she likely needed draught horses to get there. As strange as it may now seem, Elizabeth signed many of her works in her husband's name: Mrs George Parsons.

From the late 1880s, through to the twentieth century, Mrs Parsons and her family lived at St Ruan in Charnwood Road, St Kilda (the building is still there). She was a well-known figure, often taking her easel to the foreshore to paint St Kilda Beach. What has not been reported until now was her passionate opposition to the execution of Louisa Collins.

There is nothing in any archive to explain how or why Mrs Parsons became involved in the campaign to save Louisa, nor even how she came to know about the case — one assumes that she read about it in Melbourne's *Argus*, which carried a number of reports from Sydney. Nevertheless, within weeks of the sentence of death being handed down, Elizabeth had gone around to every one of her female neighbours in Charnwood Road and into the surrounding streets of cosmopolitan St Kilda to drum up support for the cause.

She also placed an advertisement in the *Argus*: 'Will those women who are opposed to capital punishment kindly sign petition lying at Mr Hutcheson's, 16 Collins street west, for the reprieve of Louisa Collins.'[13]

Elizabeth's petition — the so-called Petition of the Women of Victoria — would ultimately be signed by more than 500 women. It perhaps goes without saying that it was beautifully worded and the handwriting exquisite. In her covering letter to Lord Carrington, Mrs Parsons said: 'I have the honour to forward herewith ... a petition from the Women of Victoria praying that the sentence of death passed on Louisa Collins may be commuted.'

She added:

While loathing the crime for which this woman has been condemned we regarded the punishment of death as a barbarous method of executing justice and as demoralising both to the individuals who have to perform the execution and to the society by whose sanction the sentence is carried out, and as opposed

to the spirit of modern civilisation. We question also
whether the punishment by death has any greater
deterrent effect upon the criminal classes than other
modes which savour less of revenge and from which
the idea of reformation is not utterly excluded.[14]

The first signature on the petition is Elizabeth's own.
Some of the names that follow include Victoria Elizabeth
Talbot, a Merry Lloyd, an Emily Dowd, plus there is a
Mrs Hyde, a Mrs Strickland, a Mrs Nicolls, Mrs Roberts,
White, Dickson, Williams and Howells, and hundreds
more over many pages.

How did the public react to this intervention? With
the same scorn as had been reserved for the women of New
South Wales, when they began to protest. Shortly after the
petition from the 'Women of Victoria' had been delivered
to Lord Carrington, the following editorial, originally
from the *Brisbane Courier*, was re-published in the *Sydney
Morning Herald*:

One has happily, to go back a long way in the
annals of Australian crime to meet with a case of
such cold-blooded atrocity as the career of Louisa
Collins.

This is what makes the fact that a petition has
been got up in her favour, first from the women
of New South Wales, and now by their sisters of
Victoria, so inexplicable. Can one seriously accept
an agitation like this as emanating from any
feeling of a principle at stake, or is it only born of

a sentimental folly? Can the ladies of New South Wales and Victoria be aware of the sort of woman that they are so anxious to keep among us? Too often women seem to puzzle our stupid logical male intellects. They rise up as vehement champions of some convicted criminal … quite unrealised by their unsophisticated friends.[15]

Who, indeed, did these women think they were, daring to have a point of view in a matter so serious as the hanging of a mother of ten, including four children still under the age of twelve? Why, it's almost as if women thought they should have a stake in the way things were done in the colony, or some influence over their own lives.

In response, Lord Carrington promised to give the petition 'every consideration'. More than that, he could not promise.[16]

CHAPTER 16

The New Evidence:
Too little too late

Three days after Louisa Collins hanged, the *Bulletin* would publish a graphic and terrible cartoon depicting the New South Wales governor, Lord Carrington, yawning while Louisa dangled from the gallows by her neck.

The caption described Lord Carrington as the 'yawning guvn'r' — the implication being that he had been too idle, or perhaps too indifferent, to lift a finger to try to save this woman's life.[1]

The description was unfair. As has been shown, Lord Carrington was keenly aware of Louisa's plight. He was also honestly engaged with the question of whether to exercise the royal prerogative and commute her sentence to life imprisonment.

The degree to which Lord Carrington was involved is revealed in correspondence both to and from his office during the last week of December 1888, and the first week of January 1889 (which is to say, in the fortnight before Louisa was hanged).

Correspondence from that period is stored at State Records New South Wales, in a folder so fat it has been tied up with string in order to hold it all together. The file is stamped with the seal of Government House — even after all this time, the ink used to make that famous lion and unicorn is still blood red — and it is stuffed with letters from ordinary members of the public and from interested barristers, doctors and even parliamentarians, all weighing in on the case.[2]

The evidence suggests that Lord Carrington not only read all of these letters, but acted on those that suggested ways in which the trial might have gone awry, resulting in an injustice.

Some of the letters are quite passionate. For example, there is one from an Ernest Llewellyn, which lists all the reasons why Louisa mustn't be allowed to hang:

> [Louisa] did not go to any place and purchase any poison;
>
> There is no proof whatever that she had or got the poison and took it home to her house;
>
> There is no proof to show that the poison was not in the house when she first went to live there;
>
> There is no proof at all to show that the poison was given to her husband by her own hand;
>
> No one saw her do it.[3]

Some women also wrote with their reasons for not wanting to see Louisa hang. Mrs Rachel Elliot of Mayne Street, Gulgong (by chance, her home was on the street where the Gulgong Pioneers Museum and Historical Society stands today) said: 'I hope you will extend mercy to Louisa Collins. I do not think she is guilty of poisoning her husbands and my opinion is that no one should be hung on circumstantial evidence.'[4] Mrs Elliot also declared that 'our father in heaven considers that the pains of labour are the pains of hell, and if so that poor woman has travelled through hell five times'.[5]

William Hogan of Underwood Station urged Lord Carrington to defy Sir Henry Parkes and simply 'refuse to sign her death warrant ... the woman would then be incarcerated for life'.[6]

Mr Ellard, who had attended the Town Hall meeting, saw injustice rooted in class, saying: 'In the case of Kirwan, the husband accused of the murder of his beautifully faithless wife was saved from the gallows because he was well connected ... Louisa Collins [will be] hanged because she was poor, and friendless, and because a portion of the press in Sydney and in Victoria shrieked for her blood.'[7] (This letter would appear to refer to a famous Irish case of 1852, in which William Burke Kirwan was convicted of the murder of his wife, Sarah Maria, sentenced to death, reprieved and then released. Many people believed in his innocence.[8])

Some people wrote to support Lord Carrington as he went about the awful business of deciding whether to interfere with the court's decision. A telegram from a Mr Henry Stibbings said: 'Kindly convey to his Excellency respectful sincere sympathy re: Louisa Collins. Assure him loyal and staunch support of great majority of people of

New South Wales as [he goes about] honestly supporting the law.'[9]

A barrister, A (for Archibald) Nugent Robertson, wrote that while he hoped that he would not be credited with any 'maudlin sympathy' with the criminal, there was good reason to give an eleventh-hour reprieve. The problem, as he saw it, was that evidence about the death of Charles Andrews should not have been admissible at Louisa's trial for the murder of Michael Collins.

'The fact that Charles Andrews died of arsenical poisoning was not proved and therefore not a relevant fact at the trial,' he wrote. 'If improperly admitted, the convict ought to be at least reprieved.'[10]

At first glance, this argument seems to be the same as the one that had already been put forward at the appeal, but it is different in an important way: Mr Robertson was arguing that the cause of death of Charles Andrews had never been conclusively proven, and therefore the jury shouldn't have been allowed to hear that Charles had died of arsenical poisoning.

All of these letters are interesting, but none attracted as much attention as the letter from the firm of solicitors known as Slattery and Heydon.[11] Now, Louisa Collins's trial had been the most important criminal matter to come before the courts in the centenary year. It had attracted a huge amount of attention in the press. Solicitors, clerks, bewigged and begowned barristers — everyone had an opinion. Most of these men, if not all, belonged to the same gentlemen's clubs and worked from the same chambers. All knew that Louisa's barrister — a Scotsman by way of New Zealand, soon to be struck from the roll — had been hopelessly outmanoeuvred by barristers assembled on behalf of the Crown. And now Louisa stood just steps from the gallows.

Should something be done? Could something be done? Two solicitors working at Slattery and Heydon decided to at least try. Working for nothing other than a desire to save Louisa's life (well, perhaps also for the thrill of being involved in such an important case) they looked again at all the evidence. Was there a weak link? If so, where might it be found? Michael Collins had clearly been poisoned. The question in court had always been: by whom? But what if that were the wrong question? What if the question was not by whom — but by *what*?

Everyone — even Louisa's own counsel — seemed to accept that the poison had been arsenic, either from the box of Rough on Rats, or from the tainted sheep skins, but what if Michael had in fact been poisoned by something else?

Now their attention turned to medical texts, fat tomes sourced from eminent doctors who had lugged them from London, along with surgical tools in leather bags. Into the night they worked, by lamplight, and for no pay, until, finally, there it was, staring them in the face.

Bismuth. Michael Collins had taken bismuth.

Collins had actually been *prescribed* bismuth by Dr Marshall — and, as every good doctor knows, bismuth is not only a close cousin of arsenic, it can in some circumstances behave like arsenic, and in the nineteenth century, was often contaminated *with* arsenic.

The lawyers were excited — but would they be too late? Louisa was but days from being hanged, but if they worked quickly, perhaps she could be saved. Fountain pens came out. Medical texts too. There was nothing to do but write.

'Your Excellency, Lord Carrington ...'

The letter is long, and beautifully written, but in essence, it explained the following: Michael Collins had been prescribed bismuth for his illness. Bismuth — also known commercially as Pearl White or Spanish White — had commonly been used as a cosmetic but was also often used in medicine. The letter made plain that bismuth was widely available in New South Wales and that it was frequently prescribed to 'allay irritability of the stomach and to check vomiting and diarrhoea'. It was known to have 'poisonous properties ... and some fatal cases ... have been attributed to it'. This was due to the 'existence of arsenic in it as an impurity — a frequent occurrence if great care is not taken'.

The authors quoted authoritative sources: for one, the *Notebook of Material Medical Pharmacology and Therapeutics*, which states, at pages 264 and 265 of the second edition, that sub-nitrate of bismuth had been known to cause irritation of the stomach and the intestines — and death.

Slattery and Heydon also quoted Alfred Swaine Taylor MD, a fellow of the Royal College of Physicians in London, as saying that Pearl White had been known to have caused 'the death of an adult in five days'. This man — like Michael Collins — had complained of 'a burning pain in the throat with a vomiting and purging'. Moreover, 'on inspection, the throat, windpipe and gullet were found inflamed and there was inflammatory redness in the stomach'. Not only that, when chemical tests had been done on bismuth 'obtained from a respectable retail druggist ... only two specimens out of five were found free from this poison'.

With all this in mind, wasn't it possible that Michael's symptoms were proof of poisoning not by arsenic but by bismuth? The petitioners urged Lord Carrington to have Michael's prescriptions made up again, preferably using the same supply of bismuth that had been used the first time. In the meantime, Louisa's execution would surely have to be stayed.[12]

As arguments go, it was persuasive — more persuasive, probably, than many of the arguments put forward by Louisa's own defence counsel — and it was backed by other letters, including one from an unnamed doctor, clearly writing independently, which was also published in the *Herald*: 'I should like to point out a most important item of evidence which was not elicited at the trial: whether the arsenic is not an impurity of bismuth. The medical witnesses, I believe, [said that] bismuth was employed. All medical men know that arsenic is an impurity of this drug. In the interest of justice I sincerely trust that the execution may be delayed' while this new evidence is examined.[13]

Lord Carrington was swayed. In the margin of the first letter, he — or perhaps his private secretary — instructed that the information about the bismuth, and the evidence about the death of Charles, be forwarded to the minister for justice 'for his immediate consideration'.[14]

This was a positive step. Unfortunately, it meant that Louisa's life was now in the hands of a man once described by *Town and Country Journal* as 'the most personally disliked man in the Assembly'.[15]

Mr William Clarke, the presiding minister for justice, was a chinless wonder with a Ned Kelly-style beard. Many in the colony considered him a sycophant, the kind of man that had long been desperate for a role in the Parkes ministry and therefore not likely to take on Sir Henry. He was also — and this was apparently not uncommon — not averse to using his fists to win an argument, having once been involved in what was described as a 'vigorous if unscientific' fist fight behind the Speaker's chair in Parliament House.

Now he would decide Louisa's fate. Slattery and Heydon's letter about the bismuth, and the other complaint regarding the propensity evidence, was sent to him. We know this, because Mr Clarke replied to Lord Carrington about both matters. He could, and perhaps should, have said: 'Your Excellency, it does seem to me that a great many people in the colony, medical doctors and lawyers included, have doubts about this woman's guilt. The public's mood is against a hanging. Perhaps it's best that we — or, rather, you — commute the sentence to life imprisonment.' Instead, he said the opposite.

In the process, Mr Clarke revealed what everyone suspected: despite Sir Henry's claims about the judiciary's independence from parliament, there was no real separation of church and state in nineteenth-century New South Wales. All the main players, up to and including the chief justice, had discussed Louisa's case behind closed doors, and the evidence suggests that they had decided among themselves that she would hang.

In his letter in reply to Lord Carrington, Mr Clarke dealt first with the argument that evidence about the death of Charles should not have been admissible, saying he had already considered it his duty 'to bring the point raised under the notice of His Honour, the Chief Justice'.[16]

In other words, he — the justice minister — had discussed the matter with a judge of the highest court in the land, who was, moreover, the same judge that had sentenced Louisa to death.

Mr Clarke's letter went on: '[He] informed me that proof had been produced at the trial showing that Andrews had died of arsenical poisoning' and therefore 'the point could not have any weight'.[17]

Anyone who had been closely following the case would know that this was not true: Louisa Collins had never been convicted of the murder of her first husband; she had been tried, and the jury had been unable to reach a verdict. Small grains of arsenic had been found in the mud and slush and body parts removed from the coffin in which Charles had lain for more than a year, but there was no concrete evidence as to what had killed him. In fact, the death certificate, issued by Dr Martin, said he died of acute gastritis (although, of course, Dr Martin had later changed his mind). It was certainly true that a jury at an inquest had declared that Charles had died of arsenical poisoning, but no court had done likewise, and Louisa was never found guilty of that offence.

Still, having neatly dispensed with that argument, Mr Clarke now had to deal with the argument that bismuth might have accounted for Michael's death by poison. To this end, he made inquiries of the government analyst, Mr William Hamlet. Was it possible that bismuth, not arsenic, had killed Michael Collins?

Mr Hamlet was able to put his mind at rest. The fact that Michael Collins had taken bismuth for his illness had been raised at one of the trials, although not in great detail. Mr Lusk had not pursued it with much vigour, but Mr Hamlet had taken it upon himself to test samples of the bismuth that had been used in the medicine given to both Charles and Michael. Of course, had this matter been raised in detail in court, any decent defence barrister would have made a meal of it: Michael's prescription had been made up in July, and it was August before Mr Hamlet managed to get samples from the pharmacy. The chain of custody was broken, and contamination was almost guaranteed.

But Louisa Collins had not had a decent defence barrister. She'd had Mr Lusk.

Mr Clarke's letter to Lord Carrington continued: 'Mr Hamlet [says] that the sub-nitrate of bismuth [used in] the prescription for both Andrews and Collins medicines had been subjected to chemical analysis and found to be pure, containing no trace of arsenic whatever.'[18]

To advance this claim, Mr Clarke enclosed a letter from Mr Hamlet, saying much the same:

Sir,

In reply to your question as to the presence of arsenic in samples of bismuth nitrate, I have the honour to state that many years ago, it was not an uncommon occurrence to find traces of arsenic in commercial bismuth preparations, especially in those used as cosmetics.

In other words, yes, there was a long tradition of including arsenic in bismuth.

Mr Hamlet went on:

This fact is mentioned in the older editions of Taylor [an official guide to poisons and medicine] and other works on poisons. At the present time, however, it is rare to find even traces of arsenic in bismuth nitrate or carbonate used in medicine.

Rare — but not unheard of.

In the case of Mrs Collins, the coroner directed Sub-Inspector Hyam to obtain some bismuth from the same lot, and from the same bottle, as that used in making up the prescriptions for both Andrews and Collins medicines.

Accordingly, on the 6th of August last [about a month after Michael died] sub-inspector George H. Hyam brought a sealed package containing 1 ounce of bismuth nitrate and handed the same to me for analysis.

Mr Hamlet analysed the sample and, in his letter to Lord Carrington, revealed his findings, saying the 'pure nitrate of bismuth contained no traces of arsenic whatever'.

The pharmacist who dispensed the medicine said
in his evidence that the bismuth was obtained
from Messrs Howard and Sons of Stratford near
London — a name that carries great weight as a
guarantee of purity.[19]

As was customary, Mr Hamlet signed the letter: 'I have
the honour to be, sir, yours faithfully, William M. Hamlet,
Government Analyst' — and with those flourishes, the
argument was over.

For his part, in his own letter, Mr Clarke revealed that
he'd spoken to the chief justice about the bismuth, too:

I also consulted His Honour, the Chief Justice
respecting this point, who informed me that the
evidence at the trial made it clear that no useful
purpose would be served by carrying out the
suggestions referred to in Messrs' Slattery and
Heydon's letter.[20]

One useful purpose may have been to save Louisa's life.

To a reader at this distance, it seems that Lord
Carrington put those two matters before the minister for
justice for a reason. A woman — a mother — was going to
hang. Here was a way out, and perhaps they should take it.
But no, Mr Clarke's answer was polite, but firm: move on,
there is nothing to see here.

Lawyers were not alone in the pricking of conscience.
Another letter in the pile of correspondence to Lord

Carrington suggests the torment felt by the surgeon Dr Frederick Milford, who had cut into the raw, inflamed stomach of Michael Collins in search of signs of poison. His letter, on letterhead marked with his address — 3 Clarence Terrace — and written in his own shaky hand on tiny sheets of notepaper, says:

> Your Excellency,
>
> I made the post-mortem examination on the body of [Michael] Collins and was therefore present during the four trials.
>
> In my opinion — and I had considerable opportunity of listening to the details — there was nothing brought out which directly connected the prisoner with the administration of the arsenic.
>
> The box of Rough on Rats was exposed on the shelf in the kitchen where anybody — <u>one of the children</u> [Milford's underline] — might have given it to him.
>
> Please excuse me, my Lord, troubling you in this matter but I assure you I couldn't remain quiet without letting you know this, my individual opinion, probably it is of little significance, but I had exceptional opportunities ... and I thought it my duty to let you know.[21]

So now both the prosecutor in the second trial — Mr Cohen — and the man who carried out the post-mortem on one of the victims were in agreement: Louisa might well have done it ... but the case had not been proved.

CHAPTER 17

'Pray have mercy and pity ... Spare my life'

Louisa Collins would spend a little under six months in Darlinghurst Gaol between the day of her arrest and the morning of her execution. During that time she was a model prisoner, admired by the female wardens in particular, who would weep when she died.

The gaol chaplain, the Reverend Canon Rich, admired her, too. Where others saw a cold heart, he saw a strong exterior. On the inside, he knew, Louisa was afraid. Canon Rich spent many hours — days, weeks, months — praying with Louisa before she died and, as the day of her execution approached, his efforts extended to pleading with the governor on her behalf.

As was customary at the time, Louisa was also permitted to plead for mercy. The gaol sheriff arranged for writing paper and a fountain pen to be delivered and on 7 January 1889 — the eve of her execution — Louisa Collins picked up that pen and wrote to Lord Carrington. Make no mistake: Louisa used what were some of her last hours on earth to beg for her life. Every inch of the paper is covered with her pleas, except for those parts already printed with the letterhead — Darlinghurst Gaol — and the headline, which reads: 'Prisoner's Application or Statement'.

Next to the words 'From Prisoner' Louisa has filled in her name. In the subject line, she has written: 'Asking that the death sentence in her case be not carried out.' In the space for the address, she wrote:

> To his Excellence, the Right Honourable Lord
> Carrington KLM
> Governor and Commander-in-Chief
> The Colony of New South Wales

Then, in clear, cursive script, with pen and ink, she begins:

> Oh my Lord. Pray have Mercy and Pity. Spare my life. I beg and implore you ... have Mercy on me for my children's sake ... I have seven children ... the two youngest only seven and five years old ... spare me, oh my Lord, for their sake ... show your Mercy to me ... spare my poor children ... oh my Lord my life is in your hands ... I must again implore and humbly beg you to spare me my life ...

The writing fills the whole page, with the same words written over and over: 'Oh my Lord, spare me. I beg and implore you ...'

The letter was marked 'Urgent'. Some scribbled notes along the margin suggest that it was forwarded to 'the Sheriff, John Lovett, deputy governor of the Sydney Gaol', and the time stamp suggests that it was received by the governor at 1.23 p.m. on 7 January 1889. Louisa was to die at nine a.m. the following day.[1]

With just hours now before the scheduled execution, Louisa's supporters were gripped by desperation. What could be done?

There was one last attempt to whip up public support for Louisa. Besides writing furiously to newspapers and to politicians, Canon Rich, the phrenologist Mr Besomo and Mr Frederick Lee, had organised a 'women's petition' of their own, which by now had 1000 signatures. This exercise was not without controversy, with one letter writer telling the *Herald* that he had seen Mr Lee (or Mr Lee's men) soliciting for signatures and, being curious, had stopped to watch. By his account, four girls, the eldest of whom couldn't have been more than eleven, were encouraged to sign, and then a woman who had 'been suffering from the intense heat of the day, so much so that she could barely hold the pen' was also signed up.

> The man who was holding the petition then took the pen and signed a few more names to the pad, and when a bystander asked him why he was signing he said: 'Oh, those women miss a line, and I just fill them in myself.' I wonder what the petition was even worth.[2]

It must have been worth at least a try. The petition said that it was 'abhorrent to every feeling of humanity and a shock to the sentiments of the 19th century that a woman should suffer death at the hands of a hangman'. Moreover, it was contrary to practice in the Mother Country to try a prisoner three, and practically four times for the same offence. There was no positive proof of the prisoner's guilt; other women had been spared the death sentence.

Armed with this petition, a new deputation, led by Mr Besomo and Mr Lee, waited upon Lord Carrington at Government House on the afternoon of Monday, 7 January 1889. When the governor came into the reception hall to meet them, they presented the petition 'in favour of the commutation of the sentence on Louisa Collins'.

Mr Besomo explained that the petition was the one he had taken to the Domain, where it had been 'signed by one thousand persons' and its purpose was to show that many in the colony believed that Louisa — 'the unfortunate woman' — was not responsible for her actions, because she was suffering from 'poison monomania' (a kind of made-up psychiatric disorder, typical of diagnoses given by phrenologists, that compelled Louisa to repeatedly poison people).

Mr Lee said that His Excellency might think it unprecedented 'for ladies to sign' a petition but it was not. He spoke of the 'great degradation that was perpetrated when a woman was hanged by a man', and he argued that the Supreme Court appeal judges had failed in their duty to give Louisa another hearing. Important points raised on the prisoner's behalf could not be argued because they had not been raised at the trial. Somewhat generously, he acknowledged 'the great care' exercised by Mr Lusk, but argued that in such a serious case, the Crown should have provided the prisoner with sufficient money to enable her to secure the best barrister at the bar for her defence.

Lord Carrington sat and patiently listened. He explained that he had received many letters and petitions and he had already given his 'certain answer'. While he 'quite understood' the feelings of the deputation, 'nothing had transpired since Friday that would authorise him to change his opinion. What he had said on Friday he was bound to say [again] and that was, that nothing had happened to prevent him from taking the advice of the Executive Council' which still recommended that Louisa be executed for that was 'the sentence of the law'. And so, 'with regret', he had to repeat what he'd said on Friday: there was nothing he could do.[3]

The situation seemed hopeless, and yet Louisa's supporters still had one more card to play. They'd hoped never to have to play it. That card was Louisa's children. One, two, three, or even all of her children could go to Government House to beg for their mother's life.

It was Canon Rich who organised it. He got down to May's level. Did she think that she could do it? Could she speak up to the governor and say: please don't hang my mother?

She could.

The record doesn't make clear whether it was Canon Rich who took May to Government House on that day before her mother was hanged (although of course it probably was him and perhaps his wife). Some reports suggest that two of the children went together, and others say three, but all agree that May was in the group.

May had by this stage turned eleven but the gates to Government House must still have seemed enormous to her. The front door — designed to be wide enough to take a grand piano — would have dwarfed this child.

The aim, according to news reports, was to 'implore His Excellency to grant a reprieve'.[4] It was Louisa's last chance. It must have taken much courage — and it was such a waste of time. The governor wouldn't even come out to see them. Lord Carrington — his wife by then pregnant with what he liked to describe as his 'own fine specimen of an Australian baby',[5] a girl who would be named Sydney Myee (Myee is Aboriginal for 'native born') — instead sent his private secretary, Mr Wallington, to receive the group.[6]

The *Evening News* described the meeting thus:

> Lord Carrington felt himself unequal to the task of receiving the children, who were therefore interviewed by his Excellency's private secretary, who told the little ones that he was sorry they had come, and that it cost him a very severe struggle to have to tell them that nothing could be done on behalf of their unfortunate mother. The little ones left Government House sobbing as if their little hearts would break.[7]

The *Singleton Argus* agreed that the children were terribly upset, saying: 'The little ones left Government House sobbing bitterly.'[8]

Louisa's children were taken from Government House to see their mother one last time. Her eldest son, Herbert, was there, as was May, and the middle son, Frederick (as far as can be deduced from the record, no effort was made to ensure that Louisa's youngest boys, Charles and Edwin, saw their mother before she died).

In recounting this final meeting, the *Evening News* reminded readers that Louisa had remained calm, and perhaps even optimistic, during her many trials, at one point even 'handing one of the court officials a veil, which she explained that she would wear when she left the court, in order that the public might not recognise her'.[9] She would occasionally 'bestow a glance and a smile of recognition upon some of her acquaintances in court' and from time to time, she had leaned forward to speak to Mr Lusk, 'but beyond that would remain quiescent in the extreme ... [and] very rarely indeed did she cease from toying with the small sprig of heliotrope she invariably carried with her'.[10]

Not much had changed upon Louisa being sentenced to hang: although kept in a special cell in the women's division, under the constant watch of female guards, she still managed to eat well and, according to the *Evening News*, she also slept 'remarkably well, and is chatty and affable to those around her'.

The exception, it seems, was on those occasions when she was permitted to see her children.

'The terrible position in which her mother is placed is most acutely felt by the fair-haired tiny girl, May,' the *News* said. 'This little thing wept most bitterly on her first visit, and was with difficulty removed from the cell at the termination of her interview. The youngest boy, Fred, was also much distressed.'[11]

Now it was time for the final visit, of which the newspapers simply said: 'She [Louisa] was broken down for a time, but she soon recovered herself.'[12]

She was *broken down for a time*.

What could this mean? We don't know. But probably it means that in her final hours, Louisa wept.

All that remained for Louisa after that visit was a night to get through. She did not spend it alone. Canon Rich stayed with her. Together, they prayed:

> Our Father which art in heaven
> Hallowed be thy name.
> Thy kingdom come, thy will be done on earth, as it is in
>   heaven.
> Give us this day our daily bread
> And forgive us our sins, as we forgive those who
>   have sinned against us
> And lead us not into temptation, but deliver us from
>   evil:
> For thine is the kingdom, and the power, and the
>   glory, for ever.
> Amen.

Canon Rich also went over the Order for the Burial of the Dead, to prepare Louisa for what she would hear the next morning:

> Man that is born of a woman hath but a short time
> to live, and is full of misery. He cometh up and
> is cut down like a flower ... In the midst of life
> we be in death: of whom may we seek for succour
> but of thee, O Lord, which for our sins justly art
> displeased? Yet, O Lord God most holy, O Lord
> most mighty, O holy and most merciful saviour,
> deliver us not into the bitter pains of eternal
> death ... spare us Lord most holy, O God most
> mighty, O holy and merciful saviour ... suffer us not
> at our last hour for any pains of death ...

At some point, Louisa slept. Canon Rich retreated, but he returned to the cell before dawn, and there he remained as the sun rose above the heavy prison walls. As the first rays of sunlight spilled across the gaol courtyard, the bell tolled the hour.

CHAPTER 18

The Execution

Louisa Collins was executed at Darlinghurst Gaol shortly after nine a.m. on Tuesday, 8 January 1889. Twelve people attended, including five members of the press, all of whom agreed that death came swiftly, and savagely.

While some newspaper reports suggested that only a few groups gathered outside the court, others said there 'was a crowd in the vicinity of the gaol from an early hour' and 'fully two thousand persons' immediately outside, 'principally of the lower classes'.[1]

The crowd could see nothing 'but were smitten with a morbid desire to be present during the time of the execution' and 'many climbed the trees in order to try and look over, but the police interfered and prevented them'.[2]

Inside the gaol at around eight a.m., Louisa was taken from her cell in the women's section to the condemned prisoner's cell, which was a distance of just yards from the gallows and therefore only a few seconds' walk. The press and other parties — the sheriff, Mr Charles Cowper, and his deputy, Mr Maybury; a visiting gaol surgeon,

Dr Maurice O'Connor, and his colleague, Dr Brownless, who was acting in the role of government medical officer; and the police sub-inspector, Mr Hyam, who had overseen the exhumation of the bodies of Charles and baby John — were led through an underground passage from Central Criminal Court into the gaol yard 'where the sun was shining brightly and flower beds in the courtyard looked doubly bright in contrast to the gloom'.[3]

Shortly after nine a.m., the door to Louisa's cell was opened. She was dressed in the 'usual prison clothes of dark wincey material' and her 'head [was] resting on her breast and her eyes were on the ground, her face composed but grief-worn, her cheeks flushed'. She was escorted to the gallows by Canon Rich, who had been praying with Louisa since before dawn, and two female wardens, one each side, with a hand on each arm. One was weeping. Louisa's arms were pinioned at the elbows, but she could move her hands. Her eyes were partly closed as she walked 'slowly but firmly toward the door which led to the scaffold'.[4] To some newspapers, she 'appeared very weak and completely broken down' while to others she appeared 'quite self-possessed', and still others said 'the appearance of the woman was painful ... those who had seen her during her many trials could not but notice the careworn expression of her features and stooping shoulders, denoting the mental agony of the past few days had quite crushed the hardihood that was manifested when [she was] before the judge and jury'.[5]

Behind Louisa came the executioner, Robert 'Nosey Bob' Howard, and his assistant. Upon stepping onto the scaffold, which faced a small exercise yard, Louisa gave 'a brief look to the representatives of the press', but otherwise 'there was no facial change, although a slight twitch of the hands was noticeable'.

One of the first things Louisa would have seen when she did look up at the gallows was a chair, upon which somebody had placed a piece of carpet, on which lay the noose. Did she know why the chair was there? Perhaps she thought it was there to rest the noose upon. In fact, the sheriff had been concerned that Louisa — being a woman, and therefore weak — might collapse or faint upon the scaffold. Nosey Bob's solution then would have been to strap her into the wooden chair, place the noose around her neck, and send her through the trap seated, with her arms tied to the armrests.

The chair was not needed. Louisa seemed calm. As soon as she was directly below the beam, Canon Rich, who stood with an open Bible in his hands, pronounced the words of the burial service: 'Man that is born of a woman hath but a short time to live ...'

Quietly, Louisa said: 'Amen.'

Then Canon Rich was done, and there was nothing left to do, and no prayers left to say. Canon Rich stepped forward and whispered something to Louisa that she 'slightly inclined her head to hear' and then she nodded. Canon Rich took a step back. The assistant hangman handed the white cotton cap to Nosey Bob, who placed it over Louisa's head. She raised her right hand slightly, as if to assist him. Other than that, Louisa 'never moved or trembled'. Her feet were planted firmly on the ground.[6]

The executioner gave the signal. His assistant — appointed just the night before after Nosey Bob's regular assistant refused to have anything to do with the execution of a woman — pulled the lever. The action should have allowed the trap to open. But even after several attempts, the trap did not fall, for it was somehow stuck.

Hurriedly 'the whisper was given to procure a mallet'. Meanwhile, Louisa was 'giving way under the strain'. Having moments earlier been standing 'perfectly upright and motionless', Louisa's hands were now working nervously, and 'the hangman provided her with support from behind'.[7]

The bungling 'sent a thrill of pain through all who heard the strokes of the mallet doing their deadly task'. Nosey Bob used the time to tighten the rope around Louisa's neck. Louisa trembled slightly 'and then, to the immense relief of the horrified spectators', the bolt gave and the trap opened.

Louisa fell through with such ferocity that her head was almost severed and her windpipe left exposed. For a brief moment, she was perpendicular, with her face facing toward the ground, but then her body straightened, and she was left hanging by her vertebrae.

Some minutes passed. Louisa's hands turned purple. There was a 'slight spurt of blood followed by a thin stream which ran down the dress and spotted the floor beneath'. Louisa's body turned slowly on the rope until it partly faced the doorway 'and there it remained stationary until lowered by the executioner onto a wicker bier' (a wooden frame, on which a coffin is normally placed) and conveyed to the inquest room.[8]

Upon the plinth, Louisa's face presented 'a quiet and peaceful appearance', and except for the ghastly wound in the throat and neck 'it might have been imagined that she died in a quiet and ordinary manner'.[9]

CHAPTER 19

Equal Rights, Equal Justice

Louisa Collins's body was left to hang for twenty minutes after the execution to ensure that she was dead. After she was taken down and her corpse removed for autopsy, the press gathered around Canon Rich, clamouring for the details of any confession she might have made.

According to the *Herald*'s report, Canon Rich was somewhat vague on the point. He explained that he had 'attended the condemned woman daily, and sometimes twice a day' in the lead-up to her execution, and that she had always been 'most earnest' in her prayers. 'She fully recognised her awful position,' Canon Rich said, 'and always expressed her preparedness, and resignation to her fate.' Asked directly if she had made any confession, Canon Rich said that Louisa had 'confessed her sins to Almighty God and has supplicated for forgiveness'.[1]

As to whether any of this added up to a confession, well, the newspapers would make up their own minds. One report on the following day said that Louisa had 'told

Canon Rich that she had confessed to God and had nothing to say to him', and that she had 'made other remarks which leave no doubt that she murdered both husbands'.[2]

Several of the colony's newspapers also reported the results of the autopsy on Louisa's body: it had been conducted by the visiting surgeon to the Darlinghurst Gaol, Dr MJ O'Connor (who had tested Louisa for pregnancy back when she was first condemned to death), in the company of the acting coroner, Mr JC Moore, and a gaol official, Mr John Longford, who had also attended every day of the trials. All agreed that there had been a 'clean fracture of the vertebrae' and that Louisa's windpipe had been severed. In fact, 'the neck was torn along the front under the chin, from which blood was still oozing'.[3]

Louisa's family did not claim her body. Her corpse was taken from the plinth by two female wardens who washed and prepared her body for burial, before the coffin was taken to the railway station and then, by train, to Rookwood Cemetery, where it was buried in an untitled plot, paid for by an unnamed benefactor, in the Church of England section.[4]

A little over a week later, the Parkes ministry fell, leaving Louisa's main supporter at the Town Hall meeting, Mr George Dibbs, to form a minority administration until new elections could be held. To be clear, Mr Dibbs wouldn't hold the office of premier for long — Sir Henry would be back in the role by March — but still, had the collapse of the Parkes administration come just a week earlier, Dibbs certainly would have been there long enough to save Louisa. But then, such is life.

As to Louisa's legacy, well, just one day after she died, the following advertisement appeared in the Amusements section of the *Evening News:*

AUSTRALIAN WAXWORKS,
Opposite the Cathedral.
Just Added,
Mrs. LOUISA COLLINS,
THE BOTANY MURDERESS.

Admission, 1s; children, 6d. Open 9 a.m. till 10 p.m.[5]

Louisa had become a waxy attraction in a macabre show, alongside a figure of Jesus Christ and a replica of a hunk of gold known as the Welcome Nugget.

For more than 100 years, Louisa Collins would be remembered only in the context of the crime of which she was eventually convicted. In truth, though, the story of Louisa's life did not end there, for the story of Australian womanhood does not end there. That story — our story — is still being written.

The debate about Louisa Collins — in particular, the fairness of her trial and the question of whether she should be hanged — had inspired many Australian women to take a stand on a justice issue for the first time in their lives. They did so despite the fact that women were discouraged — actively, and in almost every other conceivable way — from having a say in how things were done.

Standing up for what is right can be scary, but it's also intoxicating, and before long, many of the women who had stood firm for Louisa were also standing up for women's rights more generally.

Such as the vote.

Such as the right to work in jobs that paid the same as jobs for men.

Such as the right not to lose their children to their husbands after divorce.

Of course it was not only the travesty of justice that was the trial of Louisa Collins that spurred women toward the suffrage movement. It was also the poverty in so many women's homes (especially the homes of deserted wives, and widows). It was the violence that so many women suffered at the hands of drunken men (inescapable violence, since there was nowhere to go, and no work they could do that would pay enough to cover the rent and feed the children). It was the backyard abortions women suffered, as they tried to avoid having more children; it was the injustice of working at jobs that paid a third of the male wage; it was the stifling and smothering of women's ambition; it was everything.

The debate about women's rights came to Australia shortly before the debate about Federation. This proved a nice confluence of events: Sir Henry Parkes, among others, was convinced by the early 1890s that the Australian colonies were mature enough to govern in their own right as an independent nation, a Commonwealth of Australia; Australia's first suffragettes couldn't see how a new nation could rise without giving full citizenship — meaning the vote, among other rights — to women.

The blue-eyed, pink-cheeked Eliza Pottie was one of those who moved quickly from campaigning for Louisa's life to campaigning for the vote. She gave her first public speech about women's suffrage during a meeting of the Women's Christian Temperance Union about a year after Louisa's death, in March 1890 and, in the same year, she placed an advertisement in local newspapers to see how many other women wanted to join the cause.

The record suggests that fewer than twenty women attended the first meeting of the Women's Suffrage League but, as everyone knows, from little things, big things grow. By May of the following year — 1891 — the suffrage movement had become extremely fashionable to join (other branches in other colonies were also experiencing fast growth). Members of the New South Wales group now included Mrs Pottie (a founding member); Justice Windeyer's wife, Lady Mary Windeyer (also a founding member and the league's first president); and the Anglican arch-deacon, Mr Francis B Boyce (whose wife had campaigned for Louisa).

Also on board was one of the nineteenth century's finest feminists, Louisa Lawson. If the name sounds familiar, it is: Mrs Lawson was Henry Lawson's mother, and she taught Henry to read by the light of a kerosene lamp. After seventeen years of marriage, Mrs Lawson separated from Henry's father, Peter, and moved to Sydney with three of their four children (Henry, who was sixteen, Peter, ten, and Gertrude, six). In an effort to make ends meet, she opened a boarding house and took in sewing. By 1888, she was publishing Australia's first newspaper for women, that was also written, edited and published by women. She called it *The Dawn*, and it lasted seventeen years, folding only because Mrs Lawson's health failed.

In her first editorial, Mrs Lawson promised to fight for women's rights, and fight she did, campaigning for the vote, but also for laws that would have given wives a legal right to part of their husband's earnings. In her many fiery editorials, Mrs Lawson argued that many women married simply because they had no alternative, and that women's wages should be increased to the level of men's wages, so women didn't get stuck in marriages to men they loathed.

Twentieth-century feminist Audrey Oldfield, who wrote the book on women's suffrage (literally — it was called *Woman Suffrage in Australia — a Gift or a Struggle?*), described how Louisa Lawson formed the Dawn Club for women in 1889, to campaign for the vote. In what must be regarded as an extremely deft move, she invited Miss Margaret Windeyer — Justice Windeyer's daughter — to give a paper at the first meeting.

Mrs Lawson herself also spoke, saying: 'Here in New South Wales, every man may vote, let his character be bad, his judgement purchasable, and his intellect of the weakest, but an honourable, thoughtful and good woman may be laughed at by such men. They can carry what laws they please in spite of her.'[6]

Like the Dawn Club, the Women's Suffrage League campaigned for 'equal justice, equal privileges in marriage and divorce, rights to property, and the custody of children in divorce'. They printed and distributed pamphlets —

usually on Mrs Lawson's press — that gave several reasons why other women (and men, especially men in power) should support women's suffrage, among them:

> Because it is the foundation of all political liberty
> Because those who obey the law should be able to
> have a voice in choosing who makes the law
> Because a government of the people for the people
> should mean all the people and not one half
> Because laws which affect women are now passed
> without consulting women
> Because large numbers of intelligent, thoughtful,
> hard working women desire it
> Because objections raised against it are not based on
> reason
> Because, to sum up all reasons in one, it is right.[7]

There's not a lot there with which to argue.

Mrs Lawson managed to weave the case for women's rights into many of her *Dawn* editorials. One example, on the 'Relative Value of Girl Babies', published in 1896, states:

> Many a mother dreads to bring forth a girl infant.
> Not that her affection would be less, but she fears
> the disappointment of a husband who, in a daughter,
> would see no proper heir to his fortune ...
> There are thousands of little feminine creatures
> who have become shy and sensitive from frequently
> hearing: 'What a pity she is not a boy!' or 'Poor

little girl! No chance of her making a mark in the world.'

One of the staunchest suffragists I ever met, a woman of magnificent mental and physical qualities, said: 'I became a believer in equal rights of women at the age of seven. At that time my only brother, a year younger than myself, was called [to God] ... Silently one by one the mourners entered: they gazed upon the marble features of my dead brother, and, shaking their heads, I heard them murmur: 'What a pity it was the boy. If the girl could have so easily been spared!' Oh God! I can never forget the anguish that quivered through my little frame ... From that moment I resolved to devote every effort of my life to place women in a position where they would be considered socially, morally, and politically, the equals of men.[8]

Two other groups deserve a mention for the work they did to secure rights for Australian women: the Sydney Women's Literary Society, which was formed in the years immediately following Louisa's execution; and the Young Women's Christian Association, now the much-loved YWCA, whose first employment agency for women opened in 1890. (By 1904, the YWCA boasted the first savings bank for women and, by 1912, the first women's gym.)

Interestingly, one of the key founders of the Literary Society was Mrs Matilda Curnow, who was the wife of the *Herald*'s editor, Mr William Curnow. Mrs Curnow's other achievements on behalf of women include helping to establish free kindergartens, as well as the Women's College at the University of Sydney. That the Literary Society was populated by early suffragettes can hardly be in doubt: one of the first members was also one of the Women's Suffrage League's first members, Mrs Dora Montefiore, whose conversion to the feminist cause came during a meeting with the trustees of her husband's will, after she had been left widowed in 1889, with two young children.

'One lawyer remarked to me, when explaining the terms of the Will, "As your late husband says nothing about the guardianship of the children, they will remain in your care,"' she would later report. Mrs Montefiore was amazed. 'I restrained my anger and replied: "Naturally, my husband would never have thought of leaving anyone else as their guardian." But the Trustee went on: "As there is a difference in your religions, he might very well have left someone of his own religion as their guardian."'

Mrs Montefiore thought: 'What!? MY children? The children I bore, left to the guardianship of somebody else?' She told the Trustee: 'I don't think the idea would ever have entered his mind ... Children belong even more to a mother than to a father!'

'Not in law,' the trustee said. 'In law, the child has only one parent, and that is the father.' From that moment, Mrs Montefiore said, 'I was a suffragette, determined to alter the law.'[9]

Of course, no change was possible without the support of men. They held the reins of power in the state parliaments, and it was they who would have to agree to extend the vote to women as Australia federated. Sir Henry Parkes had been an early supporter, telling the New South Wales parliament in 1887 that he would consider votes for women or, as he put it, 'a provision to enable the ladies of the country to vote', since they were 'half the human family' and had to obey the laws of the community in which they lived, without being able to make them.[10] (Where was this sentiment when Louisa was upon the gallows? We shall never know.)

Sir Henry's nemesis, Mr Dibbs, on the other hand, was utterly opposed to women's suffrage, saying that his wife and daughters belonged at home. However, Mr Dibbs and his like were swimming against a rising tide: by 1891, the Victorian parliament had received what soon became known as the 'monster petition' — a suffrage petition containing 30,000 signatures — demanding the vote for women, who increasingly wanted more say over how they lived their lives.

Leading the charge in Melbourne was the quite remarkable Mrs Harrison Lee, also known as Bessie Lee, who would in time become one of the most passionate and articulate sponsors of suffrage. In fact, she toured the world, giving speeches, and her letters and pamphlets were published around the globe. Mrs Lee campaigned not only for a woman's right to vote, but also for her right not to have children and even not to have sex with her husband (at that time, rape in marriage did not exist as a crime; women had to submit, whether they wanted sex or not).

For expressing these views, Mrs Lee was abused, in person and in print. Among other things, she was called a 'sour abstainer' and a 'grim melancholy child avoider' but Mrs Lee was nothing if not willing to stand her ground. Writing to her local newspaper in the working-class Melbourne suburb of Footscray, Mrs Lee explained that it was to her mind 'weakly, wickedly wrong' for women to have children that were 'unwished for and unwanted'.

'Again, I fearlessly say: If you don't want children don't have them,' she said, before revealing that 'again and again, women have said to me, sighingly: "I didn't want another" and I have said, gently "Well, why have one?" The look of surprise has generally been followed by the question "Do you believe in remedies?"'

Mrs Lee's 'indignant reply' was always the same: no, she did not believe in 'remedies' (abortion, or other means of birth control). She simply believed that women who didn't want or couldn't afford any more children shouldn't have sex. 'I know the ideal is too lofty to be understood or tried by one couple out of a hundred,' Mrs Lee said, but she fervently believed that many women would happily abstain from sex in marriage, except that 'too often would the man claim his mastéry'.[11]

Lest anyone think she wasn't serious, in 1890 Mrs Lee published a whole booklet on the subject of dodging sex. She called it *Marriage and Heredity*, and in it she argued what is today taken for granted: that every woman should have 'sole right over her body', and 'the woman who works and suffers for her children should have the right to say whether she will have little ones or not'.[12] It's perhaps worth noting that Mrs Lee had long been married when this pamphlet was published — and that she had no children.

By 1891, Mrs Lee's attention had turned to suffrage. In an essay titled 'A Woman's Plea' published in July of that year, she stated her reasons as to why women should get the vote:

> 1st — Because it is their right.
> 2nd — Because I feel assured they will use the
> privilege wisely and well.
> 3rd — Because they so intensely desire it.
> ... They [women] will use their power to advance
> public morality, to protect woman's kingdom — the
> home — to shield the weak, to denounce the wrong,
> and in every way uplift and ennoble the individual
> and the nation ... They desire it because they are
> part of the nation, bound by its laws, taxed by its
> Government, responsible for its welfare. [They are]
> allowed to share the burdens ... yet not allowed
> the one privilege of voting. They desire it now
> because they are powerless to protect their homes
> or children. With the vote they would have a voice
> in making laws for their own and their family's
> defence.[13]

Mrs Lee was not alone in singing from this song sheet. Thousands more were becoming agitated and had started to talk about campaigning against those men who would oppose them. Back in New South Wales, one of the leading lights of the suffrage movement, feminist Rose Scott, was energising crowds of women with her passionate arguments. 'Can it be good for a boy ... to feel that he has a voice in the government of the country — and that his mother has none?' Ms Scott would say in one of her most famous addresses. 'His father teaches him to be manly … to battle, to fight and to carve for himself a place in the world … His mother would teach him to cultivate his affections, to be unselfish, generous and moral. Is not hers the higher teaching? … In fact, gentlemen, to raise women is to raise yourselves!'[14]

By 1894, South Australian women had become some of the first in the world to be given what should always have been theirs: the right to vote. Western Australian women followed in 1899 and, by 1902, the same right had been extended to women in Victoria, and then in New South Wales. (When the vote came to the floor of the New South Wales Upper House, one old man complained that women should not vote because her position was the same as 'the hen in the fowl yard. She had to keep silence when the cock crew'. Mrs Lawson retorted: 'Truly an argument with no more weight than a feather.'[15])

By December 1903, Australian women were voting in a federal election. Mrs Lawson described the granting of voting rights to women as 'tardy granting of justice to half the population' — and as a gift to all women: to mothers, sisters, wives, and daughters, indeed, to everyone, from birth, through childhood and the child-rearing years, into old age.

Lest any of these women be confused about what to do with their new powers, Mrs Lawson addressed them in a letter in her own newspaper, *The Dawn*:

To the Women of New South Wales, I am not
addressing men. To those who have had the poll
ever since they came of age what I have to say is as
the A.B.C. of politics. I do not write for them, but
for those who have only just entered that school and
are yet in the infant class.

I am not going to give you any instructions, nor
even offer any advice, as to WHOM you should
vote for nor in any way to discuss party politics. You
may vote for any candidate you choose; naturally
that will be the one you think is the best man.

I want to put before you very plainly:

(1) the conditions on which you may vote;

(2) what steps it is necessary to take beforehand
to secure your vote;

(3) and what you have to do at the time of an
election.[16]

Mrs Lawson went on to explain how to get on an electoral
roll and what to do in a voting booth. 'There are separate
rolls for men and women, the women's on white paper, the
men's on blue paper ...'

If Mrs Lawson was delighted, then Mrs Pottie was too.
She had spent years urging men to understand that the vote
could 'not fail to be used for good if placed in the hands
of women'. She had heard every argument against it, and
had long been ready with a rebuttal: 'Some will argue that
women are so easily influenced that a large number would
vote as the tool of man,' Mrs Pottie said, but she knew
better. Women would vote as men did: on the basis of their

own intelligence and experience, and in line with their own beliefs.[17]

Whether Elizabeth Parsons played a role in the suffrage movement isn't entirely clear but she certainly continued to work on behalf of female artists and art students in Melbourne. In the process, she had to put up with an awful lot of condescension. In one typical review of her work, critic James Smith of the *Argus* noted that her watercolours were 'very solid and free for a lady's hand'.[18] Still, she managed to get elected as the first woman council member of the Victorian Academy of Arts, against what her biographer calls 'considerable opposition'[19] from men, who didn't want women to join.

There's no question — and it's probably no surprise — that almost all of the women who worked so hard in the nineteenth century to gain so much for women have disappeared from view. We rarely find their names in our history books — and the women themselves predicted this: in 1902, New South Wales suffragettes held a 'joy meeting' at the Sydney Art School to celebrate women getting the vote. The platform was crowded with men who wanted take the credit. Feminist Rose Scott told those men that their names would live 'not only in the history of Australia, but in that of the world' while the names of the women would be forgotten.[20]

Still, to know anything of the Australian character is to understand that lack of recognition won't keep a good woman down, and so it wasn't long before Australian women, emboldened by their progress at home, had set off overseas to spread the message of freedom.

In 1908, a 28-year-old woman named Muriel Matters of South Australia — she really ought to be better known — boarded a passenger ship for London where she proceeded to raise hell. By mid-October 1908, Muriel was dragging a 'Votes for Women' caravan around the English countryside. Later that same year, she bolted herself — literally, she bolted herself — to the notorious 'Grille', a hideous piece of ironwork in the so-called Ladies' Gallery at Parliament House that was designed to obscure the women's view of proceedings, to demonstrate its stupidity. A blacksmith had to be fetched to cut her loose, but this lady was not for turning: just a year later, there was King Edward, doing his best to formally open parliament for the coming year and look, up there, in the sky — there was the magnificent Muriel hovering overhead. She had hired a blimp (technically, a dirigible) from which she had intended to drop yet another load of pamphlets. Unfortunately, she was blown off course but, still, the point was made.

Back home, progress continued apace: in 1920, Western Australia passed legislation to enable women to stand for election. Edith Cowan not only stood, she won a stunning victory over the attorney general. Then, in 1947, more than half a century after Louisa was hanged, women in New South Wales finally won the right to take a seat on a jury (although only in those places where there were women's toilets was it considered practicable).

The second half of the twentieth century saw many more gains: in 1987, Mary Gaudron QC became the first woman appointed to the High Court; in 1991, Roma Mitchell in Adelaide became the first woman governor in an Australian state (she was also the first woman to become a judge, a Queen's Counsel, and a chancellor of an Australian university). And so it came to pass, just as those gutsy women of the late nineteenth century always said it would: women were elected to parliament; women were accepted on juries; women served in court. One, then two, then five women became state premiers. One became prime minister, another governor general.

A thousand flowers had bloomed.

Epilogue

One of the best things about doing historical research is discovering how close behind our past really is. Sometimes, it's just at the end of the telephone.

Louisa Collins and her first husband, Charles Andrews, had nine children, seven of whom survived infancy. Was it possible that descendants of those children still walked among us? And what of the descendants of the other people in this story: did Eliza Pottie's great-grandchildren have any idea just how wonderful a woman she was?

The answer to both those questions is yes!

Careful readers will remember that Louisa's eldest son, Herbert Andrews, went away to Adamstown, near Newcastle, in the late 1880s to try to find work. New South Wales was by then on the verge of a terrible recession but Herbert's father, Charles, had been a butcher, and Herbert was able to gain a position as an apprentice butcher.

Adamstown in the 1880s was accessible only by rough bush tracks. There was no sewerage and residents had to collect drinking water either from the well, or from Newcastle, by horse and cart. The main industry was mining; there were also a few brickyards. Life must have been difficult, and yet Herbert must have loved the little rural hamlet because he would never leave, except to return to Sydney in the first week of 1889 to visit his mother in gaol.

What then became of him?

Well, in 1893, Herbert Andrews married his sweetheart, Annie Henry, to whom he would stay married for the rest of his life. (When Herbert died after a long illness in 1935, Annie posted an obituary in the *Newcastle Herald*, saying: 'My dear husband left me. Heaven to gain.' They had been together for more than forty years.)

Herbert and Annie had three children: Frederick, who was born in 1897, but who died aged two in 1899; and two girls, Mabel and Pearl.

Both girls loved their dad. When Herbert died, Pearl's obituary, also in the *Newcastle Herald*, read:

> In loving memory of our dear father
> Memories are treasures no one can steal
> Death is a wound no one can heal
> Life is eternal, love will remain
> In God's own time we shall meet again.[1]

The record suggests that Pearl married a man called Stanley Lee, and they had at least one son, Stanley.

Herbert's other daughter, Mabel, married a man called Tom Civill in 1918. They had a son, Douglas, who had two boys — twins, actually — called Howard and Arthur.

Howard is sadly deceased — but Arthur is alive and well and still lives in the Newcastle area. It wasn't hard to find him. There just aren't that many Civills in the New South Wales telephone book.

I rang them all — there were only two — and asked the same question: are you by any chance descended from a Mr Herbert Andrews of Adamstown?

The first lot of Civills said no, sorry, that's not us.

But the second call? Bingo. Arthur Civill's wife, Barbara, when she picked up the phone, said: 'Yes, that's my Arthur. Mabel was his grandmother, and he had a great aunty Pearl. Would you like to speak to him?'

Would I? Oh yes! But what to say? How much would Mr Civill know about Herbert — and, indeed, about Louisa? Had anyone ever told him that his great-great-grandmother was the last woman executed in New South Wales? Did he know that she'd been tried for the murder of his great-great-grandfather, Charles?

Nothing was ever proven in that regard, and doubt remains as to whether she was guilty of anything, but I still wasn't sure how to ask, and so when Mr Civill came to the phone, I simply said: 'Mr Civill, did your grandmother Mabel ever talk to you about your family history?'

'No,' he said. Mr Civill has one of the best, old-fashioned Australian accents you've ever heard. 'I can't say she did. Why do you ask?'

'Well …' I said, coming over all shy. 'Would you mind if I wrote you a letter?'

'A letter?' he said. 'No, I suppose that would be all right.'

And so I wrote it all down, just as I've written it here — shorter, of course — posted it, and then, nervously, I waited.

I really didn't know what Mr Civill would say.

I was in Queensland visiting my own family when the telephone rang.

'Is that you, Caroline? It's Arthur Civill here.'

My heart was pounding. My best guess was that Mr Civill might say: we want nothing to do with this. Don't link us to your story. But, no, what Mr Civill actually said, in the nicest possible way, was: 'Well, you've got everyone here talking, haven't you?'

I was so pleased.

Mr Civill went on: 'You said he was a butcher? Louisa's husband, Charles Andrews?'

'That's right — he was a butcher.'

'Well, you won't believe this,' Mr Civill said. 'I was involved with the meat trade all of my life.'

No way!

'Yes. And I never even knew.'

'I don't know if Louisa did kill Charles, Mr Civill,' I said. 'I don't think anyone does. I do know Charles Andrews was a good man. Everyone said so. He worked hard and never let his children go hungry. And these were tough times. And his son, Herbert — your great-grandfather — was a gentle giant. He came all the way from Newcastle to take the little ones to see their mother for the last time, just before Louisa was hanged.'

There was a pause on the line, and then Mr Civill said: 'Well, you don't need to tell me that Herbert was a good man. I knew his daughter, Mabel. She was my grandmother. And I have the most wonderful memories of Mabel and her sister, Pearl. They were lovely people. And they always spoke fondly of their father.'

Then he dropped a bombshell. 'Now, you won't believe what I've got in front of me,' he said.

'I won't? What is it?'

'It's an old family photograph of Herbert. Would you like to see it?'

Oh yes, I said. I would *love* to see it.

'Well, I'll ask my daughter to take it to the Kodak store for you,' Mr Civill said, 'and I'll see if we can't get a nice copy.'

Less than a week later, a copy of that photograph landed on my desk, and for the longest time, I couldn't stop looking at it (you can see the image for yourself, in the picture section of the book). There was Herbert Andrews, son of Louisa Collins, all grown up with the love of his life, Annie, and their two beautiful daughters, both in white. Nobody knows when the photograph was taken but, just looking at them, you can see that this was a good family. A happy family. Herbert Andrews and his children made a good, solid life for themselves.

As testament to that, and as incredible as it seems, Mr Civill lived for a time in the house that Herbert built and left to Mabel and Pearl (the house still stands on Mackie Avenue, in Newcastle).

Mr Civill particularly remembered Mabel: 'I had a lot to do with both those ladies when I was boy,' he said. 'They never told me the story that you've told me, but I suppose in those days people didn't. But now that you've told me, I've had a think back, and I think Pearl might have known. She never said anything directly, but one or two things have come back to me. People didn't used to talk about that kind of thing. They put it away, and tried to make the best of things. And all I remember is two lovely ladies.'

Barbara Civill said: 'My Arthur comes from that stock. He's a very lovely man. A very kind man. So when you called and explained what Herbert had done, taking in the children [to see Louisa in her cell before the execution], I thought, that's my Arthur.'

So that's what happened to Herbert — but what about the rest of Louisa's children, and what about the other people in this book? Much of the women's history has been lost. There's barely a photograph of any of them left. By contrast, many of the men — in particular, the politicians and judges — live on, either in formal histories of the colony, or in oil paintings that hang in parliament, law courts and private schools. Many have streets — and even grand hotels, or whole electorates — named in their honour.

It hardly seems fair, but in any case, as best as I could find out, this is what happened next.

Reuben Andrews

Shortly after Louisa Collins was hanged, the *Evening News* provided its readers with an update on the welfare of her children:

> Since the home was so unhappily and tragically broken up, the children were scattered. Herbert and Reuben continued to reside at Maitland where the former, at least, is in the employ of a local butcher;

> Arthur and Fred have both been taken care of and
> found employment by a gentleman near Windsor;
> May, since the trial, has been kept close handy in
> case her further testimony might be required; and
> the two youngest, Edwin and Charles, are safely
> housed at the Sydney Benevolent Asylum.[2]

How accurate are these details? Well, the historical record suggests that Reuben did at some stage join Herbert in Adamstown but I was unable to find any record of his marriage, his death or any children born to him.

Arthur Andrews
Arthur Andrews married Alice in 1903; they had several children but Arthur didn't have a long life, dying of pneumonia in a Sydney hospital at the age of forty-five.

Frederick Andrews
Frederick Andrews married a girl also called Alice, and they lived in Adamstown, near Herbert, all their lives. Both Herbert and Frederick are now buried at Sandgate Cemetery, near Newcastle. (Incredibly, Fred would live through the death of his father, the hanging of his mother, two world wars, the Great Depression, and the death of his beloved Alice, before he died in 1962 at the grand old age of eighty-six.)

Edwin Andrews and Charles Andrews
An *Evening News* report suggests that the two youngest boys, Edwin, eight, and Charles, five, were sent to the

Benevolent Asylum in Randwick in July 1888. A second
newspaper report claims that Constable Jeffes provided for
their education but it seems that only the first report is true.

The Randwick Asylum's Admission and Discharge
Register confirms that both Edwin and Charles were
admitted in July 1888, immediately after the death of
Michael Collins. In the space beside their names, an
official wrote:

> The father, Charles Andrews, died ten months
> ago under suspicious circumstances. The mother,
> Louisa Andrews, afterwards married Michael
> Peter Collins and the woman was yesterday
> committed for trial on a charge of having poisoned
> him. The children have two brothers (21 years
> and 19 years of age) residing at Adamstown,
> Newcastle; there are also two brothers and a sister
> (17, 14, and 11) still residing at 1 Pople's Terrace,
> Botany Road, Botany, from which address Mrs
> Collins was removed into custody.[3]

Clearly, this suggests that both Herbert and Reuben
had, by this stage, moved to Adamstown, while Arthur,
Frederick and May were still in Botany.

The Randwick Asylum was an awful place. The
building still stands, as part of the Prince of Wales
Hospital. It opened as an asylum in 1852, initially for
eighty boys (girls came later). Children ended up in
Randwick for a variety of reasons: their mothers had died
in childbirth and their fathers couldn't cope; or else their

mothers had been abandoned and had to look for work. Some parents paid the asylum to take their children in. The asylum received no government subsidy. It relied on benefactors and donations. By the time Louisa's boys went to live there, it was home to more than 800 children, most of them aged between three and ten, who ate, slept and laboured in large dormitories until the age of twelve, when they were apprenticed to people 'desirous of employing them'. Boys went into trades or onto farms, and girls into domestic service. According to some reports, the demand for the girls was 'very great owing to the useful character of their training', meaning they were taught 'house-keeping, cleaning, cooking, laundry work, and sewing'. The *Illustrated Sydney News*, which published a report on the asylum in 1900, was certainly impressed, saying: 'The children looked intelligent, clean, tidy, bright, and happy.'[4] Other reports suggest that the asylum was rampant with disease and that more than 200 children were buried in mass graves there.

Edwin's card from Randwick is missing from the files. Charles was discharged on 18 September 1888 (that is, well before Louisa's second trial, which suggests that nobody in officialdom ever thought she'd go free). He was at first 'boarded out' — or sent to live — with a Mr John Gilby, who was a pioneer in the town of Crookwell. By most accounts, Mr Gilby was a good man: when the *Goulburn Evening Penny Post* reported the death on 17 April 1929, they described him as a man 'widely known and held in high esteem', who had for fifty years been employed as the town's maintenance man.[5]

Records from the Randwick Asylum suggest that Charles stayed with the Gilby family until 1894, when he went to live with another Crookwell pioneer, Mr Samuel Grimson, at a beautiful property called the Rose Farm (later called Rose Leigh). The Grimsons were active in the Salvation Army and, by all accounts, they were good people, too.

May Andrews

What became of May? That is the question that everyone who knows the story of Louisa wants answered. What happened to the little girl forced to give testimony against her mother? Did she ever find any peace?

The answer is: perhaps.

On Saturday, 12 January 1889, the following item appeared on page four of the *Windsor and Richmond Gazette:*

> A Good Action — We understand that Mr James
> Geehan and his good wife has determined upon
> adopting the little girl, May Andrews, daughter of
> Louisa Collins. The child is pretty and intelligent,
> and Mr and Mrs Geehan are to be complimented
> on the kindness of heart which prompted them to
> do so good and worthy an action. May Andrews is
> at present under Mrs Geehan's care.[6]

There is no doubt that this story is accurate: the *Windsor and Richmond Gazette* was the Geehans' local newspaper. They lived on a large property called Freeman's Reach on

Wilberforce Road, just outside Richmond, and the paper had reported on the family's struggles — and its many sorrows — for decades.

The family patriarch, Mr James Geehan, was born in England in 1829, meaning he was nearly seventy when his wife, Mrs Mary Ann Geehan, stepped up to take in May.

As to why they did so, the following should make it obvious: both James and Mary Ann were devout Catholics, and active in their community. Cuttings from the local paper show that James served on a number of local boards, helping to promote the Richmond region and its produce, while Mary Ann used to take her dried peaches, quinces and apples to the Hawkesbury Show, along with some of James's pumpkins, and she would occasionally win a prize.

That said, bad luck seemed to plague all areas of their life. In 1863, the *Sydney Morning Herald* reported a fire at the Geehans' property, resulting in 'the total destruction of a large barn, storeroom, and stables, containing 600 bushels of corn, several tons of hay, a quantity of flour, threshing machines, ploughs, and other farming implements'.

The only saving grace was that James and Mary Ann were absent, attending, as ever, a service at the local Catholic church.[7]

Like all good Catholics — and Protestants, and everyone else! — in nineteenth-century Australia, the Geehans had many children. In fact, they had nine. As noted above, it wasn't unusual for children to die at birth or infancy. However, Mrs Geehan's loss was greater than most: she gave birth to nine children, and by the time May came to live with her, she had lost all but one.

The closest Catholic cemetery to the Geehans' property is the Windsor Cemetery, bounded by Macquarie and George Streets and Richmond Road. It has been in use since 1822, and there are slightly more than 400 graves there. One in every fifty bears the name Geehan. There is also a group headstone that reads:

In Memory of
HUGH GEEHAN
DIED DECEMBER 29 1854
AGED 1 YEAR 9 MONTHS
WILLIAM THOMAS GEEHAN
DIED FEBRUARY 21 1859
AGED 1 YEAR 2 MONTHS
THOMAS HUBERT GEEHAN
DIED JANUARY 5 1861
AGED 1 YEAR 1 MONTH
THERESA HELENA GEEHAN
DIED MARCH 7 1863
AGED 1 YEAR 5 MONTHS
AGNES MARY ALICE GEEHAN
DIED JANUARY 3 1868
AGED 3 YEARS
EUGNIE MATILDA GEEHAN
DIED JUNE 28 1876
AGED 2 YEARS 3 MONTHS

Another child, Mary Alice, born in 1865, also died at age three, from diphtheria.

By the year of Louisa's trials — 1888 — just two of the Geehans' nine children were still living. You would be forgiven for thinking that the Grim Reaper was finished with this family, but you would be wrong: in May of the same year, the younger of those two, Norbert, twenty-one, died of consumption, leaving the Geehans with just one living (and ailing) son.

The *Gazette* report of Norbert's death makes for painful reading:

> Norbert Geehan was a quiet, affectionate, well-behaved lad — quite a noteworthy circumstance in these days ... just entering upon manhood [he was] the hope of his parents, the admired of his immediate acquaintances, and the esteemed of all. [He] seemingly had years of promise before him [but] the germs of that fatal disease — consumption — had been laid.

The whole town turned out for the funeral, which was described as 'the largest we have seen in the district. The procession left Mr Geehan's residence, Freeman's Reach at 2 p.m. ... in it were all creeds and classes, mounted, in vehicles, and on foot.'

Norbert's parents chose the most beautiful coffin they could find in the colony — polished cedar with 'white metal ornaments, covered with white flowers, in wreaths, crosses — and the *Gazette* was sure to remind all readers that his body went into the ground 'alongside sisters and brothers — seven in number — who had preceded him years ago, and now the bereaved parents have but one child left to them out of nine.

'We regret to say that the death has so completely prostrated Mrs Geehan that she is now very seriously indisposed,' the paper added. 'If sympathy for both father and mother will help in any way to soften their distress, we are confident that they have it from all classes throughout the district.'[8]

The one child left to the Geehans was their eldest boy, Raymond, who still lived at Freeman's Reach, which must have been some comfort to them, but how the Geehans must have ached for the laughter of little children (not only their own, but grandchildren! James was by this time already seventy, and yet they had none).

There is nothing on the record to explain how the Geehans came to know May. They were Catholic; her family was not. They lived on a rural property many miles from Sydney; May lived in Botany. However, if the article in the *Evening News* is correct, two of May's brothers, Frederick and Arthur, had found work in Windsor after their mother's trial, and Windsor is quite close to Richmond, so perhaps they asked around for somebody to take May.

In any case, by January 1889, May had gone to live at Freeman's Reach, and although she was by then twelve years old, the article from the *Gazette* doesn't say that she went there to take up a position as a domestic, or to work as a maid or servant. It says she was adopted: she went to the Geehans as their little girl.

Just seven years later, on 10 October 1896, Mary Ann Geehan died at the age of sixty-five.[9] A devout Catholic all her life, she was buried at the Catholic Windsor Cemetery, along with eight of her nine children. Mrs Geehan's obituary in the *Windsor and Richmond Gazette*, read:

GEEHAN —
In loving memory of Mary Geehan, who died at Wilberforce, October 10, 1896. May her soul rest in peace. Inserted by her loving Husband and Son.
We miss thy kind and willing hand,
Thy fond and earnest care:
Our home is dark without thee —
We miss thee everywhere.[10]

Then, in 1903, the only surviving Geehan child, Raymond, was involved in some kind of accident on the Windsor Bridge, and from that day forward suffered from the seizures that would eventually kill him. On Boxing Day 1904, Raymond left the house early to plough the fields, working until eleven o'clock, when he rode his favourite pony down to the river to water all the horses.

Half an hour later, the pony came home without him. He was found buried face down in the sand, at just thirty-three years of age. His death left James Geehan alone on his property, and his health soon began to fail. In September 1907, he died of a heart attack. James Geehan's belongings were sold the same month. A yearling filly raised eleven pounds and a brown saddle mare sixteen pounds.

Yes, but what of May? Well, at some point, May changed her name, at least briefly, to Mabel Andrews. As Mabel she appears twice in the *Windsor and Richmond*

Gazette, once being praised for her needlework, and once for a display of wax flowers that she entered in a local show.

Then, in 1894, she appears again, this time as a seventeen-year-old victim of a terrible assault by an older, married woman:

> Beatrice Tierney was charged that she did on
> the 3rd April beat and assault Mabel Andrews at
> Freeman's Reach ... Mabel Andrews deposed that
> she resided with Mrs Geehan at Freeman's Reach;
> on the 3rd of April, [the] defendant, Mrs Tierney,
> came into the yard at Mrs Geehan's ... and beat her
> on the face with her hands, blackening both eyes
> ... blood was coming from her nose [but she] did
> not fall from the blows; [Mabel] saw the doctor on
> Thursday evening, concerning her black eye and the
> bruises she had received.[11]

The reason for the fight is not entirely clear, although it seems that May — or Mabel, as she was then known — had earlier been fighting with Mrs Tierney's little sister, Ettie, for giving her 'impudence'. (Mrs Tierney pleaded guilty, and paid a small fine.)[12]

Then, in the late 1890s, Mabel moved to Wallsend, near Newcastle, presumably to be closer to her eldest brother, Herbert.

In 1898, she married a fettler on the railways, John McGuiness, in Lambton, which is a suburb of Newcastle. In the first few years of the new century, they had a little boy, Edward, and a little girl, Alice, whose middle name was Louisa (this, more than anything, suggests that May continued to love and mourn her mother, long after Louisa had been hanged).

Sadly, both Alice and Edward died when they were infants,[13] but May went on to have a third child, Thelma, who was born in 1909.[14]

Tragically, she did not live to see this little girl grow up. According to records, May died of 'natural causes, viz heart failure' just two years later, at the age of thirty-three.[15]

According to May's descendants, Thelma was in bed with May when May finally passed away. She was buried at the West Wallsend Cemetery, in a grave that can still be visited today, at the end of a long, gravel track.

As for Thelma, well, it seems that her dad, John, thought that he wouldn't be able to cope with her on his own, and so gave her to his own mum to raise. Thelma grew up with the lady she called 'Granny'.[16]

Then, when Thelma turned sixteen in 1925, she married into the robust Cairney family.[17] Thelma and her husband, Jim, had two daughters: Margaret, who is still alive; and Mabel, who married Rupert Thompson of Wallsend in 1949. They also had three sons: John, who died in 1982; James; and Victor.

Mabel died just last year (in June 2013) aged eighty-six, but her two daughters, Janis and Bev Thompson, still live in the Newcastle area; as does Margaret, who is eighty-nine years old, and still going strong; and plenty of other descendants.

The family are very close, and although Janis and Bev didn't know it until this book was written, they are

Louisa's great-great-grandchildren, and they have proudly
provided a photograph of Thelma, for the picture section
of this book.

Constable George Jeffes

Constable Jeffes enjoyed a long career in the New South
Wales police force. He was promoted to senior constable,
and then sergeant, and was for years especially active
around the opium dens of Chinatown, rescuing girls from
prostitution. In one particularly engaging interview with
the *Sunday Times*, he described the dens:

> They are, of course, in a terribly dirty condition for
> there is no one to clean them up. The windows are
> never opened, and the doors only when someone
> enters ... I have often felt sick myself when I have
> entered them. As a rule, they have about four rooms,
> which are occupied on an average by from twelve to
> fifteen persons ... The occupants include men and
> women of every color — Chinamen, black fellows,
> and white men, with women to match. All colors
> occupy the same room. The only furniture which
> they possess are trestles with ordinary floor mats on
> them, and it is upon these they sleep. In the cold
> weather they may use a rug or two for covering ...
> most [are] young girls who have been ruined, and
> who do not care to face anyone they know. Once
> the opium gets hold of them there is very little
> chance of curing them. Some of them are splendidly
> educated, and of very good parents, who have been

broken-hearted. On one visit I went into a cellar
where I saw a woman stripped and conversing with
a Chinaman. I told her that she must leave with
me at once, and I waited in the adjoining room
until she was dressed. You can imagine my surprise
when a most attractive woman in a nurse's uniform
entered … She was a genuine nurse, and when I
questioned her, she could not tell me how she got
there, except that she remembered having had a few
drinks. She was restored to her people.[18]

Sergeant Jeffes seems to have been a good man, with his
heart in the right place, and yet tragedy befell his family as
it might befall any family, when, in 1909, Constable Jeffes'
own daughter, Catherine Margaret Jeffes, was murdered
in the streets of Sydney. Reports say she was just twenty-
one years old and working as a waitress when she met a
35-year-old cook, Felix Perrier, a native of Montreal, at a
small café called Glenrock, in Pitt Street. They exchanged
a few letters but Catherine called it off, telling her father
that Perrier seemed unhinged and kept pestering her. It
seems that Perrier lay in wait for her one afternoon near
Goulburn and George Streets, shooting her twice — in
the left arm and below the right breast. She was taken to
Sydney Hospital and while the injuries didn't at first seem
life-threatening, she 'suffered greatly from shock and loss
of sleep … she gradually grew weaker, and passed away'.
Perrier shot himself dead.[19]

On Saturday, 26 June 1909, a Sydney newspaper
reported that 'the wounded girl in a recent tragedy

in Sydney was a daughter of the late Louisa Collins, of Botany notoriety'.[20] This is not correct. The girl in question was not Louisa's daughter, but Constable Jeffes' daughter, Catherine, born in 1888, who was in the aforementioned incident in June 1909, and died shortly afterwards.

Sergeant Jeffes continued to work as a policeman for several years after the death of his daughter but then, on 3 November 1911, the *Evening News* reported that Jeffes himself had been knocked down by a tram and killed on one of Sydney's busy streets:

> Sergeant George Jeffes died in Sydney Hospital early this morning as the result of a tram accident. He was on duty … inspecting pawn shops in the No. 2 Police District yesterday afternoon, and while crossing Castlereagh-street at the corner of Campbell-street, he was knocked down by tram No. 81 … He [was] conveyed … to the hospital where he was admitted with a fractured skull. He was operated on and a clot of blood was removed from his brain but he never rallied.[21]

He was given a police funeral, with colleagues lining the road and saluting the casket. He is buried at Rookwood, the same cemetery as both Michael Collins and Charles Andrews. Mourners noted with sorrow that he could have retired six months earlier but 'being still strong, he was, at his own desire, allowed to continue and was working in plain clothes on light duty among the poor'.[22]

Lieutenant Colonel Thomas Morgan Martin

Dr Thomas M Martin, who tended to Charles Andrews on his deathbed, became an Australian hero. He was placed in the reserve of officers for the Australian Army Medical Corps in 1897 as lieutenant, rising to the rank of captain in 1900, major in 1903, and lieutenant colonel in 1911.[23] By 1916, he was in command of the No. 2 Australian General Hospital in Egypt. When he died in 1928, the *Sydney Morning Herald* said this:

> When the milestones ended for Dr. Morgan Martin and he was being laid to rest, there was no mistaking the profound grief that prevailed among all classes who crowded into St John's, Darlinghurst, and overflowed on to the sidewalks.
>
> The tear-stained faces and broken voices of hundreds of his old patients bore testimony to their grief at losing not only their much depended-on doctor, but a dear and valued friend. Many of the mourners had been attended by him for over forty years, and their children, and again their children after them, whom he not only knew, but was personally interested in, through life. So intensely human and sympathetic was he that his patients confided their joys and sorrows alike to him as a matter of course.
>
> He served all his patients, irrespective of class or creed, to the utmost of his efficient ability. Often amidst poor surroundings he battled the whole night through to beat back the Grim Reaper, snatching

what little rest he could get on an uncomfortable sofa.

Small wonder they came with reverent steps to his flower-covered casket to take their last farewell ... Medical comrades and soldiers who served with him in the Boer War were there to pay their last tribute of respect, along with the younger generation who served under him at No. 2 Australian General Hospital.

He never spared himself; ill as he was, he attended a last unimportant case, saying it would be a load off his mind; and that was the keynote of his whole life, nothing neglected, no patient unattended at the end of the day.

During the influenza epidemic in 1919 for weeks he worked from ten to twelve hours a day, his meals often consisting of a few sandwiches eaten in his cab.

Dr Martin travelled in many lands, but never for pleasure or profit. The will of the physician to save, combined with the soldier blood in him, made it impossible for him to keep out of the struggle when the Empire was in danger ... Now he has gone to his regard and eternal rest: Thomas Morgan Martin, physician, soldier, and man.[24]

Lieutenant Colonel George Archibald Marshall

Dr George Marshall, who treated Michael Collins in his rooms at Elizabeth Street and on his sickbed in Botany, was appointed a second lieutenant to the Army Medical

Corps in 1892. In 1903 he attained the rank of major and in 1909 he was given the rank of lieutenant colonel. He saw active service in the South African campaign, leaving Sydney with 'A' Battery, and was awarded the Queen's Medal with clasps. He left Sydney again during World War One with the headquarters staff of the First Expeditionary Force as deputy assistant director of medical services. He was injured on the tenth day at Gallipoli, was invalided to England, but died of his injuries at his home in Darling Point on Christmas Eve, 1916. His obituary, published in the *Sydney Morning Herald* on Christmas Day, described Dr Marshall as a hero of the Australian people, who also had a 'high reputation in the profession, and his genial nature won for him much respect and esteem amongst his many patients'.[25] Dr Marshall left a widow and four daughters. His only son died at the age of three. He is buried at Waverley Cemetery.

William Mogford Hamlet

Having served as New South Wales government analyst for more than half a century, Mr Hamlet retired in 1915 to pursue his passion — walking. As co-founder of the Warragamba Walking Club (sadly now defunct) he walked twice from Brisbane to Sydney (1907 and 1913) and from Sydney to Melbourne along the Princes Highway, covering some 750 miles (1200 kilometres) in thirty-three days. His lifelong habit of eating in moderation and walking every day worked for him: when Mr Hamlet died at his residence in pretty Glenbrook, he was eighty-one years old.

City Coroner Mr Henry Shiell JP

Mr Henry Shiell JP died just three weeks after Louisa Collins was hanged at Darlinghurst Gaol and just a year after his marriage to young Agnes Olive (they'd married in 1887, when Henry was sixty-one and she just twenty-seven).[26]

Having always been bad with money, it's probably no surprise to learn that Mr Shiell died destitute. On 12 April 1889, Agnes wrote to Lord Carrington, saying that she was broke and needed some kind of special pension. Mrs Shiell said that Henry had 'contracted the illness which proved fatal to him in the discharge of his official duties', and that it had been 'aggravated by his forced attendance at an important inquiry [the case of Louisa Collins]'.

She reminded Lord Carrington of Henry's 'long service to the government, the length of service, the able way in which he discharged his arduous duties [including working] without any public holiday [and having to respond to] police reports on Sundays.

'I, his widow have been left totally impoverished,' she said, 'and pray that his Excellency the governor may be pleased to grant me the sum of 150 pounds in order to pay my late husband's debts.'[27]

As to whether she was ever granted the pension, the minutes of the Executive Council from February 1889 show that the government had already considered the question of whether Mrs Shiell should be given some kind of special, one-off payment of 325 pounds.

In response, Mrs Shiell swore to the terribleness of her circumstances:

I, Agnes Shiell, of 30 Upper Fort Street
That I am the widow of the late Henry Shiell, city
coroner, who died at his residence Upper Fort Street
Sydney on the 30th day of January last year.

My late husband left no property nor was his
life insurance [sic].

He left no will and I have not applied for [funds
from his estate].

I have no children.

With the exception of household furniture
the value of which is about 80 pounds I am left
absolutely without any means of support and have
no private means of any kind.[28]

There is a pencil note on the statement, in which a clerk of
some kind wonders where the money for a one-off payment
should come from, but it seems that it was found.

Justice William John Foster

Justice Foster, who presided over Louisa's first trial, died
at Valley Heights on 16 August 1909 from what was
then known as 'senile decay'. He is buried in Waverley
Cemetery. Predeceased by his wife Matilda Sophia, née
Williams, he was survived by six sons and two daughters.
He left an estate of 10,000 pounds.[29]

William Henry Coffey

The Crown prosecutor from the first trial became a district
court judge. He was sitting in Taree one Tuesday in 1899
when he was seized by paralysis. He did not recover. The

Wagga Wagga Advertiser, which reported his death, said the news would be received 'with universal regret, the deceased gentleman being one of the most honourable, upright and fearless judges on the bench'.[30]

Mr Hugh Hart (HH) Lusk

In 1889 — just a year after Louisa's trial — her barrister, Mr HH Lusk, wrote *A History of Australia for Schools,*[31] which not only won a £300 prize, but was later used as a textbook for children attending Sydney's public schools. The book contains maps and hand-written notes, and is today regarded by many as wrong in several respects.

By 1894, Mr Lusk had become the first barrister to be struck off the rolls in New South Wales, accused by a client of withholding money without doing any work. Called to appear before the Full Court to explain himself (the case was heard by both Chief Justice Darley and Justice Windeyer), Mr Lusk failed to attend, not once, but three times. He claimed he was sick, telling the court: 'Your Honour, I exceedingly regret that I am laid up with an attack of a somewhat dangerous illness ... This has rendered it quite impossible either to complete an affidavit ... or to appear personally before the Court.'[32]

The court gave Mr Lusk another week, but when he still didn't appear, the Full Bench had no choice other than to strike his name from the roll for dishonesty and deception. A client was able to show that he had paid Mr Lusk 200 pounds to complete some work that was never done, and when he asked about the delay Mr Lusk told him he was in financial difficulties, and had no money to go on with the case. Only later was it revealed that Mr Lusk had form: in 1877, when living in New Zealand, he was found to have taken a bribe and was fined fifty pounds.

Mr Lusk returned to literature, and under the pseudonym Owen Hall he wrote two Australian novels, including one called *Eureka* (1899), in which the protagonist uses ancient documents to discover a hidden city, settled by Alexander the Great, in Australia. (Eureka is the name of a princess in the book. She dies.) *Eureka* is now regarded as one of the earliest examples of Australian science fiction. Mr Lusk also wrote a convict novel, *The Track of a Storm*. By the late 1890s, he was living in New York, where he gave lectures on politics. He later returned to New Zealand, where he died in Auckland in 1926.[33]

Justice William Charles Windeyer and Lady Mary Windeyer

The second trial judge, Justice Windeyer, visited England in 1896 for what was then described as 'rest'. He retired from the bench the following year, and although he wanted to keep working in some capacity, he died of paralysis of the heart on 12 September 1897 in Bologna, Italy. He was survived by his wife, three sons and five daughters. His estate was valued for probate at 18,733 pounds.

Lady Windeyer was a pioneer of women's rights in New South Wales. In 1895, she helped found the Women's Hospital on Crown Street, and became president of the Womanhood Suffrage League of New South Wales. She was also prominent in the organisation of the Women's

Industrial Exhibition in 1888 and in the Women's Christian Temperance Union of New South Wales.[34]

In 1992, the *Sydney Morning Herald* carried an article noting the service of six generations of the Windeyer family to the justice system in New South Wales. 'William (Bill) Victor Windeyer, now a Master of the Supreme Court, will be sworn in as Justice Windeyer on Tuesday,' the article said. 'His father, Sir Victor, was a High Court judge, his great-grandfather, Sir William Charles, a Supreme Court judge and his great-great-great-grandfather, Charles Windeyer, was the first police magistrate in New South Wales.'[35]

Sir Joseph George Innes

Sir Joseph Innes, who presided over the third trial, visited England in 1889 to restore his health and take up grouse shooting. He died on 28 October 1896, leaving an estate of 34,414 pounds to the 'unfettered discretion' of his wife, who survived him with five sons and one daughter. His son, Reginald Heath Innes, became chief judge in equity of the New South Wales Supreme Court.[36]

Charles Gilbert Heydon

The former Crown prosecutor contested Legislative Assembly seats twice, unsuccessfully. After the resignation of (Sir) Edmund Barton, he accepted the attorney generalship in the Dibbs ministry and was appointed to the Legislative Council on 15 December 1893. He later became a judge of the District Court and, in what was known as the Sawmillers' case, he crafted the basis for a minimum wage to enable 'every worker however humble ... to lead a human life, to marry and bring up a family and maintain them and himself with at any rate some small degree of comfort'. On 8 November 1909 at Mosman he married a 28-year-old art student, Sybil Russell. Heydon died at his home at Potts Point on 6 March 1932 and was buried in the Field of Mars Cemetery. He was survived by his second wife and by his son, George, who served with the Australian Army Medical Corps and was awarded the Military Cross.[37]

Chief Justice Frederick Darley

Upon the retirement of Sir Alfred Stephen in 1891, Chief Justice Darley was appointed lieutenant governor of New South Wales. He visited England in 1902 and was appointed a member of the Privy Council in 1905, and in 1909 was granted the honour of dining with King Edward. In August 1888 — which is to say, between the first two of Louisa's four trials — Sir Frederick had purchased over 11 acres of land adjacent to Echo Point in Katoomba where he built the mansion — now guesthouse — known as Lilianfels, designed by architect Varney Parkes (son of Sir Henry). The property was used for a summer residence and for many years, nearly every noted visitor to Australia — royalty included — stayed there. Sir Frederick died in London on 4 January 1910, at the age of seventy-nine.

Eliza Pottie

As awful as it is to report, Eliza Pottie developed dementia and died in November 1907 of burns that she inflicted upon herself after secretly playing with matches. An inquest into her death found that Mrs Pottie went to bed at her mansion, St Ives, in Manly, at around six p.m. (her normal time). Her daughter, who was caring for her, was at pains to ensure that no lamp was left in the room.

Shortly before midnight, Mrs Pottie's daughter heard a little cry in the hall, followed by a second cry, and she went out and saw her mother in the passage with her nightdress on fire.

The daughter grabbed a quilt and wrapped it around her mother, but Mrs Pottie was badly burned, and yet seemed not able to feel the pain.

According to the report in the *Herald*, 'she was childish, and delighted to play with matches, which were in consequence kept from her'. Afterwards, Miss Pottie found 'two boxes all burned on [the] deceased's chest of drawers. They were a different brand of matches from what were used in the house.'[38]

The cause of death was ruled as shock resulting from burns accidentally received. It's little consolation, but Mrs Pottie was given a grand obituary in the *Newsletter: an Australian Paper for Australian People*. It was headlined: 'The Late Eliza Pottie — Benefactress'.

A most estimable woman, and unostentatious benefactress, Mrs Eliza Pottie, wife of Mr John Pottie, veterinary surgeon, has passed away at her residence, 'St. Ives,' Manly. Born in Belfast, Ireland ... [she] came out to Sydney with her parents and two brothers. Nearly fifty years ago she married Mr John Pottie ... [and] from that time began her life work of ministering to the sick, distressed, and poor, befriending many homeless ones from foreign lands. Regular visitations were made to the Public Hospitals, Newington Asylum, and the Aboriginals' camp at La Perouse. One of her greatest life efforts was the undertaking to improve the conditions of the Newington Asylum ... Mrs Pottie was one of the originators of the Sydney Female Mission Home, on whose committee she remained for some thirty-one years. She was also President of the Women's Christian Temperance Union, Ladies Sanitary Association ... Flower Mission, and vice-president of the Ladies Committee of the Sydney City Mission from its foundation. She took a very keen interest in the Boer War, lecturing on the 'Horrors of War.' Sir George Dibbs and Sir Henry Parkes repeatedly sought Mrs Pottie's advice with regard to questions on charitable institutions. She was a frequent contributor to the papers on social and philanthropic topics [and] every Monday before Xmas day she entertained at tea upwards of 100 widows and their families. On leaving each woman received her Christmas parcel of tea, flour, sugar and a Xmas cake, and each child a toy.[39]

Eliza Pottie is buried in Waverley Cemetery.

As to her family, Mrs Pottie was survived by her husband, John, who is to this day regarded as one of the finest veterinarians ever to work in New South Wales. His responsibilities included the health of the New South Wales police horses — it's said that no police horse died under

Pottie's care — and he worked hard to ensure that New South Wales sheep remained free of disease (safeguarding the New South Wales economy in the process).

Besides working closely with the animals themselves, Mr Pottie — who kept his own private zoo in Bondi — wrote important books on animal care, including two — *The Horse in Health* and *Pottie's Horse Guide* — that remain in use today.

His company, John Pottie & Son, which produced a variety of products for horses and cattle, was being managed in the early 1970s by a great-grandson, Bruce Pottie, who handed the reins to his son, Richard Pottie, who now lives in Manildra, in country New South Wales. Richard picks up the history: 'John Pottie had a son, Stuart, who had Bruce, who had three sons: Hugh, Graeme, and myself, so I'm his great-grandson. Our family has always been very proud of the name, although of course we always knew a lot more about John Pottie than we did about Eliza.'

Of his great-grandmother, Eliza, he says: 'We have known for a long time that she was involved in good works. She was also a very strong Quaker. They had these meetings where nobody would speak until moved to do so — it could go on for hours, the silence!

'My father used to speak very highly of her. She was a strong and compassionate woman, and we are all proud of that.'

Elizabeth Parsons

A short history of Elizabeth Parsons hardly does her justice: during the late 1870s and 1880s, she travelled across Victoria, New South Wales and Tasmania and to remote areas of New Zealand, sketching the landscape as she saw it. Most of her journeys were made by boat, coach, and then by horse, or horse and cart, and many of the areas she visited were so truly remote that she was the first to capture them.

Despite widespread discrimination against women artists, Mrs Parsons did manage to show her works: two of her oils and three watercolours were accepted for the International Exhibition in Sydney in 1879–1880; three oils were exhibited at the Melbourne International Exhibition in 1880–1881; and six of her watercolours were accepted for inclusion in the Victorian Jubilee Exhibition in 1884. In 1882, she published a set of lithographed drawing books on Australian landscape, in three parts.

Despite this success, Mrs Parsons' biographer, Mr Andrew Mackenzie,[40] believes she never achieved the fame that was her due. 'Like so many of the women artists of this period, Elizabeth Parsons has become one of the forgotten artists,' Mr Mackenzie wrote in the online journal *In the Artist's Footsteps*. 'Little is known of her work, which is mostly held in private collections, and in keeping with the social conventions of the day, she exhibited under the name Mrs George Parsons.'

The State Library of Victoria is thought to hold some of her works, and her correspondence.[41]

JF Archibald

Friends used to say that JF Archibald had no social life. Instead, he had the *Bulletin*. It's true that the magazine was his obsession: Mr Archibald took only the briefest fishing holidays and on them he paced around restlessly. He 'come[s] back looking ten years older, but completely recovers his old form after a week's work', Henry Lawson apparently said.[42]

Perhaps it was the relentless pace, perhaps something else entirely, but at some point, Mr Archibald went mad. He ended up in Callan Park Asylum where he stayed for some years before making a complete recovery.

His return to the community was triumphant: in the final decade of his life, Mr Archibald became a trustee of the Art Gallery of New South Wales and, when he died, he made sure to leave money for the creation of an impressive public fountain (the bronze Apollo, surrounded by horses' heads, dolphins and tortoises that now stands in Hyde Park; the sculptor was French, of course). Archibald also endowed an annual prize for portrait painting, now known as the Archibald Prize. A significant portion of his estate went to those he loved best: distressed journalists, who turned in their hour of need to the Benevolent Fund of the Australian Journalists' Association. Mr Archibald died at St Vincent's Hospital on 10 September 1919. He was buried in the Catholic section of the Waverley Cemetery — quite near Nosey Bob.[43]

Sir Henry Parkes

Sir Henry Parkes occupies a special place in Australia's political history. He was an early advocate of free, secular, public education, and he was the most prominent of our.

Founding Fathers — the wind beneath the wings of
Federation — which he would not live to see.

Besides being a man of great political strengths,
Sir Henry was a man of grand passions. He was married for
the first time in 1936 to Clarinda Varney. They mourned
the loss of two children — Thomas, aged seventeen days,
and Clarinda, aged one day — before they boarded the
ship for Australia. Their third child, also Clarinda, was
born just two days after they landed.

The first Lady Parkes died in 1888 — the same year
as Louisa's trial — and by 1889, Sir Henry was married
again. His bride this time was Eleanor Dixon, and they
had five children, including three — Sydney, Kenilworth,
and Aurora — born *before* the marriage, when Eleanor was
Sir Henry's mistress.

Eleanor would not live long. She died in July 1895, at
age thirty-six, when the youngest of her children, Cobden,
was only three years old.

Just three months later, Sir Henry married for the
third time, and this time his bride was his 23-year-old
housekeeper, Julia Lynch, which apparently didn't go
down all that well in the family:

FAMILY DISGUSTED
Sir Henry Parkes was married to Miss Julia Lynch,
at Parramatta yesterday. The bride had for years
been employed in Sir Henry's house. She is 23 years
of age, and is very prepossessing in appearance.
Sir Henry, who is 82 years of age, lost his second
wife on July 11 last. Sir Henry's family are disgusted

with the marriage. Two of his daughters have left
home and the family governess has resigned her
situation and left the house.[44]

A little over a year later, in 1896, Sir Henry contracted
pneumonia. His death was reported thus:

> The little ones were brought by the bedside of their
> father to take what none of them then realised was
> the last look at him. At about 3 o'clock chicken
> broth and brandy were administered. Then there
> came a slight rally, but just at the hour of 4 o'clock
> the dying man reached out his hands and grasped
> those of his wife and … quietly passed away without
> pain. The last coherent words of Sir Henry Parkes
> addressed to any one were to Lady Parkes, to
> whom he said: 'You have been a good mother to my
> children. Like a good mother never desert them.'
> Lady Parkes shows signs of complete collapse.[45]

The widowed Lady (Julia) Parkes had been left penniless, a
situation the government sought to resolve by granting her
a pension worth 100 pounds a year. It wasn't much, as the
Clarence and Richmond Examiner explained:

> Lady Parkes has to pay for (the house) out of her
> £100. As this house costs £80 a year she is thus left
> with £20, just about housemaid's wages for looking
> after Sir Henry's children … It is sincerely to be
> hoped that this disgraceful state of things will be

> taken up in the proper quarter. It is safe to say that
> it couldn't have existed in any other country in the
> world. Here is the widow of the senior Knight of
> Australia, and as such the first lady in the land …
> reduced to the beggarly pittance of a few shillings a
> week … It is a scandal, a living national scandal.[46]

Lady Parkes never gave up her promise to care for Sir Henry's children, one of whom, Cobden, became a soldier: he enlisted in the Australian Imperial Force in August 1914, embarked for Egypt with the 1st Battalion, and was wounded at Gallipoli (three fingers of his right hand were amputated).[47] Cobden returned to New South Wales to become government architect. Among other important buildings, he designed the magnificent reading room of the State Library of New South Wales, where so many of his father's papers may now be accessed.

Sir George Dibbs

Sir George Dibbs served as premier of New South Wales on three occasions between 7 October 1885 and 2 August 1894, and was colonial secretary on three occasions between 5 January 1883 and 2 August 1894. He was a member of the Legislative Assembly between 16 December 1874 and 5 July 1895. Upon his retirement from politics, Sir George was appointed managing trustee of the Savings Bank of New South Wales.

He held this position until his death in 1904. He was survived by Lady Dibbs, two sons and nine daughters.[48] As befits a man of his achievements, the funeral was enormous, and reverential: Sir George was buried in a polished cedar coffin with silver embellishments and the inscription 'George Richard Dibbs, KCMG, died 5th August, aged 69'. The body was conveyed by steamer to Milson's Point, where the cortege, headed by mounted police, was formed. The hearse was drawn by four horses, and crowds formed along the route. The funeral was attended by Chief Justice Sir Frederick Darley, who had passed the sentence of death upon Louisa, and wreaths were received from Messrs John Fairfax and Sons, directors of Sydney Hospital, members of the Australian Club, officers, non-commissioned officers, and the men of the Metropolitan Police.[49] Sir George is buried at St Thomas's Cemetery, North Sydney. Descendants of the Dibbs family continue to reside in Sydney, and were special guests in the gallery of the state parliament in 2008.[50]

Fun fact for New South Wales readers: the grand mansion in which he lived toward the end of his life, Passy, in Sydney's Hunter's Hill, is now the home of former New South Wales parliamentarian Eddie Obeid.

Charles Frederick Lindeman

Charles was one of the twelve men on the fourth and final jury. He was also one of five sons of Dr John Henry Lindeman, who settled the Hunter Valley wine region in 1843, and who is today widely regarded as a founder of the immensely successful Australian wine industry. Charles took over the company upon his father's death, and when he retired in 1918, his son Eric Lindeman took over the company. Lindeman's to this day produces a range called

Dr Henry's Sons — which includes a 'Charles's Floral and Crisp Riesling', named for Charles Lindeman.

Archibald Nugent Robertson

The British-born barrister who tried to convince Lord Carrington to commute Louisa's death sentence to life imprisonment on the grounds that evidence about the death of Charles should have been inadmissible at her trial was, by 1905, embroiled in a legal dispute of his own.

In June of that year, Mr Robertson and his companion, an elocution teacher named Miss Mercia Murray, decided to take a ride on a ferry but, after entering the wharf at Circular Quay via a turnstile, they found that the last ferry had departed, and yet they were told that they would have to pay a penny each to exit. Mr Robertson refused, and the resulting altercation prompted him to sue the ferry company for false imprisonment. He initially obtained 100 pounds in damages but the High Court and the Privy Council, in *Robertson v The Balmain New Ferry Company Ltd*, overturned the verdict, and Mr Robertson is now famous in legal circles as the man who sued for a penny and lost. In his private life, Mr Robertson chalked up thirty-one years of service as a (paid) visitor to the New South Wales system of hospitals for the insane. He also wrote a bodice-ripper, called *Her Last Appearance*, which was published in 1914.

Pasquale Besomo

A decade after Louisa's trial, the phrenologist who so lovingly painted a word portrait of her head found himself in court fighting one of the colony's more amusing defamation actions. The case was insanely complicated, but involved a man — an 'old German' — who claimed to have paid Mr Besomo to meet a potential bride, only to find that the lass was a lad dressed in women's clothing (or, in the words of the court document, the 'woman was a man with a veil over his face'). According to the 'old German', Mr Besomo then expected him to pay 126 pounds not to have to go through with the marriage. Mr Besomo said it was all a lie and sued for defamation. In cross-examination, the following exchange took place:

> Question to Mr Besomo: Do you not engage in palm-reading and fortune-telling?
>
> Mr Besomo: Not for 13 or 14 years. I am a pure scientist. Phrenology and homoeopathy are science, and you must not insinuate anything against me.
>
> Question: But pure science does not pay, does it?
>
> Mr Besomo: That is because people are so dull that they don't understand what it means.

He lost the case.[51]

Lord Carrington

In 1889, a year after Louisa Collins was hanged, Lady Carrington gave birth to what her husband liked to describe as his 'fine specimen of an Australian baby'.

Lord Carrington spent the last two years of his post gently encouraging Australia toward Federation. He developed a warm friendship with Sir Henry Parkes, who would lead the charge in his absence. When Lord and Lady Carrington left Sydney in 1890, they received an 'unprecedented farewell, with thousands lining the streets and showering flowers on their carriage'. In his parting speech, Lord Carrington declared they would leave 'half their hearts behind'.[52]

Carrington returned to England, where he became lord chamberlain under King Edward and King George. When his 'fine specimen of an Australian baby' got married in 1909, both the King and Queen attended, and newspapers declared that 'no prettier wedding [had] been seen during the present London season' and his Majesty was reportedly 'one of the merriest of the wedding party'.[53]

Lord Carrington died on 13 June 1928. He was survived by his wife and four of their five daughters; his only son, Albert Edward Charles Robert Wynn Carrington, had been killed in World War I. A number of buildings in New South Wales still bear his name — including The Carrington Hotel in Katoomba, renamed for him in 1886, and once described as the only rival to Raffles within the Empire.

Robert Rice Howard ('Nosey Bob')

The bungled execution of Louisa Collins did not go unnoticed by the press.

A report in the *Brisbane Courier*, filed by what the newspaper described as 'our own correspondent, by electric telegraph', criticised the way Bob had asked the assistant to pull the lever, and how the trap had failed to fall, prompting a warden to have to run for the mallet to pound on the bolt, all while Louisa stood there trembling.

'The woman fell with a thud,' the paper noted, 'the rope breaking her neck right open and completely severing the windpipe.'[54]

A report in the *Kerang Times and Swan Hill Gazette* was also highly critical: 'When the sign was given to draw the bolt, it was found that it would not come away ... The hangman's assistant showered blow after blow upon the pin with a tall wooden mallet while the poor woman began to tremble, and a horrible catastrophe seemed imminent.'[55]

The Clarence and Richmond Examiner, whose report was headlined 'The Doomed Woman's Last Minutes — The Final Scene', said that Louisa's head seemed at one point to be 'parting from the body' and it was only on close examination that spectators realised that 'there was an unusually large gaping wound in the throat, and that the windpipe was torn right through'.[56]

The *Launceston Examiner* was likewise appalled: 'The body fell the full length of the drop ... and immediately a horrible sight was presented. The whole of the front of the neck was torn open almost from ear to ear, the blood spurting from the gaping wound.'[57]

Even the *Sydney Morning Herald*, which had been campaigning for Louisa's death throughout the month of December, turned on Nosey Bob: 'Why bungling occurs at executions is a question that is asked over and over again,' the paper said, but unfortunately, the question always seemed to be asked when 'it is too late to set things right. The machinery for the death service is not complicated. It is indeed the simplest that could be used, and such scenes as that which occurred yesterday morning at the execution of

Louisa Collins are a disgrace to the officials concerned ... There can be no excuse for such bungling.'

Lest anyone think the *Herald*'s next step would be toward a campaign for the abolition of capital punishment ... well, no. What the *Herald* wanted to see was an orderly execution: 'Hanging when properly conducted answers ... the purposes of capital punishment better than any other means of death,' the paper said. 'If this form of execution cannot be performed without such revolting experiences as occur here and elsewhere, it should be abandoned for some other which would be more decisive and more certain in its action.'[58]

Nosey Bob did not respond — at least, not in print — to these remonstrances, but the sheriff, Mr Charles Cowper, was offended. He immediately wrote back to the *Herald*, criticising those who had complained about the bungling. As he understood it, a good execution was one that caused 'instantaneous death' and in that regard, Louisa's had been 'most successful'. Still, he had done his best to find out what had gone wrong, and had in fact already submitted a report to the under-secretary for justice, in which blame was laid not at the feet of Nosey Bob but at his assistant, who was employed in turn not by Nosey Bob, but by the sheriff:

> I experienced some difficulty in getting an assistant. The man I had engaged refused to act, and I only succeeded in engaging another at the last moment. He promised to be a most suitable person, and not nervous; but, from some unaccountable reason,

while pulling the bolt he kept his hand on the lever which held the bolt tight. As I am informed that he went with the chief executioner and tested the gallows early in the morning; so that he ought to have understood his work. When the bolt would not answer to his pull, a warder standing near, instead of seeing that he had his hand on the lever and removing it, undoubtedly with the very best intention ran for a small wooden mallet, and gave two or three taps with it … The delay was only that of a few seconds, and might happen under any system.

(Signed) CHARLES COWPER, Sheriff.[59]

Still, it was thought that heads might roll, and they did. On Friday, 11 January 1888, the *Evening News* reported that Sheriff Cowper had found a new assistant hangman, who 'promises to be a most capable person and is not nervous'.[60]

Lest anyone think Nosey Bob ever got any better at his job after all that criticism, the answer is no. To pick an example of a hanging at random: three years after the ghastly execution of Louisa Collins, Nosey made a hash of the execution of the murderer George Martin Walker Archer by creating a noose that was far too large for his head.[61]

The public's contempt for his profession never faded: a short history of Nosey Bob's life, kept at the Waverley Library, says that 'even his pigs [kept in his back yard in Bondi] had to be sold cheaper than the going rate because of his social stigma'.[62]

Nosey Bob retired in May 1904, and spent much of his retirement fishing. In an anecdote likely to terrify local swimmers, he used to set bait just offshore at Bondi, 'and when the shark was hooked, he would wade in, grab it by the tail, fasten a rope to his old horse, and drag it out of the water'.[63] A collection of the largest shark jaws was littered around his garden.

When Nosey died in 1906, the *Newsletter: an Australian Paper for Australian People* reported his death as follows:

Hangman Howard Dead.
A REMARKABLE CHARACTER.
The retired hangman of New South Wales, Robert Howard, died last Saturday at his seaside residence at Bondi, at the ripe age of seventy-four years. He took the lives of about thirty-four persons [actually more than seventy], including Captain Moonlight, the four Mount Rennie boys, and Louisa Collins, so he deserves a well-earned rest from his labours. Howard was formerly a cabman in Sydney, but was not popular, owing to his being minus his nose — a feature which earned him the title of Nosey Bob. Howard was lean and gaunt, and had a most repulsive look. 'Nosey Bob' always did his work for the sheriff well, and was able to retire some time ago with a neat bank balance, and a small pension. Of later years Howard has not been seen about, owing largely to the public scowling at him wherever and whenever he appeared.[64]

Nosey Bob is buried at Waverley Cemetery — Grave 82/83, Church of England Ordinary Section 2 — with his wife, Jane.

Mrs Harrison Lee Cowie (Bessie Lee)

One of the best books you'll ever read — and one of the hardest to find — about the lives of Australian women in the nineteenth century is *One of Australia's Daughters: An Autobiography*.

Published in 1906, it was written by the formidable suffragette and celibate Mrs Harrison Lee. It tells the story of her birth, in June 1860, in Daylesford, Victoria, to Henry Vickery, a butcher, and Emma Susan, née Dungey, who died of consumption in 1868.

Little Bessie was sent to live in Melbourne with relatives who drank and mistreated her. She received little formal schooling but read voraciously, and became a devout Christian.

In 1880, Bessie was introduced to a miner, Harrison Lee, who married her at St Peter's Church of England in Melbourne. The couple lived in Richmond, where Harrison took up shiftwork with the railways, but they were so poor that Bessie decided never to have children (which in turn meant that she stopped having sex, if indeed she ever had sex at all).

By the late 1890s, Bessie had started Sunday school classes for poor children, and was visiting prisoners in gaol. She had also become an accomplished public speaker on the subjects of both women's suffrage and temperance (it must be said that many of the early suffragettes wanted little to do with her, because of her stand on celibacy and strict temperance).

When Bessie's first husband died on 17 January 1908, she was approached, by letter, by a New Zealand farmer, Andrew Cowie, who had heard of her many achievements, understood her stance, and offered his hand. The wedding took place at Winton on 17 November 1908, after which Auckland became the new Mrs Lee Cowie's headquarters for the next twenty years, until the death of Andrew in December 1928 at the age of eighty-two.

Bessie had by then already written her best-known works, including *Marriage and Heredity* (1893) and her autobiography. In June 1930, on medical advice, Bessie moved to Honolulu and, when women were advised to leave Hawaii during World War II, she went to California, where she took up picketing bars as part of the temperance movement. She died at Pasadena on 18 April 1950.

John Berry, of Berry's paddock

May Andrews saw her first box of Rough on Rats at her father's house, 'when we lived at the paddock' — meaning Berry's paddock, near Berry's bone-dust factory.

John Berry wasn't called to testify at Louisa's trial, but it's worth telling something of his story, to illustrate how tough life was for women in nineteenth-century Sydney.

Mr Berry had a daughter, Sarah Jane Wright, who, by the age of just twenty-three, had been both married and widowed. With no other means of support, she moved back home with her father, while dating a local boy named Harry Deeper.

Less than a year later, she was dead. The city coroner, Mr Henry Shiell, presided over the inquest. He found that Sarah Jane had gone to a local chemist to look for a 'potion' to deal with 'a certain situation' (this was code for pregnancy).

Later that day, she began vomiting. Mr Berry, who was still in the dark about the baby, told her to take some castor oil. 'I thought she was suffering from a bilious attack,' he said. 'She complained of inward pains. I had not the slightest suspicion.'

After several days, he called a doctor, who attended to Sarah Jane. He told the coroner that she had spent the last days of her life bathed in perspiration.

'She was perfectly sensible and collected, but in reply to my inquiries would assign no cause for her ailments,' he said. Only later did he discover that Sarah Jane had done more to end the pregnancy than take a potion; somebody had 'used an instrument on her'. The poor girl's womb was perforated, and she died in great agony.[65]

Belltrees

The more things change, the more they stay the same: Belltrees is today the home of the White family, just as it was when Louisa was born.

The importance of Belltrees to Australia's economic development in the nineteenth century can't be overstated: the White brothers came to Australia with just a dream — to develop the merino wool industry — and, after purchasing the land from fellow pastoralist William Charles Wentworth, they succeeded in ways too numerous to count, in the process making themselves, and the nation, rich beyond anyone's wildest dreams.

In the 1950s, the family's key enterprise shifted from sheep. The White family today grazes 5000 head of beef cattle, and most days you'll still find Antony or Peter White, with their hats, dogs and some stockmen, working the station on horseback.

Dr Judy White, the family's matriarch and historian and the mother of five sons and two daughters, is an artist, historian and writer who has produced several books, including a history of Belltrees and a history of horses in the Hunter. Dr White represents the seventh generation of the dynasty to live on the land, and it wasn't all that long ago — 2013, to be exact — that she celebrated her eightieth birthday in the woolshed with hay bales and a bush band.

Dr White tends the family's archives as lovingly as if they were her own children. The property itself is also in remarkable shape: preserved by the family is the homestead (built 1908); the St James Chapel (built 1887); the original colonial homestead (built 1880); the trading store (built 1837) and the magnificent shearing shed (built 1880). Visitors are welcome for overnight stays, booked in advance.

Besides remaining active in Australia's farming industry, three of the White family's descendants — William, Alec and Jasper White — now play polo at a competitive level in England, Argentina, New Zealand and Australia.

Rough on Rats

Sometime after the death of Michael Collins and many others from arsenical poisoning, the *Sydney Morning Herald* began a campaign to have the poison sold only under licence: 'For some time, the colony has been suffering from a sort of epidemic of suicide by the use of Rough on Rats,' it said in one typical article, noting with approval that authorities were moving to 'render it more difficult to get possession of this rat poison'.[66] Indeed, the legislature was considering bringing the sale of Rough on Rats — and other arsenic-based poisons — under the *Poisons Act* of 1876, which would make it more difficult to obtain (such poisons, fly poison papers and other mixtures used to control vermin had deliberately been excised from the original legislation, given the problem of vermin in the colony).

Once under the *Poisons Act*, Rough on Rats would be restricted for sale by anyone other than persons who had a certificate from the Board of Pharmacy, who would in turn only be able to sell it to people who gave their name and occupation. Penalties for the unregulated sale of poisons were as high as fifty pounds.

As ever, there was some opposition to the state meddling in such affairs: libertarian columnists complained that if restrictions were placed on the sale of poisons, where would the government stop? 'Should a law be passed to prohibit the use of a razor by anyone who does not hold a certificate of competency?' asked one such correspondent. 'Should we require the attachment of a label "not to be lighted" to every vessel containing kerosene?' Increasing the list of poisons could 'cause serious inconvenience'.[67]

In June 1889, the *Newcastle Morning Herald & Miners' Advocate* reported restrictions on the sale of Rough on Rats, saying: 'In view of the large number of suicides in New

South Wales from taking Rough on Rats the Government have decided to extend the provisions of the sale of the *Poisons Act* to that preparation.'[68]

Nevertheless, at least until 1892, people were still using it to kill themselves. In May of that year, local newspapers reported 'A Suicide at Parramatta' where a young man, Arthur Cosier, 'on Friday was found suffering from arsenical poisoning at his mother's residence in Parramatta [having] succumbed to the effects of the irritant poison'. He had been found 'lying in bed greatly collapsed, with cold extremities and almost pulseless and occasionally vomiting'. The box was found in his dresser with about half a teaspoon missing.[69]

As for the inventor, the *New York Times* in March 1913 reported the death of Ephraim S Wells at the home of his son, Edgar Wells, in Glenmore, Mercer County, in his seventy-second year.

The Darlinghurst Gaol

The last hanging at Darlinghurst Gaol took place in 1907, and the gaol ceased taking prisoners soon after. In 1914 it became the East Sydney Technical College and many acclaimed artists, including Margaret Olley, John Olsen and Max Dupain, studied there. The building still stands and is today the National Art School. The online history credits Katherine Hepburn and Robert Helpmann with starting a fund to turn the old cells into a dramatic theatrical venue, although 'the impression of the old cells still lingers with traces of the curved stone staircases climbing three stories high, the narrow barred windows, the rough sandstone edges that mark the cells and the solid iron doorway. This makes for a very unique venue for many different types of events'.[70]

Capital Punishment

Louisa Collins was the last woman executed in New South Wales. Hangings of men — and of women in other states — continued for many more decades. The last person executed in New South Wales was the murderer John Trevor Kelly, on 24 August 1939 at Long Bay Gaol. The last woman to be executed in Australia was the murderer Jean Lee in Melbourne in 1951 (Lee became hysterical on the morning of her execution, was sedated, and strapped semi-conscious to a chair for the hanging — just as the plan had been for Louisa). The last person hanged in Australia was Ronald Ryan, at Melbourne's Pentridge Prison in 1967.

New South Wales became one of the first states to formally abolish the death penalty in 1954, with Premier Cahill saying that judges were, at that time, bound to sentence to death some persons convicted of murder, rape and some other crimes, although the Executive Council would then automatically commute the sentence to imprisonment. Under the new legislation, the maximum penalty would not be death but life imprisonment. The opposition, led by Murray Robson, objected on the grounds that women and children were still being 'subject to vicious attacks, including murder' but the Anglican bishop, the Right Reverend WG Hilliard, said: 'I don't think the death penalty is necessarily the strongest deterrent against crime. In days where the death penalty existed for a large number of offences in England, there was far more violent crime than there is today.'[71]

The ineffectiveness of the death penalty as a deterrent to crime is borne out in statistics: capital punishment was abolished in all Australian states in 1985 and, according to the National Homicide Monitoring Program, which has compiled and analysed homicide data since 1989, there has been a steady decrease in homicide since the abolition of the death penalty, with rates now at historic lows.[72]

Afterword

By every account — and there were many — Louisa's first husband, Charles Andrews, was a good man. He had suffered two significant personal tragedies before they married: the death of his first wife, and then of his father, who cut his own throat, yet he never hit the bottle, or became a layabout. Louisa was a handful, yet he stayed married to her for more than two decades. She bore him nine children, seven of whom survived infancy, and although they were at times poor, Charles always did what he could to provide for all of them. Often, the work he had to do was awful: he'd been a butcher, which is dirty and bloody; and a wool washer, which is dirty and back-breaking.

There is not much on the record from his children, but Charles had earned their love and respect. His eldest son, Herbert, was devastated when he heard that his father had died; he could hardly believe that his mother was sitting in their little cottage with another man just months after the burial. Plus, the money was gone. Charles had taken the precaution of insuring his life for a significant sum —

it would not have been cheap to do so — and so provide for his family in the event that some calamity befell him. Another son, Reuben, expressed love for Charles in court: he always worked hard, he said, and he was never drunk.

Louisa's second husband, Michael Collins, started an affair with her when she was married, and very likely married her for her money, which he then spent or gambled away and, by May's account, he hit Louisa's little children with a walking stick, none of which is an excuse for anyone to take his life.

It is entirely possible that Louisa killed both Charles Andrews and Michael Collins. However, in the humble opinion of the author — shared by many good citizens of the colony, and three juries before the final one — the case was not proved beyond a reasonable doubt, and even if it had been so proved the problem is not the verdict, but the sentence. Hanging is barbaric. Some of the people who tried to save Louisa believed her to be guilty. They did not condone her actions. It is not enough to say that the life that Louisa Collins lived was miserable, for it was typical of the lives of many: she was born into poverty; barely educated; got married too early; became pregnant every other year for twenty years; knew a never-ending chain of mouths to feed, floors to scrub, and clothes to wash; and there was no hope — not ever — of breaking that cycle. Then she fell in love, but could not be with her man: she was already married, and divorce was out of the question. But misery is not an excuse for murder, and if murder is what happened here, and misery is the excuse, that is pathetic, and Louisa certainly should have been punished. The point is that she should not have been hanged: capital punishment is ghastly, and more so when guilt is in doubt, and this was one of those cases. The evidence was circumstantial. Louisa's case was hamstrung by a poor quality defence. What if she were innocent? It's a mistake that can never be undone.

A Personal Note

Careful readers will remember where this book started: at Belltrees, where Louisa was born. I'd like to take you back there.

Belltrees was at the time of Louisa's birth managed by the White family: three hard-working brothers who sailed from London to New South Wales to develop the merino sheep industry. They succeeded in ways they possibly never imagined: more than 180,000 sheep were being shorn at Belltrees every year during the first part of the twentieth century, and the wool regularly topped the prices at the London markets. The White brothers became rich beyond anyone's wildest dreams.

Given that my own mother was born in Berlin, and came to Australia only after World War II, I wouldn't have thought that I could draw a line from my own family, through Belltrees, to Louisa and her daughter, May, but I can, which in turn means that you probably can, too.

In my case, it works like this: one of the first James White's seven sons was, predictably enough for the age, also called James White.

He became the Honourable James White MLA, a rich man, able to buy and train great racehorses, among them Chester, which won the VRC Derby and the Melbourne Cup. (It's by-the-by, but James was also a legendary gambler; such was his betting, he rendered many of the colony's bookmakers bankrupt.)

Besides racehorses, James White also built, or purchased, several of Sydney's most famous mansions, including the one known as Cranbrook in Bellevue Hill.

James had no children, and so Cranbrook was sold when he died, after which it briefly became home to the New South Wales governor. (When Australia federated in 1901, it gained a governor general, who had nowhere to live, because Government House at Yarralumla had not yet been built; in an effort to solve this problem, the New South Wales government leased Cranbrook for its governor, and the new governor general moved into the house where Lord Carrington had lived.)

Then, in 1918, Cranbrook became a school — and, in 2010, my son enrolled there.

So it's true what they say: we are all of us connected. If I can draw a line back from my son through Cranbrook to James White and therefore to Louisa, and through her to little May, almost anyone can. Did you or any member of your family ever step foot in Sydney's Town Hall, or at Circular Quay? Have you ever visited the Victorian goldfields? Can you trace an ancestor back to London, to Gallipoli, or to a convict ship? Did anyone in your family ever fly into Sydney airport, on the road past what used to be called Mount Rennie? If so, you too can also draw a line straight back to Louisa Collins — and through her, to her fair-haired, tiny daughter, May.

Depending on how you read it, Louisa's story is either one of passion and murder — or one of poverty, powerlessness, and injustice. It is a personal story, but it is also a political story, about human rights, legal quandaries and moral questions.

To my mind, as well, Louisa's story is that of a young country struggling to find a new identity, not as a penal colony, where convicts were thrashed in the streets, but as a place where people could find freedom — and with that freedom, build lives of hope and happiness.

It is the story of good people trying and failing — and getting up again. It is the story of the last woman hanged in New South Wales — but it is also the story of our shared history, in this young country that we are still building, together. So yes, this is Louisa's story — but it is our story, too.

ENDNOTES

Introduction

1   'The Execution of Louisa Collins', *Sydney Morning Herald* (NSW: 1842–1954), 9 January 1889, p 7, retrieved 5 April 2014 from http://nla.gov.au/nla.news-article13709701.

2   'Central Criminal Court — Tuesday', *Sydney Morning Herald* (NSW: 1842–1954), 7 November 1888, p 6, retrieved 5 April 2014 from http://nla.gov.au/nla.news-article13702629.

3   The birth certificate for May Andrews (NSW Registry of Births, Deaths and Marriages: reference no. 1877/016403) gives her date of birth as 16 October 1877; a letter from Louisa Collins in gaol ('Conduct In Gaol', *Evening News*, 8 January 1889, p 3, retrieved 18 May 2014 from http://nla.gov.au/nla.news-article108789486) gives her daughter's date of birth as 17 October 1877. If the birth certificate is taken as correct, and the first trial of Louisa Collins was held in August 1888, May would still have been ten, and only by the time of the second trial would she have turned eleven.

Chapter 1

1   To give just two examples of the confusion surrounding Louisa's age: the record for Louisa Collins in the Gaol Description and Entrance Book for Darlinghurst Gaol (State Records NSW: NRS 2138; [3/6050], roll 5103, photograph 84) gives her date of birth as 1849; the birth certificate of her tenth-born child, William (John) Collins (NSW Registry of Births, Deaths and Marriages: no. 1888/011997) gives her age, in November 1887, as thirty, when she was actually already forty; her death certificate (Louisa Collins file, City of Botany Bay Library, barcode reference: 00894400) gives her age at her first marriage as fourteen, when she was in fact eighteen.

2 NSW Registry of Births, Deaths and Marriages: Louisa Hall, birth certificate no. V18472606 32A (1847).

3 State Records NSW: Principal Superintendent of Convicts; NRS 12212, Settler and Convict Lists, 1787–1834; entry for Henry Hall, age nineteen, date of conviction 28 June 1831; vessel *Asia*; [4/4513] and [4/4106] roll 89, class and piece No. HO11/8, p 179 (92).

4 State Records NSW: Principal Superintendent of Convicts; NRS 12212, Registers of Convicts' Applications to Marry, 1826–1851; [4/4513 p 302].

5 J. White, *The White Family of Belltrees*, Seven Mile Press, Sydney, 1981.

6 Heritage Australia Publishing, 'Scone', Australian Heritage website, retrieved 22 March 2014 from http://www.heritageaustralia.com.au/ search.php?state=NSW&region=99&view=501#a.

7 Birth certificates for children of Henry Hall and Catherine Hall show six daughters and one son born between 1843 and 1855. Source: NSW Registry of Births, Deaths and Marriages.

8 'The Botany Murder Case', *Evening News* (Sydney, NSW: 1869–1931), 8 January 1889, p 3, retrieved 22 March 2014 from http://nla. gov.au/nla.news-article108789492.

9 Charles Andrews arrived in Australia in June 1848 aged fifteen, with his father Richard, mother Charlotte, and six siblings. Source: NSW Assisted Passenger List, 'Canton', arrived Sydney 12 June 1848, retrieved from search.ancestry.com.au/browse/print_u.apx?dbid=12 04&iid=IMAUS1787_081405-0475&pid=93457; also at SRNSW: [4/4786], reel 2135.

10 ibid.

11 'The Botany Murder Case', *Evening News*, 8 January 1889, p 3.

12 When Charles Andrews married Louisa Hall, his status was listed as bachelor; however, many of the reporters who covered Louisa's case in 1888 insist that he was widowed when they met. See, for example: 'The Botany Murder Case', *Evening News*, 8 January 1889, p 3.
An exhaustive search of the NSW Registry of Births, Deaths and Marriages found no certificate of marriage for Charles's first wife; no newspaper ever reported her first name or how she died; there is no reference to any child sired by Charles before his marriage to Louisa.

13 'Metropolitan District Court', *The Sydney Morning Herald* (NSW: 1842–1954), 23 August 1860, p 4, retrieved 9 May 2014 from http:// nla.gov.au/nla.news-article13044809.

14 'Coroner's Inquest', *Empire* (Sydney, NSW: 1850–1875), 31 August
    1860, p 5, retrieved 9 May 2014 from http://nla.gov.au/nla.news-
    article60497325.

15 'The Botany Murder Case', *Evening News*, 8 January 1889, p 3.

16 NSW Registry of Births, Deaths and Marriages: Louisa Hall and
    Charles Andrews, marriage certificate no. 1865/001940.

17 'Muswellbrook', *The Maitland Mercury and Hunter River General
    Advertiser* (NSW: 1843–1893), 30 December 1876, p 9, retrieved 9
    May 2014 from http://nla.gov.au/nla.news-article18814144.

18 'Insolvency Proceedings', *The Maitland Mercury and Hunter
    River General Advertiser* (NSW: 1843–1893), 28 February 1878,
    p 4, retrieved 9 May 2014 from http://nla.gov.au/nla.news-
    article18827028.

19 'The Botany Murder Case', *Evening News*, 8 January 1889, p 3.

20 A Painter, 'The Hanging of Michael Magee', Professional Historians'
    Association website, retrieved 9 May 2014 from http://www.
    sahistorians.org.au/175/chronology/april/2-may-1838-the-hanging-
    of-michael-magee.shtml.

21 'Horrible Occurrence', *Colonial Times* (Hobart, Tas: 1828–1857), 5
    June 1838, p 6, retrieved 18 May 2014 from http://nla.gov.au/nla.
    news-article8748723.

22 ibid.

Chapter 2

1 NSW Registry of Births, Deaths and Marriages: Herbert Andrews,
    birth certificate no. 8316/1867.

2 NSW Registry of Births, Deaths and Marriages: Ernest Andrews,
    death certificate no. 5398/1872.

3 NSW Registry of Births, Deaths and Marriages: Reuben
    Andrews, birth certificate no. 13888/1871; Arthur Andrews, birth
    certificate no. 14890/1873; Frederick Andrews, birth certificate
    no. 15591/1875; May Andrews, birth certificate no. 16403/1877.

4 'The Botany Murder Case', *Evening News*, 8 January 1889, p 3.

5 No birth certificate for Louisa's son Edwin Andrews can be found,
    but he was admitted to the Benevolent Society of New South Wales
    on 27 July 1888, aged eight. A birth certificate (no. 8395/1881, NSW
    Registry of Births, Deaths and Marriages) exists for a son, David
    Andrews, who died the same year (death certificate no. 4148/1881,

NSW Registry of Births, Deaths and Marriages). A birth certificate also exists (no. 9462/1883, NSW Registry of Births, Deaths and Marriages) for Louisa's last child with Charles, the baby Charles Andrews.

6   'The Botany Murder Case', *Evening News*, 8 January 1889, p 3.

7   'An Early Sydney Zoo', *Sydney Morning Herald* (NSW: 1842–1954), 6 July 1935, p 11, retrieved 6 April 2014 from http://nla.gov.au/nla. news-article17194179.

8   'The Botany Murder', *Reporter and Illawarra Journal* (NSW: 1887–1894), 12 January 1889, p 4, retrieved 22 March 2014 from http:// nla.gov.au/nla.news-article106430237.

9   ibid.

10   ibid.

11   ibid.

12   ibid.

13   'Suspicious Deaths at Botany' *Evening News* (Sydney, NSW: 1869–1931), 3 August 1888, p 5, retrieved 18 May 2014 from http:// nla.gov.au/nla.news-article107328432.

14   'Suspicious Deaths at Botany', *Evening News* (Sydney, NSW: 1869–1931), 4 August 1888, p 4, retrieved from http://nla.gov.au/ nla.news-article107322208.

15   ibid.

16   'The Botany Murder Case', *Evening News*, 8 January 1889, p 3.

17   ibid.

18   Statement of Dr Thomas Martin, Louisa Collins file, City of Botany Bay Library, barcode 00894400, disc reference nos. DSCF0848–0851

19   Statements of Charles Sayers and Constable Jeffes, Louisa Collins file, City of Botany Bay Library, barcode 00894400, disc reference nos. DSCF0852 and DSCF0875.

20   Statement of Mrs Margaret Collis, Louisa Collins file, City of Botany Bay Library, barcode 00894400, disc reference no. DSCF1188.

21   ibid.

22   Wage comparisons are notoriously tricky, but the State Library of Victoria's Victorian Year Books (accessed at http://guides.slv.vic.gov. au/content.php?pid=14258&sid=95522) put average annual wages in 1903 at 157 pounds, meaning Charles's 200-pound life insurance

payment was equal to something like two years' pay. However, one pound in 1900 is also considered to be worth around $110 today, meaning Charles's insurance could also be calculated at around $22,000 in today's money.

23 Statement of Mr Henry Kneller, Louisa Collins file, City of Botany Bay Library, barcode 00894400, disc reference no. DSCF0976.

24 ibid.

25 Statement of Mrs Mary Law, Louisa Collins file, City of Botany Bay Library, barcode 00894400, disc reference no. DSCF0891.

26 Statement of Reuben Andrews, Louisa Collins file, City of Botany Bay Library, barcode 00894400, disc reference no. DSCF0973.

27 ibid.

28 Statement of Mrs Ellen Price, Louisa Collins file, City of Botany Bay Library, barcode 00894400, disc reference nos. DSCF0978–0979.

29 'The Botany Murder Case', *Evening News*, 8 January 1889, p 3.

30 ibid.

31 Statement of Dr Thomas Martin, disc reference nos. DSCF0848–0850.

32 K Grant, 'Prolific Inventor: Moses Doolittle Wells (1798–1878) of Morgantown, WV', ancestry.com message boards, retrieved 7 May 2014 from http://boards.ancestry.com/localities.northam.usa.states. westvirginia.counties.monongalia/4876.1.2.1/mb.ashx.

33 'Advertising', *The Maitland Mercury and Hunter River General Advertiser*, 17 December 1887, supplement, p 4, retrieved 9 February 2014 from http://nla.gov.au/nla.news-article18957141 (NSW: 1843–1893).

34 ES Wells/*Evening Journal*, 'Rough On Rats' advertisement, 1870–1890, East Carolina University digital collection, call no. 12.1.28.2, retrieved 7 May 2014 from https://digital.lib.ecu.edu/20792.

35 R Ludacer, 'Rough On Rats', Box Vox, 7 Sept 2010, retrieved 7 May 2014 from http://www.beachpackagingdesign.com/wp/2010/09/ rough-on-rats.html.

36 'Suicide in Tully', *Cortland County Democrat*, 12 May 1882, retrieved on 7 May 2014 from http://www.usgenweb.info/nycortland/vitals/ d1882.htm.

37 Author unknown, 'Willie and three other brats', Ruthless Rhymes website, retrieved 7 May 2014 from http://ruthlessrhymes.com/ little_willies/little-willie-poems/willie-and-three-other-brats.

38 'Advertising', *Burra Record* (SA: 1878–1954), 21 March 1884, p 3, retrieved 10 May 2014 from http://nla.gov.au/nla.news-article36010947.

39 'Peculiar Case of Poisoning', *South Australian Advertiser* (Adelaide, SA: 1858–1889), 25 November 1886, p 5, retrieved 26 February 2014 from http://nla.gov.au/nla.news-article37163072.

40 'The Poisoning Case', *Evening News* (Sydney, NSW: 1869–1931), 29 November 1886, p 7, retrieved 7 May 2014 from http://nla.gov.au/nla.news-article107319792.

41 'Rough on Rats', *Evening News* (Sydney, NSW: 1869–1931), 24 September 1887, p 5, retrieved 6 May 2014 from http://nla.gov.au/nla.news-article108008545.

42 'Coroner's Inquest', *The Sydney Morning Herald* (NSW: 1842-1954), 24 September 1887, p 8, retrieved 17 May 2014 from http://nla.gov.au/nla.news-article13659948.

43 ibid.

44 'The Botany Mystery', *The Sydney Morning Herald*, 4 August 1888, p 8, retrieved 10 May 2014 from http://nla.gov.au/nla.news-article28340876.

Chapter 3

1 'The Botany Murder Case', 8 January 1889, *Evening News*, p 3.

2 ibid.

3 Statement of Mrs Ellen Price, disc reference no. DSCF0979.

4 Statement of May Andrews, Louisa Collins pamphlet and file (disc), City of Botany Bay Library, barcode 00894400, disc reference no. DSCF0974.

5 Unsigned statement, Louisa Collins file, City of Botany Bay Library, barcode 00894400, disc reference no. DSCF1287.

6 Statement of Mr William Burnet, Louisa Collins file, City of Botany Bay Library, barcode 00894400, disc reference no. DSCF0982.

7 'The Botany Murder Case', 8 January 1889, *Evening News*, p 3.

8 ibid.

9 ibid.

10 ibid.

11 ibid.

12   'The Mysterious Death at Botany', *The Sydney Morning Herald*
     (NSW: 1842–1954), 14 July 1888, p 10, retrieved 27 January 2014
     from http://nla.gov.au/nla.news-article13690913.

13   Statement of Louisa Collins, Louisa Collins file, City of Botany Bay
     Library, barcode 00894400, disc reference nos. DSCF0983–1003.

14   'Central Criminal Court — Friday', *The Sydney Morning Herald*
     (NSW: 1842–1954), 8 December 1888, p 16, retrieved 18 May 2014
     from http://nla.gov.au/nla.news-article13706592.

15   Statement of Constable Jeffes, Louisa Collins file, City of Botany Bay
     Library, barcode 00894400, disc reference nos. DSCF0860–0868.

16   Statement of Dr GA Marshall, Louisa Collins file, City of Botany
     Bay Library, barcode 00894400, disc reference nos. DSCF0831–
     0847.

17   ibid.

18   ibid.

19   Statement of Dr GA Marshall, disc reference nos. DSCF0831–
     0847; also described as 'engastro-duodenal catarrh' in 'Coroner's
     Inquests', *The Sydney Morning Herald* (NSW: 1842–1954), 11 July
     1888, p 7, retrieved 10 May 2014 from http://nla.gov.au/nla.news-
     article28340956.

20   Statement of Dr GA Marshall, disc reference nos. DSCF0831–0847.

21   ibid.

22   ibid.

23   ibid.

24   Statement of Mrs Ellen Pettit, , disc reference no. DSCF1214.

25   Sdatement of Dr GA Marshall, disc reference nos. DSCF0831–
     0847.

26   Statement of Mrs Ellen Pettit, disc reference no. DSCF1215.

27   Statement of Senior Constable Sherwood, Louisa Collins file,
     City of Botany Bay Library, barcode 00894400, disc reference nos.
     DSCF1120–1137.

Chapter 4

1   'Obituary', *Freeman's Journal* (Sydney, NSW: 1850–1932), 9 August
     1902, p 19, retrieved 3 February 2014 from http://nla.gov.au/nla.
     news-article111067166; 'The Miller's Point Tragedy', *Wagga Wagga
     Advertiser* (NSW: 1875–1910), 8 July 1893, p 2, retrieved 3 February
     2014 from http://nla.gov.au/nla.news-article101832862.

2   Statement of Dr Milford, Louisa Collins file, City of Botany Bay Library, barcode 00894400, disc reference no. DSCF1076–1083.

3   'Central Criminal Court — Monday', *The Sydney Morning Herald* (NSW: 1842–1954), 7 August 1888, p 9, retrieved 5 April 2014 from http://nla.gov.au/nla.news-article13692846.

4   State Records NSW: Central Criminal Court Papers, July 1888, Inquest No. 786, *Regina v Louisa Collins* [9/6758 6-149].

5   ibid.

6   Hyde Park Barracks is today inscribed on UNESCO's World Heritage list, along with ten other key convict sites around Australia.

7   F Starr, 'A Striking Impression', Hyde Park Barracks Museum website, 3 December 2013, retrieved 7 May 2014 from http://sydneylivingmuseums.com.au/stories/striking-impression.

8   R Shiell and D Anderson, 'Henry Shiell (1827–1889)', Shiell Genealogy website, last revised May 2005, retrieved 7 May 2014 from http://www.alangullette.com/lit/shiel/family/Shiell_Henry.htm.

9   State Records NSW: Colonial Secretary's correspondence; [5/59308] letter from the widow Mrs Shiell to Lord Carrington.

10   There would not today be a jury at a coronial inquest. An inquest, as currently understood, is where the coroner alone decides both the likely cause of death and whether charges should be laid against any known person.

11   State Records NSW: Central Criminal Court Papers, July 1888, Inquest No. 786, *Regina v Louisa Collins* [9/6758 6-149].

12   HHG McKern, 'Hamlet, William Mogford (1850–1931)', *Australian Dictionary of Biography*, National Centre of Biography, Australian National University, Canberra, 2005, retrieved 2 March 2014 from http://adb.anu.edu.au/biography/hamlet-william-mogford-12962/text23429.

13   HJ Tompkins, *With Swag and Billy: Tramps by Bridle Paths and the Open Road: A Guide to Walking Trips in Tourist Districts of New South Wales* with an introduction by William M Hamlet, Government Tourist Bureau, Intelligence Department, Sydney, 1906.

14   'From Sydney to Melbourne', *Barrier Miner* (Broken Hill, NSW: 1888–1954), 22 May 1912, p 8, retrieved 21 February 2014 from http://nla.gov.au/nla.news-article45194998.

15   State Records NSW: Central Criminal Court Papers, July 1888, Inquest No. 786, *Regina v Louisa Collins* [9/6758 6-149].

16   'The Botany Murderess', *Evening News* (Sydney, NSW: 1869–1931), 2 January 1889, p 5, retrieved 2 March 2014 from http://nla.gov.au/nla.news-article108788990.

17   'Coroner's Inquests — The Botany Poisoning Case', *The Sydney Morning Herald* (NSW: 1842–1954), 18 July 1888, p 7, retrieved 18 May 2014 from http://nla.gov.au/nla.news-article13691315.

18   Statement of Mr William Hamlet, Louisa Collins file, City of Botany Bay Library, barcode 00894400, disc reference no. DSCF1105–1111.

19   ibid.

20   State Records NSW: Central Criminal Court Papers, July 1888, Inquest No. 786, *Regina v Louisa Collins* [9/6758 6-149].

21   ibid.

22   Statement of Dr Thomas Martin, disc reference nos. DSCF1114–1119.

23   ibid.

24   ibid., disc reference no. DSCF1118.

25   State Records NSW: Central Criminal Court Papers, July 1888, Inquest No. 786, *Regina v Louisa Collins* [9/6758 6-149].

26   Statement of Senior Constable Sherwood, disc reference no. DSCF1137.

27   ibid., disc reference no. DSCF1133

28   ibid., disc reference no. DSCF1134

29   'The Botany Mystery', *The Richmond River Herald and Northern Districts Advertiser* (NSW: 1886–1942), 3 August 1888, p 3, retrieved 10 May 2014, from http://nla.gov.au/nla.news-article127721878.

30   Statement of Louisa Collins, disc reference no. DSCF0983–DSCF1003.

31   ibid.

32   ibid.

33   ibid.

34   ibid.

35   ibid.

36   Statement of Edward William Pople, Louisa Collins file, City of Botany Bay Library, barcode 00894400, disc reference no. DSCF0892.

37 Statement of Louisa Collins, disc reference nos. DSCF0983–DSCF1003.

38 'The Poisoning Case in Sydney', *South Australian Weekly Chronicle* (Adelaide, SA: 1881–1889), 4 August 1888, p 12, retrieved 27 February 2014 from http://nla.gov.au/nla.news-article94761999.

39 'The Botany Poisoning Case', *The Sydney Morning Herald* (NSW: 1842–1954), 27 July 1888, p 4, retrieved 6 April 2014 from http://nla.gov.au/nla.news-article13692088.

40 Statement of Senior Constable Sherwood, disc reference no. DSCF1137.

41 ibid.

42 'The Botany Poisoning Case', *The Sydney Morning Herald*, 27 July 1888, p 4.

43 ibid.

Chapter 5

1 Statement of Mr William Hamlet, disc reference no. DSCF1041.

2 'Review', *The Sydney Morning Herald* (NSW: 1842–1954), 12 February 1889, p 10, retrieved 13 February 2014 from http://nla.gov.au/nla.news-article13713846.

3 'Suspicious Deaths at Botany', *Evening News,* 3 August 1888, p 5.

4 'The Mysterious Death at Botany', *Burrowa News* (NSW: 1874–1951), 27 July 1888, p 4, retrieved 27 February 2014 from http://nla.gov.au/nla.news-article101611405.

5 'The Botany Mystery', *The Sydney Morning Herald*, 4 August 1888 p 8.

6 'The Botany Mystery', *The Sydney Morning Herald* (NSW: 1842–1954), 6 August 1888, p 9, retrieved 5 April 2014 from http://nla.gov.au/nla.news-article28344424.

7 ibid.

8 ibid.

Chapter 6

1 KK Mcnab, 'Green, Alexander (1802—?)', *Australian Dictionary of Biography*, National Centre of Biography, Australian National University, Canberra, 2005, retrieved 5 April 2014 from http://adb.anu.edu.au/biography/green-alexander-12949/text23403.

2   Author unknown, 'Robert "Nosey Bob" Howard (1832–1906)',
     retrieved 7 May 2014 from http://www.waverley.nsw.gov.au/__data/
     assets/pdf_file/0020/8732/Robert.pdf.

3   PA Norrie, 'An analysis of the causes of death in Darlinghurst
     Gaol 1867–1914 and the fate of the homeless in nineteenth-
     century Sydney', MA thesis, University of Sydney, 2007,
     retrieved 7 May 2014 from http://ses.library.usyd.edu.au/
     bitstream/2123/1862/6/02whole.pdf.

4   'Nosey Bob', *Bowral Free Press and Berrima District Intelligence*
     (NSW: 1884–1901), 11 March 1899, p 4, retrieved 7 May 2014 from
     http://nla.gov.au/nla.news-article124504890.

5   GP Walsh, 'Governor Jimmy (1875–1901)', *Australian Dictionary
     of Biography*, National Centre of Biography, Australian National
     University, Canberra, 1983, retrieved 7 May 2014 from http://adb.
     anu.edu.au/biography/governor-jimmy-6439.

6   Author unknown, 'Robert "Nosey Bob" Howard (1832–1906)'.

7   'A Horrible Outrage', *Evening News* (Sydney, NSW: 1869–1931), 10
     September 1886, p, 4, retrieved 5 April 2014 from http://nla.gov.au/
     nla.news-article107320162.

8   Cited in T Gilling, 'Frenzy: The Story of the Mount Rennie
     Outrage', DCA thesis, University of Technology, Sydney, 2012,
     retrieved 7 May 2014 from http://epress.lib.uts.edu.au/research/
     bitstream/handle/10453/21806/02whole.pdf?sequence=2.

9   'The Hanging Judge', *The San Francisco Call*, 17 February 1896,
     p 8, retrieved 7 May 2014 from http://cdnc.ucr.edu/cgi-bin/
     cdnc?a=d&d=SFC18960217.2.98.

10   'The Mount Rennie Outrage Case', *Maitland Mercury and Hunter
     River General Advertiser* (NSW: 1843–1893), 2 December 1886, p 4,
     retrieved 5 April 2014 from http://nla.gov.au/nla.news-page156808.

11   ibid.

12   JF Archibald, *Evening News*, 10 June 1879, p 290, cited in
     T Gilling, 'Frenzy: The Story of the Mount Rennie Outrage'; 'The
     Blackfellow Executed', *Evening News* (Sydney, NSW: 1869-1931), 10
     June 1879, p 3, retrieved 5 May 2014 http://nla.gov.au/nla.news-
     article107148311.

13   JF Archibald, 'Wantabadgery Bushrangers', *Bulletin*, 31 January
     1880, p 5, cited in D Myton, 'J.F. Archibald, the *Bulletin*, and the
     Spirit of Australia', *Limina*, vol. 7, 2001, p 104.

14 'The Mount Rennie Outrage', *The Sydney Morning Herald* (NSW: 1842–1954), 8 January 1887, p 8, retrieved 5 April 2014 from http://nla.gov.au/nla.news-article28353273.

15 'Inter-Colonial', *West Australian* (Perth, WA: 1879–1954), 8 January 1887, p 3, retrieved 5 April 2014 from http://nla.gov.au/nla.news-article3764718.

16 'Execution Of A Woman', *Evening News* (Sydney, NSW: 1869–1931), 20 December 1888, p 5, retrieved 24 May 2014 from http://nla.gov.au/nla.news-article108109912; 'Condemned Mother's Final Act', *The Goulburn Post*, 21 October 2001, retrieved 24 May 2013, from http://www.goulburnpost.com.au/story/953492/condemned-mothers-final-act/.

17 'Died in Gaol', *Evening News* (Sydney, NSW: 1869–1931), 21 September 1885, p 4, retrieved 13 May 2014, from http://nla.gov.au/nla.news-article111340978.

Chapter 7

1 'Then Came The Trials' *Evening News* (Sydney, NSW: 1869–1931), 8 January 1889, p 3, retrieved 10 May 2014, from http://nla.gov.au/nla.news-article108789490.

2 'Central Criminal Court — Monday', *The Sydney Morning Herald*, 7 August 1888, p 9.

3 'Suspicious Deaths at Botany', *Evening News* (Sydney, NSW: 1869–1931), 8 August 1888, p 5, retrieved 6 April 2014 from http://nla.gov.au/nla.news-article107325771.

4 State Records NSW: NRS 2138, Photographic Description Books [Darlinghurst Gaol]; [3/6050 p 84] Louisa Collins, reel 5103.

5 'Suspicious Deaths at Botany', *Evening News*, 8 August 1888, p 5.

6 'The Botany Murderess', *Evening News* (Sydney, NSW: 1869–1931), 20 December 1888, p 5, retrieved 6 April 2014 from http://nla.gov.au/nla.news-article108109917.

7 ibid.

8 P Besomo, *A Brief History of the Most Famous Female Poisoners, Borgia Family etc: How They Killed and What They Killed With: With Phrenological and Physiognomical Sketch of Mrs Louisa Collins the Botany murderess*, Sydney, c. 1888.

9 GD Woods, *A History of Criminal Law in New South Wales*, Federation Press, Sydney, 2002, p 9; I Barker, 'Sorely Tried —

Democracy and Trial by Jury in New South Wales', paper presented to the Francis Forbes Society for Australian Legal History, 2001, retrieved 6 April 2014 from http://www.forbessociety.org.au/documents/trial_jury.pdf.

10   State Records Authority of NSW, 'William John Foster QC', State Records NSW website, retrieved 6 April 2014 from http://search.records.nsw.gov.au/persons/18.

11   *New South Wales Law Almanac*, NSW Government Printer, Sydney, 1888, retrieved 6 April 2014 from http://www.lawalmanacs.info/almanacs/nsw-law-almanac-1888.pdf?1227110993

12   'Central Criminal Court — Monday', *The Sydney Morning Herald*, 7 August 1888, p 9.

13   'The Lusk Case', *Wagga Wagga Advertiser* (NSW: 1875–1910), 24 March 1894, p 2, retrieved 6 April 2014 from http://nla.gov.au/nla.news-article101797947.

14   'Extracts from the Murderess's Letters', *Clarence and Richmond Examiner and New England Advertiser* (Grafton, NSW: 1859–1889), 12 January 1889, p 8, retrieved 6 May 2014 from http://nla.gov.au/nla.news-article62108720.

15   ibid.

16   ibid.

17   'Suspicious Deaths at Botany', *Evening News* (Sydney, NSW: 1869–1931), 7 August 1888, p 6, retrieved 6 April 2014 from http://nla.gov.au/nla.news-article107329160.

18   State Records NSW: Central Criminal Court Papers, July 1888, Inquest No. 786, *Regina v Louisa Collins* [9/6758 6-149].

19   'Central Criminal Court — Monday', *The Sydney Morning Herald*, 7 August 1888, p 9.

20   'Central Criminal Court — Tuesday', *The Sydney Morning Herald* (NSW: 1842–1954), 8 August 1888, p 4, retrieved 6 May 2014 from http://nla.gov.au/nla.news-article13692943.

21   The rules of evidence in 1888 were different; jurors could ask questions of the witnesses. That would not be permitted in court today.

22   Statement of Mr William Hamlet, disc reference no. DSCF1041.

23   Statement of Constable Jeffes, disc reference nos. DSCF0860–0868.

24   ibid.

25   ibid.

26   M Rutledge, 'Foster, William John (1831–1909)', *Australian Dictionary of Biography*, National Centre of Biography, Australian National University, Canberra, 1972, retrieved 7 May 2014 from http://adb.anu.edu.au/biography/foster-william-john-3560/text5505.

27   'The Charge Of Poisoning Against A Wife', *The South Australian Advertiser* (Adelaide, SA: 1858–1889), 8 August 1888, p 5, retrieved 13 May 2014 from http://nla.gov.au/nla.news-article36436279.

28   Statement of May Andrews, disc reference no. DSCF0884. (This statement begins with the words: 'I am eleven years old.' However, May's birth certificate gives her date of birth as 16 October 1877, which would mean that she was, at the time of the August 1888 trial, still only ten, going on eleven.)

29   State Records NSW: NRS 5968, Judges' Notebooks; [2/4212-15] Justice Foster.

30   The fact that May could read is somewhat, if not entirely, surprising: by the early 1890s, primary education was technically compulsory; most people could read. The fact that she did so is made plain in her statement (disc reference no. DSCF0886). This account of May's evidence, repeated in various forms at all four trials, is compiled from judges' notebooks; May's own statements (disc reference nos. DS0884–0886; 0962; 1219); and contemporaneous newspaper reports of the trial.

31   'Central Criminal Court — Tuesday', *The Sydney Morning Herald*, 8 August 1888, p 4.

32   ibid.

33   ibid.

34   ibid.

35   ibid.

36   'Suspicious Deaths at Botany', *Evening News*, 8 August 1888, p 5.

37   ibid.

38   ibid

39   'Central Criminal Court — Wednesday', *The Sydney Morning Herald* (NSW: 1842–1954), 9 August 1888, p 3, retrieved 6 May 2014 from http://nla.gov.au/nla.news-article13693041.

40   ibid.

41   'Suspicious Deaths at Botany', *Evening News*, 8 August 1888, p 5.

42   'Central Criminal Court — Wednesday', *The Sydney Morning Herald*, 9 August 1888, p 3.

43 ibid.

44 ibid.

45 'Suspicious Deaths at Botany', *Evening News* (Sydney, NSW: 1869–1931), 9 August 1888, p 6, retrieved 6 April 2014 from http://nla.gov.au/nla.news-article107329795.

46 ibid.

47 ibid.

48 'Central Criminal Court — Wednesday', *The Sydney Morning Herald*, 9 August 1888, p 3.

49 'Suspicious Deaths at Botany', *Evening News*, 9 August 1888, p 5.

50 ibid.

Chapter 8

1 'Then Came The Trials', *Evening News*, 8 January 1889, p 3.

2 Retrieved from http://www.dailytelegraph.com.au/news/breaking-news/third-trial-expected-over-wa-womans-death/story-fni0xqi3-1226756085227.

3 F Norton and L Mellor, 'Jury discharged after not reaching verdict on former Bundaberg-based surgeon Jayant Patel', ABC News website, 15 October 2013, retrieved 10 May 2014 from http://www.abc.net.au/news/2013-10-15/jury-discharge-after-not-reaching-verdict-on-patel/5016732.

4 'Suspicious Deaths at Botany', *Evening News* (Sydney, NSW: 1869–1931), 16 August 1888, p 6, retrieved 10 May 2014 from http://nla.gov.au/nla.news-article107322857.

5 ibid.

6 State Records NSW: Colonial Secretary; NRS 905, Letters Received 1826–1982; items [1/2886] letter no. 88/942 and [1/2715] letter no. 88/9300.

7 Louisa Collins file, City of Botany Bay Library, barcode: 00894400.

8 ibid.

9 ibid.

10 Statement of Senior Constable Sherwood, disc reference no. DSCF1213.

11 ibid.

12 Statement of Mrs Margaret Collis, disc reference no. DSCF1216.

13 Statement of Senior Constable Sherwood, disc reference no. DSCF1213.

14   ibid.

15   ibid.

16   M Dunn, 'Windeyer, William Charles', Dictionary of Sydney website, 2012, retrieved 7 May 2014 from http://dictionaryofsydney. org/entry/windeyer_william_charles

17   ibid.

18   GFJ Bergman, 'Cohen, Henry Emanuel (1840–1912)', *Australian Dictionary of Biography*, National Centre of Biography, Australian National University, Canberra, 1969, retrieved 7 May 2014 from http://adb.anu.edu.au/biography/cohen-henry-emanuel-3242/ text4895.

19   State Records NSW: NRS 5968, Judges' Notebooks; [2/7366] Justice Windeyer.

20   Statement of May Andrews, disc reference no. DSCF0885–0886.

21   ibid., disc reference no. DSCF1219.

22   'The Alleged Murders at Botany', *Evening News* (Sydney, NSW: 1869–1931), 7 November 1888, p 3, retrieved 10 May 2014 from http://nla.gov.au/nla.news-article108111946.

23   'Brevities', *Evening News* (Sydney, NSW: 1869–1931), 7 November 1888, p 6, retrieved 6 May 2014 from http://nla.gov.au/nla.news-article108111928.

24   The widespread use of arsenic in dip solutions for cattle-tick and sheep-lice control was examined by Australian authorities as recently as 2009, when a report, titled 'Management of Former Sheep Dip Sites', conducted for the ACT Legislative Assembly (retrieved from http://www.audit.act.gov.au/auditreports/reports1996/contam.pdf) found that, while arsenic-based cattle dips were removed from the market in June 1983 and the use of arsenic-based products for sheep and cattle was banned in January 1987, poisonings still occur — as in, they occur to this day because the arsenic-based products were not always disposed of properly. The report found that arsenic poisoning occurs when animals ingest the chemical or absorb it through the skin and, in areas where old arsenical dips have been pumped out, the soil still contains arsenic in a form that can be absorbed by animals (rain coupled with disturbance of the soil may produce a very attractive arsenic brew for any stock which have access, the report says).

25 'Lice And Ticks In Sheep', *Kerang Times and Swan Hill Gazette* (Vic: 1877–1889), 14 December 1886, p 4, retrieved May 10 2014 from http://nla.gov.au/nla.news-article65598229.

26 'Dipping for Ticks', *Australasian* (Melbourne, Vic: 1864–1946), 3 September 1881, p 24, retrieved 18 February 2014 from http://nla.gov.au/nla.news-article138070412.

27 'Advertising', *Australasian* (Melbourne, Vic: 1864–1946), 14 January 1882, p 4, retrieved 18 February 2014 from http://nla.gov.au/nla.news-article138074712.

28 'Central Criminal Court — Monday', *The Sydney Morning Herald* (NSW: 1842–1954), 6 November 1888, p 11, retrieved 19 May 2014 from http://nla.gov.au/nla.news-article13702502.

29 ibid.

30 'Central Criminal Court — Tuesday', *The Sydney Morning Herald*, 7 November 1888, p 6.

31 'Central Criminal Court — Wednesday', *The Sydney Morning Herald* (NSW: 1842–1954), 8 November 1888, p 5, retrieved 11 May 2014 from http://nla.gov.au/nla.news-article13702734.

32 ibid.

33 ibid.

34 ibid.

35 ibid.

36 ibid.

37 ibid.

38 ibid.

39 'The Alleged Botany Murders', *Evening News* (Sydney, NSW: 1869–1931), 8 November 1888, p 3, retrieved 14 February 2014 from http://nla.gov.au/nla.news-article108109956.

40 ibid.

41 State Records NSW: Colonial Secretary; NRS 906, Special Bundles, 1826–1982; [4/895.1 part] Louisa Collins — petitions for remission of death sentence, 1889.

42 State Records NSW: NRS 596; [2/7366].

43 'The Alleged Botany Murders', *Evening News*, 8 November 1888, p 3.

44 ibid.

45 State Records NSW: NRS 906; [4/895.1]

46   Louisa Collins, letter, Louisa Collins file, City of Botany Bay
      Library, barcode 00894400, disc reference no.

47   'Execution of the Man Hewart, Disgraceful Bungling', *Balmain
      Observer and Western Suburbs Advertiser* (NSW: 1884–1907), 15
      September 1888, p 6, retrieved 14 February 2014 from http://nla.
      gov.au/nla.news-article132303803.

48   ibid.

49   ibid.

Chapter 9

1   'The Botany Murder Case', *Evening News*, 8 January 1889, p 3.

2   'Charge of Husband Murder' *Goulburn Evening Penny Post* (NSW:
      1881–1940), 20 November 1888, p 2, retrieved May 13 2014, from
      http://nla.gov.au/nla.news-article98450405.

3   State Records NSW: Central Criminal Court Papers, July 1888,
      Inquest No. 786, *Regina v Louisa Collins* [9/6758 6-149].

4   KG Allars, 'Innes, Sir Joseph George (1834–1896)', *Australian
      Dictionary of Biography*, National Centre of Biography, Australian
      National University, Canberra, 1972, retrieved 6 April 2014 from
      http://adb.anu.edu.au/biography/innes-sir-joseph-george-3836/
      text6091.

5   'The Alleged Botany Murders', *Evening News* (Sydney, NSW:
      1869–1931), 21 November 1888, p 6, retrieved 18 May 2014 from
      http://nla.gov.au/nla.news-article108109459.

6   Statement of Johanna E Bartington, Louisa Collins file, City
      of Botany Bay Library, barcode 00894400, disc reference no.
      DSCF0963.

7   Statement of James Law, Louisa Collins file, City of Botany Bay
      Library, barcode 00894400, disc reference no. DSCF0975.

8   State Records NSW: Central Criminal Court Papers, July 1888,
      Inquest No. 786, *Regina v Louisa Collins* [9/6758 6-149].

9   'Central Criminal Court — Wednesday', *The Sydney Morning Herald*
      (NSW: 1842–1954), 22 November 1888, p 6, retrieved 13 May 2014
      from http://nla.gov.au/nla.news-article13704459.

10   ibid.

11   ibid.

12   ibid.

13   ibid.

14 'Central Criminal Court — Tuesday', *The Sydney Morning Herald* (NSW: 1842–1954), 21 November 1888, p 13, retrieved 13 May 2014 from http://nla.gov.au/nla.news-article13704417.

Chapter 10

1 'The Botany Murder Case', *Evening News*, 8 January 1889, p 3.

2 'The New Chief Justice', *Australian Town and Country Journal* (NSW: 1870–1907), 4 December 1886, p 19, retrieved 5 February 2014 from http://nla.gov.au/nla.news-article71070358.

3 'Sir Patrick Jenning to Mr. Darley', *The Maitland Mercury and Hunter River General Advertiser* (NSW: 1843–1893), 2 December 1886, p 3, retrieved 20 May 2014 from http://nla.gov.au/nla.news-article71070358.

4 'The Alleged Botany Murders', *Evening News* (Sydney, NSW: 1869–1931), 5 December 1888, p 5, retrieved 11 May 2014 from http://nla.gov.au/nla.news-article108110406.

5 State Records NSW: NRS 5968, Judges' Notebooks; [2/2873] Justice Darley.

6 Statement of Frederick Andrews, Louisa Collins file, City of Botany Bay Library, barcode 00894400.

7 State Records NSW: NRS 5968, Judges' Notebooks; [2/2874] Justice Darley.

8 Statement of May Andrews, disc reference no. DSCF0974.

9 'Central Criminal Court — Thursday', *The Sydney Morning Herald* (NSW: 1842–1954), 7 December 1888, p 4, retrieved 11 May 2014, from http://nla.gov.au/nla.news-article1370637.

10 ibid.

11 'Central Criminal Court — Friday', *The Sydney Morning Herald*, 8 December 1888, p 16.

12 ibid.

13 ibid.

14 ibid.

15 ibid.

16 ibid.

17 'Preparations for Christmas', *The Sydney Morning Herald* (NSW: 1842–1954), 8 December 1888, p 10, retrieved 5 February 2014 from http://nla.gov.au/nla.news-article13706472.

18 'The Botany Poisoning Case — Sentence Of Death', *Goulburn Herald* (NSW: 1881–1907), 11 December 1888, p 2, retrieved 13 May 2014 from http://nla.gov.au/nla.news-article100233423.

19 ibid.

20 ibid.

21 ibid.

22 ibid.

23 ibid.

24 ibid.

25 ibid.

26 'The Judge's Summing Up', *Evening News* (Sydney, NSW: 1869– 1931), 10 December 1888, p 6, retrieved 14 February 2014 from http://nla.gov.au/nla.news-article108118670.

27 ibid.

Chapter 11

1 'The Judge's Summing Up', *Evening News*, 10 December 1888, p 6.

2 *R. v. Collins* (1888) NSWSupC 2.

3 ibid.

4 ibid.

5 ibid.

6 'The Botany Murder', *The Sydney Morning Herald* (NSW: 1842– 1954), 10 December 1888, p 11, retrieved 18 May 2014 from http:// nla.gov.au/nla.news-article13706767.

7 'The Judge's Summing Up', *Evening News*, 10 December 1888, p 6.

8 ibid.

9 State Records NSW: NRS 906; [4/895.1].

10 'The Murder Near Binda — Confession of the Murderess', *The Sydney Morning Herald* (NSW: 1842–1954), 15 November 1859, p 2, retrieved 13 May 2014 from http://nla.gov.au/nla.news-article13033267.

11 'Died in Gaol', *Evening News* (Sydney, NSW: 1869–1931), 21 September 1885, p 4, retrieved 13 May 2014 from http://nla.gov.au/ nla.news-article111340978.

12 Bruce E Mansfield, 'Melville, Ninian (1843–1897)', *Australian Dictionary of Biography*, National Centre of Biography, Australian National University, Canberra, 1974, retrieved 6 April 2014 from http://adb.anu.edu.au/biography/melville-ninian-4184/text6725.

13 *NSW Parliamentary Debates*, 19 December 1886–1888, State Library of New South Wales, p 1338; 'Legislative Assembly', *The Sydney Morning Herald* (NSW: 1842–1954), 20 December 1888, p 3, retrieved 13 May 2014, from http://nla.gov.au/nla.news-article13707738.

14 ibid.

15 Author unknown, 'Sir Henry Parkes', retrieved 13 May 2014 from http://www.nnsw.com.au/tenterfield/hparkes.html.

16 Edgar F Penzig, 'Gardiner, Francis (Frank) (1830–1903)', *Australian Dictionary of Biography*, National Centre of Biography, Australian National University, Canberra, 1972, retrieved 16 May 2014 from http://adb.anu.edu.au/biography/gardiner-francis-frank-3589/text5561.

17 *NSW Parliamentary Debates*, p 1338; 'Legislative Assembly' *The Sydney Morning Herald*, 20 December 1888, p 5.

18 'Execution Of A Woman', *Evening News* (Sydney, NSW: 1869–1931), 20 December 1888, p 5, retrieved 24 May 2014 from http://nla.gov.au/nla.news-article108109912.

19 Statement of Arthur Andrews, Louisa Collins file, City of Botany Bay Library, barcode 00894400, disc reference nos. DSCF0887 and DSCF1220.

20 *NSW Parliamentary Debates*, p 1338; 'Legislative Assembly', *The Sydney Morning Herald*, 20 December 1888, p 5.

Chapter 12

1 'Advertising', *Evening News* (Sydney, NSW: 1869–1931), 27 December 1888, p 1, retrieved 3 April 2014 from http://nla.gov.au/nla.news-article108111368.

2 'Society for the Abolition of Capital Punishment', *Empire* (Sydney 1850–1875), 1 September 1869, p 3, retrieved 14 June 2014 from http://nla.gov.au/nla.news-article60896180.

3 'The Case of Louisa Collins', *The Sydney Morning Herald* (NSW: 1842–1954), 27 December 1888, p 3, retrieved 3 April 2014, from http://nla.gov.au/nla.news-article13708512.

4 'The Maitland Poisoning Case', *Goulburn Evening Penny Post* (NSW: 1881–1940), 25 April 1885, p 3, retrieved 24 May 2014 from http://nla.gov.au/nla.news-article98442243.

5   The earlier executions of women were in 1855: see 'Condemned Mother's Final Act', *The Goulburn Post*, 21 October 2001, retrieved 24 May 2013 from http://www.goulburnpost.com.au/story/953492/condemned-mothers-final-act/.

6   'The Case of Louisa Collins', *The Sydney Morning Herald*, 27 December 1888, p 3.

7   'As You Like It', *The Sydney Morning Herald* (NSW: 1842–1954), 29 December 1888, p 7, retrieved 3 April 2014 from http://nla.gov.au/nla.news-article13708791.

8   'The Case of Louisa Collins: To the Editor of the Herald', *The Sydney Morning Herald* (NSW: 1842–1954), 29 December 1888, p 8, retrieved 3 April 2014 from http://nla.gov.au/nla.news-article13708765.

9   'As You Like It', *The Sydney Morning Herald*, 29 December 1888, p 7, retrieved 3 April 2014 from http://nla.gov.au/nla.news-article13708791 (NSW: 1842–1954).

10   ibid.

11   'The Case of Louisa Collins', *The Sydney Morning Herald* (NSW: 1842–1954), 31 December 1888, p 9, retrieved 3 April 2014 from http://nla.gov.au/nla.news-article28339128.

12   'Louisa Collins', *Evening News* (Sydney, NSW: 1869–1931), 18 December 1888, p 5, retrieved 24 May 2014 from http://nla.gov.au/nla.news-article108110316.

13   'To the Editor', *Evening News* (Sydney, NSW: 1869–1931), 20 December 1888, p 5, retrieved 25 May 2014 from http://nla.gov.au/nla.news-article108109911.

14   'Louisa Collins. To the Editor of the Herald', *The Sydney Morning Herald*, 3 January 1889, p 5. retrieved 24 May 2014 from http://nla.gov.au/nla.news-article13709132 (NSW: 1842–1954).

15   'To the Editor', *Evening News*, 20 December 1888, p 5.

16   'To the Editor of the Herald', *The Sydney Morning Herald* (NSW: 1842–1954), 28 December 1888, p 4, retrieved 3 April 2014 from http://nla.gov.au/nla.news-article13708658.

17   ibid.

18   J Falk, 'Reverend Charles Hamor Rich', Cassirer and Cohen — draft family genealogy website, 17 December 2006, retrieved 7 May 2014 from http://genealogy.metastudies.net/PS06/PS06_007.HTM.

19   'Brevities', *Evening News* (Sydney, NSW: 1869–1931), 14 December
      1888, p 4, retrieved 3 April 2014 from http://nla.gov.au/nla.news-
      article108116038.
20   ibid.

Chapter 13

1   'A Merciless Murderess', *Queanbeyan Age* (NSW: 1867–1904), 15
      October 1902, p 2, retrieved from http://nla.gov.au/nla.news-
      article31093074.
2   Letter from Louisa Collins, Louisa Collins file, City of Botany Bay
      Library, barcode reference: 00894400.
3   'The Botany Murderess', *Evening News*, 2 January 1889, p 5.
4   JM Bennett, 'Rogers, Francis Edward (1841–1925)', *Australian
      Dictionary of Biography*, National Centre of Biography, Australian
      National University, Canberra, 1968, retrieved 18 June 2014 from
      http://adb.anu.edu.au/biography/rogers-francis-edward-8255.
5   'The Botany Murder', *Evening News* (Sydney: 1869–1931), 28
      December 1888, p 5, retrieved 18 June 2014 from http://nla.gov.au/
      nla.news-article108116356.
6   ibid.
7   ibid.
8   'Law Report', *The Sydney Morning Herald* (NSW: 1842–1954), 29
      December 1888, p 8, retrieved 18 June 2014 from http://nla.gov.au/
      nla.news-article13708773.
9   ibid.
10   ibid.

Chapter 14

1   'To the Editor of the Herald', *The Sydney Morning Herald* (NSW:
      1842–1954), 4 January 1889, p 3, retrieved 3 April 2014 from http://
      nla.gov.au/nla.news-article13709226.
2   ibid.
3   'To the Editor of the Herald', *The Sydney Morning Herald* (NSW:
      1842–1954), 5 January 1889, p 8, retrieved 3 April 2014 from http://
      nla.gov.au/nla.news-article28338735.
4   ibid.
5   ibid.
6   ibid.

7   'To the Editor of the Herald', *The Sydney Morning Herald*, 24
     December 1888, p 5, retrieved 3 April 2014 from http://nla.gov.au/
     nla.news-article13708213 (NSW: 1842–1954).

8   ibid.

9   'Friday, January 4, 1889', *The Sydney Morning Herald* (NSW:
     1842–1954), 4 January 1889, p 4, retrieved 3 April 2014 from http://
     nla.gov.au/nla.news-article13709276.

10   'To the Editor of the Herald', *The Sydney Morning Herald*, 5 January
     1889, p 8.

11   BE Mansfield, 'Dibbs, Sir George Richard (1834–1904)', *Australian
     Dictionary of Biography*, National Centre of Biography, Australian
     National University, Canberra, 1972, retrieved 14 June 2014 from
     http://adb.anu.edu.au/biography/dibbs-sir-george-richard-3408/
     text5179.

12   'Funeral of the Late Mr. William Ellard', *Freeman's Journal* (Sydney,
     NSW: 1850–1932), 15 February 1902, p 22, retrieved 14 June 2014
     from http://nla.gov.au/nla.news-article111070206.

13   'Louisa Collins', *Molong Express and Western District Advertiser*
     (NSW: 1887–1954), 5 January 1889, p 3, retrieved 14 June 2014 from
     http://nla.gov.au/nla.news-article140160248.

14   'The Case of Louise Collins. Public Meeting at the Town Hall',
     The Sydney Morning Herald (NSW: 1842–1954), 4 January 1889,
     p 3, retrieved 14 June 2014 from http://nla.gov.au/nla.news-
     article13709220.

15   ibid.

16   'The Botany Murderess', *Evening News* (Sydney, NSW: 1869–1931),
     4 January 1889, p 8, retrieved 14 June 2014 from http://nla.gov.au/
     nla.news-article108794672.

17   'The Case of Louisa Collins. Public Meeting at the Town Hall', *The
     Sydney Morning Herald*, 4 January 1889, p 3.

18   AW Martin, 'Carrington, Charles Robert (1843–1928)', *Australian
     Dictionary of Biography*, National Centre of Biography, Australian
     National University, Canberra, 1969, retrieved 7 May 2014 from http://
     adb.anu.edu.au/biography/carrington-charles-robert-3169/text4745.

19   'Lord Carrington At Adelaide', *Newcastle Morning Herald
     and Miners' Advocate* (NSW: 1876–1954), 10 December 1885,
     p 7, retrieved 11 May 2014 from http://nla.gov.au/nla.news-
     article139064512.

20 Author unknown, 'Cecilia Annetta Carrington, Philanthropist &
    Charity Worker (circa 1850s-?)', Museum Victoria website, retrieved
    11 May 2014 from http://museumvictoria.com.au/collections/
    themes/1884/cecilia-annetta-carrington-philanthropist-charity-
    worker-circa-1850s.

21 'Lord Carrington: An Extraordinary Rumor', *Evening News* (Sydney,
    NSW: 1869–1931), 26 September 1888, p 8, retrieved 27 January
    2014 from http://nla.gov.au/nla.news-article107323015.

22 'Rumored Resignation of Lord Carrington', *South Australian
    Weekly Chronicle* (Adelaide, SA: 1881–1889), 18 August 1888,
    p 21, retrieved 27 January 2014 from http://nla.gov.au/nla.news-
    article94762322.

23 'Lord Carrington on his Reported Resignation, *Goulburn Evening
    Penny Post* (NSW: 1881–1940), 4 October 1888, p 2, retrieved May
    11 2014 from http://nla.gov.au/nla.news-article98452306.

24 'Lord Carrington and the Prerogative of Mercy', *Morning Bulletin*
    (Rockhampton, Qld: 1878–1954), 11 January 1889, p 6, retrieved
    May 11, 2014 from http://nla.gov.au/nla.news-article52274644.

25 ibid.

26 'The Botany Murderess', *Evening News* (Sydney, NSW: 1869–1931),
    5 January 1889, p 5, retrieved 21 May 2014 from http://nla.gov.au/
    nla.news-article108786681.

27 'Lord Carrington and the Prerogative of Mercy', *Morning Bulletin*,
    11 January 1889, p 6.

28 Cited in N Cushing, 'Woman as Murderer: the defence of Louisa
    Collins', *Journal of Interdisciplinary Gender Studies*, vol. 1, no. 2, 1996,
    p. 146.

29 'Lord Carrington and the Prerogative of Mercy', *Morning Bulletin*,
    11 January 1889, p 6.

30 Letters from Lord Carrington to Sir Henry Parkes, 19 May 1888–1
    August 1889, State Library of NSW, call no. A977, digital order
    no. 855863.

Chapter 15

1   'Woman's Column', *The Newsletter: an Australian Paper for Australian
    People* (Sydney, NSW: 1900–1918), 23 August 1902, p 13, retrieved 5
    April 2014 from http://nla.gov.au/nla.news-article114724930.

2   ibid.

3   GP Walsh, 'Allen, William Bell (1812–1869)', *Australian Dictionary of Biography*, National Centre of Biography, Australian National University, Canberra, 1969, retrieved 5 April 2014 from http://adb.anu.edu.au/biography/allen-william-bell-2878/text4113.

4   'Old-age Pensions', *The Sydney Morning Herald* (NSW: 1842–1954), 6 September 1901, p 3, retrieved 5 April 2014 from http://nla.gov.au/nla.news-article14408080.

5   'Treatment of Criminals', *The Sydney Morning Herald* (NSW: 1842–1954), 29 January 1887, p 15, retrieved 5 April 2014 from http://nla.gov.au/nla.news-article13625933.

6   'The Blacks at La Perouse', *The Sydney Morning Herald* (NSW: 1842–1954), 14 July 1891, p 6, retrieved 5 April 2014 from http://nla.gov.au/nla.news-article13831179.

7   ibid.

8   'A Plea for the Flower-Sellers', *The Sydney Morning Herald* (NSW: 1842–1954), 8 July 1904, p 5, retrieved 17 February 2014 from http://nla.gov.au/nla.news-article14622580.

9   'To the Editor of the Herald', *The Sydney Morning Herald* (NSW: 1842–1954), 23 September 1903, p 10, retrieved 17 February 2014 from http://nla.gov.au/nla.news-article14548704.

10 'The Women's Meeting', *The Sydney Morning Herald* (NSW: 1842–1954), 5 January 1889, p 8, retrieved 2 March 2014 from http://nla.gov.au/nla.news-article28338743.

11 A Mackenzie, 'Elizabeth Parsons — Biography', In the Artist's Footsteps website, 2000, retrieved 2 March 2014 from http://www.artistsfootsteps.com/html/Parsons_biography.htm.

12 ibid.

13 'Advertising', *Argus* (Melbourne, Vic.: 1848–1957), 29 December 1888, p 11, retrieved 24 February 2014 from http://nla.gov.au/nla.news-article6914394.

14 State Records NSW: NRS 906; [4/895.1].

15 'The Women's Meeting', *The Sydney Morning Herald*, 5 January 1889, p 8.

16 'Latest Colonial Telegrams', *Clarence and Richmond Examiner and New England Advertiser* (Grafton, NSW: 1859–1889), 5 January 1889, p 5, retrieved 5 April 2014 from http://nla.gov.au/nla.news-article62127257.

Chapter 16

1   Cited in Cushing, p. 146.
2   State Records NSW: NRS 906; [4/895.1].
3   ibid.
4   ibid.
5   ibid.
6   ibid.
7   ibid.
8   MM Bodkin, *Famous Irish Trials*, Maunsel & Company Ltd, Dublin, 1918, pp 106–129.
9   State Records NSW: NRS 906; [4/895.1].
10 ibid.
11 ibid.
12 ibid.
13 'The Case of Louisa Collins', *The Sydney Morning Herald* (NSW: 1842–1954), 8 January 1889, p 5, retrieved 5 April 2014 from http://nla.gov.au/nla.news-article13709515.
14 State Records NSW: NRS 906; [4/895.1].
15 FM Dunn, 'Clarke, William (1843–1903)', *Australian Dictionary of Biography*, National Centre of Biography, Australian National University, Canberra, 1969, retrieved 14 June 2014 from http://adb.anu.edu.au/biography/clarke-william-3227/text 4863.
16 'The Case of Louisa Collins', *The Sydney Morning Herald*, 8 January 1889, p 5.
17 ibid.
18 ibid.
19 ibid.
20 State Records NSW: NRS 906; [4/895.1].
21 ibid.

Chapter 17

1   State Records NSW: NRS 906; [4/895.1].
2   'To the Editor of the Herald', *The Sydney Morning Herald* (NSW: 1842–1954), 3 January 1889, p 5, retrieved 16 February 2014 from http://nla.gov.au/nla.news-article13709134.
3   'The Condemned Woman Collins', *Braidwood Dispatch and Mining Journal* (NSW: 1888–1954), 9 January 1889, p 2, retrieved 21 March 2014 from http://nla.gov.au/nla.news-article99867450.

4   'The Case of Louisa Collins', *The Sydney Morning Herald*, 8 January 1889, p 5.

5   'News from Abroad', *The Inquirer and Commercial News* (Perth, WA: 1855–1901), 4 December 1889, p 5, retrieved 14 June 2014 from http://nla.gov.au/nla.news-article66931332.

6   'The Case of Louisa Collins', *The Sydney Morning Herald*, 8 January 1889, p 5.

7   'The Botany Murderess', *Evening News* (Sydney, NSW: 1869–1931), 8 January 1889, p 6, retrieved 13 May 2014 from http://nla.gov.au/nla.news-article108789588.

8   'The Case of Louisa Collins', *Singleton Argus* (NSW: 1880–1954), 9 January 1889, p 2, retrieved 24 May 2014 from http://nla.gov.au/nla.news-article82621303.

9   'The First Inquest', *Evening News* (NSW: 1869–1931), 8 January 1889, p 3, retrieved 24 May 2014 from http://nla.gov.au/nla.news-article108789487.

10 'The Botany Murderess', *Evening News*, 20 December 1888, p 5.

11 ibid.

12 'Execution Of Louisa Collins', *North Eastern Ensign* (Benalla, Vic: 1872–1938), 11 January 1889, p 3, retrieved 24 May 2014 from http://nla.gov.au/nla.news-article70081002.

Chapter 18

1   'Gross Mismanagement', *Singleton Argus* (NSW: 1880–1954), 9 January 1889, p 2, retrieved 29 March 2014 from http://nla.gov.au/nla.news-article82621305.

2   'Louisa Collins's Execution', *Horsham Times* (Vic: 1882–1954), 11 January 1889, p 4, retrieved 21 May 2014 from http://nla.gov.au/nla.news-article72875551.

3   ibid.

4   'The Execution Of Louisa Collins', *The Sydney Morning Herald*, 9 January 1889, p 7.

5   'Her Last Hours', *Evening News* (Sydney, NSW: 1869–1931), 8 January 1889, p 4, retrieved 21 May 2014 from http://nla.gov.au/nla.news-article108789472.

6   'The Execution Of Louisa Collins', *The Sydney Morning Herald*, 9 January 1889, p 7.

7   'Louisa Collins's Execution', *Horsham Times*, 11 January 1889, p 4.

8   'The Execution Of Louisa Collins' *The Sydney Morning Herald*, 9
    January 1889, p 7.

9   'Execution Of A Female Poisoner', *Colac Herald* (Vic: 1875–1918), 11
    January 1889, p 4, retrieved 24 May 2014 from http://nla.gov.au/nla.
    news-article90349914.

Chapter 19

1   'The Execution of Louisa Collins', *The Sydney Morning Herald*, 9
    January 1889, p 4.

2   'Execution of Mrs. Louisa Collins', *Daily News* (Perth, WA:
    1882–1950), 10 January 1889, p 3, retrieved 29 March 2014 from
    http://nla.gov.au/nla.news-article77375529.

3   'The Botany Murder Case', *Evening News* (Sydney, NSW: 1869–
    1931), 8 January 1889, p 6, retrieved 29 March 2014 from http://nla.
    gov.au/nla.news-article108786453.

4   'Burial of Louisa Collins', *Bendigo Advertiser* (Vic: 1855–1918), 10
    January 1889, p 3, retrieved 29 March 2014 from http://nla.gov.au/
    nla.news-article88558837.

5   'Advertising', *Evening News* (Sydney, NSW: 1869–1931), 9 January
    1889, p 1, retrieved 1 May 2014 from http://nla.gov.au/nla.news-
    page11929686.

6   A Oldfield, *Woman Suffrage in Australia: A Gift or a Struggle?*,
    Cambridge University Press, Melbourne, 1992, p 77.

7   ibid., p 188.

8   'Relative Value of Girl Babies', *Dawn* (Sydney, NSW: 1888–1905), 1
    May 1896, p 26, retrieved 6 April 2014 from http://nla.gov.au/nla.
    news-article76418416.

9   Oldfield, p 78.

10 ibid.

11 'Mrs Lee on the Marriage Question', *Independent* (Footscray, VIC:
    1883–1922), 20 October 1888, p 3, retrieved 14 June 2014 from
    http://nla.gov.au/nla.news-article73770162.

12 H Lee, *Marriage and Heredity*, JJ Howard, Melbourne, 1863.

13 'A Woman's Plea', *The Alliance Record*, 11 July 1891, p 171.

14 Oldfield, p 77.

15 'The Womanhood Suffrage Victory', *Dawn* (Sydney, NSW: 1888–
    1905), 1 September 1902, p 8, retrieved 6 April 2014 from http://
    nla.gov.au/nla.news-article77082871.

16 'How to vote', *Dawn* (Sydney: 1888–1905), 1 August 1903,
    p 7, retrieved 14 June 2014 from http://nla.gov.au/nla.news-
    article77443040.

17 'Women's Suffrage', *The Sydney Morning Herald* (NSW: 1842–1954),
    9 May 1890, p 5, retrieved 14 June 2014 from http://nla.gov.au/nla.
    news-article13786588.

18 J Smith, 'Saturday, June 25, 1870', *The Argus* (Melbourne, Vic.:
    1848–1957), 25 June, 1870, p 4, retrieved 14 June 2014 from http://
    nla.gov.au/nla.news-article5823993.

19 Mackenzie, 'Elizabeth Parsons — Biography'.

20 Oldfield, p xiii.

Epilogue

1   'In Memoriam', *Newcastle Morning Herald*, 26 December 1936,
    p 6, retrieved 14 June 2014 from http://nla.gov.au/nla.news-
    article134679358.

2   'The Issue of This Marriage', *Evening News* (Sydney, NSW:
    1869–1931), 8 January 1889, p 3, retrieved 11 May 2014 from http://
    nla.gov.au/nla.news-article108789494.

3   State Children's Relief Board, Dependent Children Registers
    1883–1923, Folio no. 5, Charles Andrews admitted 14 September
    1888; State Records NSW: [11/22097], Fiche 7028.

4   'The Randwick Asylum', *Illustrated Sydney News* (NSW: 1853–1872),
    17 April 1890, p 17, retrieved 23 February 2014 from http://nla.gov.
    au/nla.news-article63610792.

5   'Obituary', *Goulburn Evening Penny Post* (NSW: 1881–1940), 17
    April 1929, p 6, retrieved 16 February 2014 from http://nla.gov.au/
    nla.news-article99334780.

6   'Local And General', *Windsor and Richmond Gazette* (NSW: 1888–
    1954), 12 January 1889, p 4, retrieved 21 May 2014 from http://nla.
    gov.au/nla.news-article72558584.

7   'Windsor', *The Sydney Morning Herald* (NSW: 1842–1954), 25
    November 1863, p 2, retrieved 21 May 2014 from http://nla.gov.au/
    nla.news-article13091429.

8   'Large Funeral', *Hawkesbury Chronicle and Farmers Advocate*
    (Windsor, NSW: 1881–1888), 12 May 1888, p 3, retrieved 21 May
    2014 from http://nla.gov.au/nla.news-article66374808.

9   'Family Notices', *Windsor and Richmond Gazette* (NSW: 1888–1954), 17 October 1896, p 11, retrieved 16 February 2014 from http://nla. gov.au/nla.news-article72549995.

10   'Family Notices', *Windsor and Richmond Gazette* (NSW: 1888– 1954), 9 October 1897, p 4, retrieved 16 February 2014 from http://nla.gov.au/nla.news-article72553127.

11   'Windsor Police Court', *Windsor and Richmond Gazette* (NSW: 1888–1954), 14 April 1894, p 5, retrieved 18 June 2014 from http:// nla.gov.au/nla.news-article66443553.

12   ibid.

13   'Inscription for Alice L McGuiness', photographed and transcribed by R and J McDonnell, Australian Cemeteries Index website, retrieved 18 June 2014 from http://austcemindex.com/inscription. php?id=8157536.

14   NSW Registry of Births, Deaths and Marriages: Thelma McGuiness, birth certificate no. 9440/1909.

15   NSW Registry of Births, Deaths and Marriages: Mabel Theresa McGuiness, death certificate no. 1911/16783.

16   John McGuiness died in a mine accident in 1930. Source: 'In Memoriam', *Newcastle Morning Herald and Miner's Advocate* (1876– 1954), 19 December 1931, retrieved 23 August 2014 from http://nla. gov.au/nla.news-article135632867.

17   NSW Registry of Births, Deaths and Marriages: Thelma McGuiness and James Cairney, marriage certificate no. 2789/1925.

18   'Girls in Opium Dens', *Sunday Times* (Sydney, NSW: 1895–1930), 25 August 1901, p 7, retrieved 21 May 2014 from http://nla.gov.au/ nla.news-article125886828.

19   'The George-St. Tragedy', *Evening News* (Sydney, NSW: 1869– 1931), 9 July 1909, p 3, retrieved 18 February 2014 from http://nla. gov.au/nla.news-article114771401.

20   'Sporting Items', *The Newsletter: an Australian Paper for Australian People* (Sydney, NSW: 1900–1918), 26 June 1909, p 9, retrieved 17 July 2014 from http://nla.gov.au/nla.news-article102794441.

21   Sergeant Jeffes Killed, *Evening News* (Sydney, NSW: 1869–1931), 3 November 1911, p 9, retrieved 21 May 2014 from http://nla.gov.au/ nla.news-article115281632.

22   ibid.

23 'Australian Honoured', *The Sydney Morning Herald* (NSW: 1842–1954), 29 January 1916, p 10, retrieved 26 February 2014 from http://nla.gov.au/nla.news-article28782298.

24 'An Appreciation', *The Sydney Morning Herald* (NSW: 1842–1954), 16 June 1928, p 8, retrieved 26 February 2014 from http://nla.gov.au/nla.news-article16472584.

25 'Death of Lieut.-Colonel Marshall', *The Sydney Morning Herald* (NSW: 1842–1954), 25 December 1916, p 6, retrieved 2 March 2014 from http://nla.gov.au/nla.news-article15679583.

26 Shiell and Anderson, 'Henry Shiell (1827–1889)'.

27 State Records NSW: Colonial Secretary; NRS 906; [5/59308] Letter from the widow of Mr Henry Shiell to Lord Carrington.

28 ibid.

29 Rutledge, 'Foster, William John (1831–1909)'.

30 'Death of Judge Coffey', *Wagga Wagga Advertiser* (NSW: 1875–1910), 4 November 1899, p 2, retrieved 24 February 2014 from http://nla.gov.au/nla.news-article101843588.

31 HH Lusk, *History of Australia for Schools*, George Stephan Chapman, Acting Govt Printer, Sydney, 1891.

32 'Action Against a Barrister', *Newcastle Morning Herald and Miners' Advocate* (NSW: 1876–1954), 16 March 1894, p 5, retrieved 19 February 2014 from http://nla.gov.au/nla.news-article137182147.

33 Author record, Hugh H Lusk, AustLit, 2002, retrieved 7 May 2014 from http://www.austlit.edu.au/austlit/page/A92281.

34 'Windeyer, Sir William Charles (1834–1897)', *Australian Dictionary of Biography*, National Centre of Biography, Australian National University, Canberra, 1976, retrieved on 7 May 2014 from http://adb.anu.edu.au/biography/windeyer-sir-william-charles-1062/text8145.

35 T Stephens, 'Windeyer's Law: Keep It All in the Family', *The Sydney Morning Herald*, 8 April 1992, retrieved 7 May 2014 from http://www.legaldictionary.com.au/legal-dictionary-articles/1992/4/8/windeyers-law-keep-it-all-in-the-family/.

36 KG Allars, 'Innes, Sir Joseph George (1834–1896)', *Australian Dictionary of Biography*, National Centre of Biography, Australian National University, Canberra, 1972, retrieved 2 March 2014 from http://adb.anu.edu.au/biography/innes-sir-joseph-george-3836/text6091.

37 JM Bennett and M Rutledge, 'Heydon, Louis Francis (1848-1918)'
    Australian Dictionary of Biography, National Centre of Biography,
    Australian National University, Canberra, 1972, retrieved 21
    May 2014 from http://adb.anu.edu.au/biography/heydon-louis-
    francis-1104/text11469.

38 'Inquests', *The Sydney Morning Herald* (NSW: 1842–1954), 21
    November 1907, p 4, retrieved 11 May 2014 from http://nla.gov.au/
    nla.news-article14899576.

39 'The Late Eliza Pottie, Benefactress', *The Newsletter: an Australian
    Paper for Australian People* (Sydney, NSW: 1900–1918), 7 December
    1907, p 4, retrieved 31 March 2014 from http://nla.gov.au/nla.news-
    article103243743.

40 A Mackenzie, 'Andrew Mackenzie', In the Artist's Footsteps
    website, 2000, retrieved 7 May 2014 from http://www.
    artistsfootsteps.com/html/Mackenzie_cv.htm.

41 Mackenzie, 'Elizabeth Parsons — Biography'.

42 S Lawson, 'Archibald, Jules François (1856–1919)', *Australian Dictionary
    of Biography*, National Centre of Biography, Australian National
    University, Canberra, 1969, retrieved 1 March 2014 from http://adb.
    anu.edu.au/biography/archibald-jules-francois-2896/text4155.

43 ibid.

44 'New South Wales', *Daily News* (Perth, WA: 1882–1950), 25
    October 1895, p 3, retrieved 19 February 2014 from http://nla.gov.
    au/nla.news-article81384238.

45 'Death Of Sir Henry Parkes', *South Australian Register* (Adelaide,
    SA: 1839–1900), 28 April 1896, p 5, retrieved 21 May 2014 from
    http://nla.gov.au/nla.news-article53687974.

46 'Lady Parkes' Allowance', *Clarence and Richmond Examiner* (Grafton,
    NSW: 1889–1915), 4 December 1900, p 4, retrieved 19 February
    2014 from http://nla.gov.au/nla.news-article61256966.

47 P Reynolds, 'Parkes, Cobden (1892–1978)', *Australian Dictionary
    of Biography*, National Centre of Biography, Australian National
    University, Canberra, 2000, retrieved 19 February 2014 from http://
    adb.anu.edu.au/biography/parkes-cobden-11342/text20257.

48 BE Mansfield, 'Dibbs, Sir George Richard (1834–1904)'.

49 'The Late Sir George Dibbs', *The Sydney Morning Herald* (NSW:
    1842–1954), 8 August 1904, p 5, retrieved 2 March 2014 from
    http://nla.gov.au/nla.news-article14627178.

50 GR Torbay, 'Sir George Dibbs, a Former Premier of New South Wales', Legislative Assembly, 7 May 2008, retrieved 7 May 2014 from http://www.parliament.nsw.gov.au/prod/parlment/hansart.nsf/V3Key/LA20080507009.

51 *Besomo v Keating* (1895) NSWSupC 1, retrieved 7 May 2014 from http://www.law.mq.edu.au/research/colonial_case_law/nsw/cases/case_index/1895/besomo_v_keating/.

52 AW Martin, 'Carrington, Charles Robert (1843–1928)', *Australian Dictionary of Biography*, National Centre of Biography, Australian National University, Canberra, 1969, retrieved 7 May 2014 from http://adb.anu.edu.au/biography/carrington-charles-robert-3169/text4745.

53 'King at a Wedding', *Mullumbimby Star* (NSW: 1906–1936), 2 September 1909, p 8, retrieved 20 August 2014 from http://nla.gov.au/nla.news-article12519059.

54 'Execution of Louisa Collins', *The Brisbane Courier* (Qld.: 1864–1933), 9 January 1889, p 5, retrieved 17 July 2014 from http://nla.gov.au/nla.news-article3490943.

55 'The Execution of Louisa Collins', *Kerang Times and Swan Hill Gazette* (Vic.: 1877–1889), 11 January 1889, p 5, retrieved 17 July 2014 from http://nla.gov.au/nla.news-article65606554.

56 'Execution of Louisa Collins', *Clarence and Richmond Examiner and New England Advertiser* (Grafton, NSW: 1859–1889), 12 January 1889, p 8, retrieved 17 July 2014 from http://nla.gov.au/nla.news-article62127427.

57 'Echoes of the Street', Launceston Examiner (Tas.: 1842–1899), 16 January 1889, p 3, retrieved 17 July 2014 from http://nla.gov.au/nla.news-article38342270.

58 'Wednesday, January 9, 1889', *The Sydney Morning Herald* (NSW: 1842–1954), 9 January 1889, p 6, retrieved 27 January 2014 from http://nla.gov.au/nla.news-article13709693.

59 'The Recent Execution at Darlinghurst', *The Sydney Morning Herald* (NSW: 1842–1954), 11 January 1889, p 3, retrieved 27 January 2014 from http://nla.gov.au/nla.news-article13709903.

60 'Brevities', *Evening News* (Sydney, NSW: 1869–1931), 11 January 1889, p 4, retrieved 23 February 2014 from http://nla.gov.au/nla.news-article108785864.

61 'Archer's Last Moments', *Evening News* (Sydney, NSW: 1869–1931),
    12 July 1893, p 6, retrieved 15 February 2014 from http://nla.gov.au/
    nla.news-article113727840.

62 Author unknown, 'Robert "Nosey Bob" Howard (1832–1906)'.

63 ibid.

64 'Hangman Howard Dead', *The Newsletter: an Australian Paper for
    Australian People* (Sydney, NSW: 1900–1918), 10 February 1906,
    p 5, retrieved 17 July 2014 from http://nla.gov.au/nla.news-
    article102707783.

65 'The Suspicious Death of a Woman at Botany', *Kiama Independent
    and Shoalhaven Advertiser* (NSW: 1863–1947), 25 November 1884,
    p 4, retrieved 29 March 2014 from http://nla.gov.au/nla.news-
    article101640285.

66 'Friday, March 2, 1889', *The Sydney Morning Herald* (NSW: 1842–
    1954), 2 March 1888, p 6, retrieved 17 July 2014 from http://nla.gov.
    au/nla.news-article28347551.

67 ibid.

68 'South Australia', *Newcastle Morning Herald and Miners' Advocate*
    (NSW: 1876–1954), 3 June 1889, p 6, retrieved 17 July 2014 from
    http://nla.gov.au/nla.news-article138927681.

69 'Suicide at Parramatta', The Sydney Morning Herald (NSW:
    1842–1954), 23 May 1892, p 6, retrieved 17 July 2014 from http://
    nla.gov.au/nla.news-article13868821.

70 'National Art School–The Cell Block', retrieved 7 May 2014 from
    http://www.laissez.com.au/Venues/The-National-Art-School/Venue-
    Information/National-Art-School-venue.

71 'NSW Legislation Will Abolish Capital Punishment', *The
    Sydney Morning Herald* (NSW: 1842–1954), 26 October 1954,
    p 1, retrieved 20 August 2014 from http://nla.gov.au/nla.news-
    page1083254.

72 A Chan and J Payne, 'Homicide in Australia: 2008–10, National
    Homicide Monitoring Program Annual Report', Australian Institute
    of Criminology, Canberra, February 2013, retrieved 7 May 2014
    from http://www.aic.gov.au/publications/current%20series/mr/21-
    40/mr21/04_homicide.html.

PICTURE CREDITS

page 1: 'The Botany Mystery', *Australian Town and Country Journal* (Sydney, NSW: 1870–1907), 11 August 1888, retrieved from http://nla.gov.au/nla.news-article71100980.

page 2: State Records NSW: NRS 2138; [3/6050]; roll 5103, photograph 84.

page 3 top: Darlinghurst Gaol and Court House, Sydney, 1870 by Charles Pickering/State Library of NSW (SPF/253, a089253).

page 3 bottom: State Records NSW: Central Criminal Court Papers, July 1888, Inquest No. 786, *Regina v Louisa Collins* [9/6758 6-149].

page 4: P. Besomo, *A Brief History of the Most Famous Female Poisoners, Borgia Family etc: How They Killed and What They Killed With: With Phrenological and Physiognomical Sketch of Mrs Louisa Collins the Botany murderess*, Sydney, c. 1888.

page 5 top: 'Springvale and Floodvale, the wool-washing and fellmongering establishments of Geddes Brothers, at Botany, New South Wales', *Australian Town and Country Journal* (Sydney, NSW: 1870–1907), 3 Decemeber 1881, p 24, retrieved from http://nla.gov.au/nla.news-article70963012.

page 5 middle: 'Rough On Rats', Box Vox website, retrieved from http://www.beachpackagingdesign.com/wp/2010/09/rough-on-rats.html

page 5 bottom: State Records NSW: Central Criminal Court Papers, July 1888, Inquest No. 786, *Regina v Louisa Collins* [9/6758 6-149].

page 6 top: 'Parkes, Henry', Dictionary of Sydney website, retrieved from http://www.dictionaryofsydney.org/entry/parkes_henry

page 6 middle: Parsons' family collection, retrieved from http://www.artistsfootsteps.com/html/Parsons_biography.htm

page 6 bottom: 'The Late Eliza Pottie, Benefactress', *The Newsletter: an Australian paper for Australian people* (NSW:1900–1918), 7 December 1907, p 4, retrieved from http://nla.gov.au/nla.news-article103243743.

page 7 top: P. Besomo, *A Brief History of the Most Famous Female Poisoners.*

page 7 bottom: 'People's Summer Fun Special', *People* magazine, 1984, p.8.

page 8 top: Courtesy of Mr Arthur Civill, great-great grandson of Louisa Collins.

page 8 bottom: Courtesy of Janis and Bev Thompson.

FURTHER REFERENCES

Allen, J., *Sex and Secrets: Crimes involving Australian women since 1880*, Oxford University Press, Melbourne, 1990.

Beck, D., *Hope in Hell: a history of Darlinghurst Gaol and the National Art School*, Allen and Unwin, Sydney, 2005.

Blaikie, G., 'The Borgia of Botany Bay', *Great Australian Scandals*, Rigby, Adelaide, 1979.

Campbell, N., *Femme Fatale: The female criminal*, Historic Houses Trust of New South Wales, Sydney, 2008.

Dobash, R.P., Dobash, R.E. and Gutteridge, S., *The Imprisonment of Women*, B. Blackwell, Oxford, 1986.

Holledge, J., *Australia's Wicked Women*, Horwitz Publications, Melbourne, 1963.

Kukulies-Smith, W. and Priest, S., '"No Hope of Mercy" for the Borgia of Botany Bay: Lousia May Collins, the last woman executed in NSW, 1889', *Canberra Law Review*, Vol. 10, Issue 2, 2011.

Sharp, A., *The Giant Book of Crimes That Shocked Australia*, The Book Company, Sydney, 1994.

White S and P, 'About Belltrees', Belltrees website, www.belltrees.com.

ACKNOWLEDGEMENTS

This is the first book to be written about Louisa Collins. As such, it depends heavily on original sources. I don't doubt that there will be mistakes. There always are. You try to catch them all and you never can. I hope that those readers who find them will point them out to me, so I can correct the record.

I would like to express my thanks to those people — librarians, researchers, archivists — who helped track the material down, including the staff at State Records NSW (especially Gail Davis) and at the state libraries of NSW and Victoria; to Ron Smith and Shirley Baines-Smith for assistance with information about Elizabeth Parsons; to the National Gallery of Australia for assistance in locating many of the photographs; to Beryl Chesterton, Terri McCormack, Heather Garnsey and Martyn Killion, for their assistance with locating specific documents, such as the ledger showing the date of admission of Louisa's children to the Randwick Asylum; to Amruta Slee and Shona Martyn at HarperCollins for embracing the project with such enthusiasm; and to my editors, Rachel Dennis and Jude McGee. I also thank the descendants of Eliza Pottie, who provided such wonderful background on their feisty ancestor; Dr Judy White of Belltrees for reminding me how important are the original sources in understanding of the past (and for correcting the record on Cranbrook for me before publication); Rebecca Pettit, whose enthusiasm for the story is greater even than my own, and whose passion for it has kept the story alive into the twenty-first century; to the descendants of May Andrews, who filled my heart with joy when they produced a photograph of dear, sweet Thelma; and to the wonderful Arthur Civill, great-great-grandson of Louisa Collins, and his loving wife, Barbara. Mr Civill, I can't tell you how happy you made me that day, when I picked up the phone, and it was you.

Also, much love and thanks to Katrin Schwab, for taking to the project with precision and gusto, even whilst working on a computer balanced on an upturned casserole dish.

To my own family: I love you. Always have, always will.